The Purest Mo:

MW00633507

Monotheistic Islam. Polytheistic Muslims.*

Eeshat Ansari

* All Muslims are not polytheists. Inspired by verse 12:106 and Hadith of 73 sects.

Dedicated to

My Mother and Father
Whom I remember as
Ammi and Abba

*They taught me how to love,
how to think and find the truth,
and how to have courage to say what is true.*

**My Lord! Have mercy on them (parents) as they cared for me when
I was little** [17:24]

Table of Contents

CHAPTER 1

WHAT DOES GOD LOOK LIKE?

How does God/god look like? About half a millennium before Christ,
a Greek philosopher, and poet, Xenophanes of Colophon (d–circa
478 BCE), answered this question with pinpoint accuracy.

> Mortals deem that gods are begotten as they are,
> and have clothes like theirs and voice and form...
> yes, and if oxen and horses or lions had hands,
> and could paint with their hands,
> and produce works of art as men do,
> horses would paint the forms of gods like horses,
> and oxen like oxen
> the Ethiopians make their gods black and snub-nosed:
> the Thracians say theirs have blue eyes and red hair[1]

Xenophanes made perfect sense. A horse will think like a horse. A lion has
no choice but to think like a lion. Of course, a human is bound to see the
mythological world only from a human point of view. This is not by choice,
but it is a necessary part of being human.

Even when we think out of the box, we are still constrained by the
limitations of our human mind. For example, the human mind cannot
comfortably imagine the infinite size of space surrounding the universe, or
time that continues forever. Similarly, the human mind cannot imagine any
object that is not similar to any other known entity. Based on this
understanding, it is easy to predict what will happen when religion is created

1

or altered by human imagination. Gods will not only look like humans, but will also have male and female genders. Just like humans, the gods and goddesses will give birth to offspring. Following human patterns, gods will also wear clothes and use language to communicate.

The race and ethnicity of worshippers are also carried over to their gods. No wonder the African god Amun was dark-skinned, while the Norse goddess Iounn of Scandinavian mythology had blond hair. According to spiritual author Eckhart Tolle, "Man made 'God' in his own image. The eternal, the infinite, the unnamable was reduced to a mental idol that you had to believe in and worship as 'my god' or 'our god.' "[2]

Many religions claim to be monotheistic, but the Islamic concept of God is unique. Among the Abrahamic religions, in the context of monotheism, Judaism comes closest to Islam. To illustrate the uniqueness of Islamic monotheism, let us study the following excerpts from the Jewish Publication Societies' English Translation of the Jewish Bible, the Tanakh, 1917, the chapter of Genesis.[3]

> 32:25 And Jacob was left alone; and there wrestled a man with him until the breaking of the day.
>
> 32:26 And when he saw that he prevailed not against him, he touched the hollow of his thigh; and the hollow of Jacob's thigh was strained, as he wrestled with him.
>
> 32:27 And he said: 'Let me go, for the day breaketh.' And he said: 'I will not let thee go, except thou bless me.'
>
> 32:28 And he said unto him: 'What is thy name?' And be said: 'Jacob.'
>
> 32:29 And he said: 'Thy name shall be called no more Jacob, but Israel; for thou hast striven with God and with men and hast prevailed.'
>
> 32:30 And Jacob asked him and said: 'Tell me, I pray thee, thy name.' And he said: 'Wherefore is it that thou dost ask after my name?' And he blessed him there.
>
> 32:31 And Jacob called the name of the place Peniel: 'for I have seen God face to face and my life is preserved.'

According to these excerpts, God changed into human form and wrestled with Prophet Jacob[PBUH] (superscript PBUH stands for *peace be upon him*). However, this interpretation is controversial. According to the Encyclopedia Britannica, "Jacob wrestled with a mysterious stranger, a *divine being* who changed Jacob's name to Israel."[4] Another interpretation says, "Jacob ultimately succeeded in pinning the *angel*, refusing to free him until he gives him a blessing."[5]

NO ANTHROPOMORPHISM IN ISLAM

ISLAM STANDS OUT 1: GOD NEVER CONVERTS TO MAN

Islam is not a new religion. The very first human, Adam, was a Prophet of Islam. The Quran says: **"O Prophet [Muhammad^PBUH], We [Allah] have sent many messengers before you"** (40:78).

> NOTE:
> In this verse, Allah uses the pronoun 'We' instead of 'I' for Himself. Several languages, like Arabic, Urdu, Hindi, and English, sometimes use the majestic plural, when the plural pronoun is used to refer to a single person of authority. Such usage in English is called the 'royal we.'[6] For example: *We, the king of England . . .*

Prophet Muhammad^PBUH was the last Prophet, with 124,000 Prophets of Islam preceding him. It must be noted that *every single Prophet was a human.*[7] These Prophets were sent to different geographical regions during different periods.

Allah also gave holy books to some Prophets. **"He [Allah] sent down the Taurat (Torah) and the Injeel (Gospel)"** (3:3). Muslims believe that parts of the old books (before the Quran) have been corrupted or lost. All Prophets were Muslims, and they preached only the religion of Islam. However, over time, their books—and even the name of their religion—changed.

The Quran mentions only 25 Prophets, including Abraham, Jacob, Moses, Jesus, and Muhammad PBUT (peace be upon them). Prophet Jacob^PBUH is among those few individuals who are not only named but are also praised in the Quran. **"Commemorate Our [Allah's] servants Abraham, Isaac, and *Jacob* (PBUT), possessors of Power and Vision"** (38:45).

It is interesting to note that the above-mentioned wrestling between Prophet Jacob^PBUH and God (or an angel or other divine-being) is *not* found in the Quran. Allah never takes the shape of a human anywhere in the Quran—not symbolically, figuratively, or metaphorically. Islam is free of anthropomorphism. Islam has one and exactly one divine being, and that is Allah.

HUMAN CONTROL OVER DESTINY

Since prehistoric times, humans have longed to become the masters of their destiny, by wresting control away from the ever-unpredictable, all-powerful, unseen, and at times frightening and unknowable divine. One option is, as Xenophanes suggested, to believe in a god that holds human form. Such belief immediately removes the unseen and unknown aspects, and places the god fully within reach of human imagination. It allows idols and pictures of the god/gods to be used in worship. Worshippers then have no problem imagining what the god looks like.

The strong desire to visualize the divine in the form of a human-god has profoundly influenced believers of both polytheistic and monotheistic religions. There are three distinct ways humans have visualized sharing divinity with gods.

Anthropomorphic Case 1: Scriptured-god

In this type of human-god overlap, the religious scripture or mythology states that a god took the shape of a created being. If a god or goddess appears as a human, an animal, or a combination of both, it serves as powerful attraction because the infinite and invisible power of the Creator would become accessible in imagination and dreams. It seems easier to relate to and worship a human-god. This overlap is also called anthropomorphism, incarnation, personification or manifestation of a god. Egyptian mythology has many gods and goddesses who look human. This is the only case in which the initiative of human-god overlap comes from religious scripture or mythology and is *not* initiated in any manner by believers themselves.

Anthropomorphic Case 2: Believer-projected-god

Sometimes the desire to worship a human-god motivates believers. In that case, devotees project onto their favorite priest the status of god, *without the priest's consent*. Imagine that High Priest Asklepios, of the city temple, is uniquely gifted. His profound religious knowledge and moving sermons attract thousands of devotees. He attends to the individual problems of his devotees by making emotional and passionate prayers to the idol of the temple god, which brings the devotees to tears. Instead of relating to the lifeless statue of the temple god, it is far more fulfilling to engage in two-way communication with Asklepios, who can answer questions, cry, offer an embrace, and provide moral support. As a result, interacting with an inspirational priest can be more rewarding than praying to idols.

How can the temple god ignore the intercession of a perfect worshipper like Asklepios? When Asklepios prayed for someone and the prayers were answered, then the believer would credit Asklepios, who acted as an intercessor to plead their case to the temple god. Many worshippers started to believe that the temple god's help was not possible without the intervention of High Priest Asklepios. This is similar to the situation in which the fictional Aladdin possesses a magic lamp, and he is on your side. As a result, you can control the otherwise uncontrollable genie.

In this case, Asklepios never claimed to be the controller of the temple god. Instead, *the believers were responsible*. The believers wanted to make sure that the temple god accepted their prayers; they preferred a compassionate human intercessor to praying to a lifeless statue. After the death of Asklepios, his transformation from a priest to an intercessor to a god became even easier. Asklepios becomes an icon with legendary success stories. Believers pray to the *soul* of Asklepios to act as an intercessor to the temple god.

Unlike a petition from an ordinary believer, the temple god cannot refuse Asklepios. In other words, Asklepios is believed to be the *controlling-intercessor* to the temple god. As far as inner perception is concerned, Asklepios is a god, and while seeking his help, even mentioning the name of the temple god is no longer necessary.

The only way to raise Asklepios' status from man to god is to encourage his followers to repeatedly *praise and love* him. Here it should be noted that the praise-and-love cycle plays a critical role of its own. Loving the holy man develops a sense of closeness with and trust in him, while showering him with exaggerated praise makes the holy man appear superior to ordinary humans. In the context of religion, excessive praise-and-love reinforced by Asklepios' miracles stories play the role of powerful stimulants.

After several sessions of praise-and-love cycles, the followers raise the status of the holy man far above ordinary humans, and gradually the idea of his divinity becomes part of their belief. The entire process bears a striking resemblance to the custom of 'ancestor veneration' practiced in many cultures.

Anthropomorphic Case 3: Self-proclaimed-god

Sometimes, instead of the believers, Asklepios himself can exploit an opportunity by claiming that he is the controlling-intercessor, and the temple god cannot refuse his prayers. In other words, Asklepios self-proclaims his own divinity. He can even start a cult of his own. For example, for centuries, the Egyptian pharaohs claimed to be gods.

ISLAM STANDS OUT 2: PREVENTING BELIEVER-PROJECTED-GOD AND SELF-PROCLAIMED-GOD

Since the Prophets brought Islam to the people, there was always the risk that Muslims of later generations would be tempted to empower their favorite Prophet or holy man with divinity. Amazingly, the Quran emphatically prohibits this on several levels. The verse: "**Surely our Lord's Majesty is exalted: He has neither taken a *wife nor a son***" (72:3) rules out any possibility of the believer-projected-god scenario, in which followers promote a Prophet or holy man as an offspring of God or make a holy woman God's spouse.

The Quran not only describes Prophets as human, but also points out their human limitations, thus guiding people to stay in touch with reality and avoid the believer-projected-god scenario. According to the Quran, all humanity, including all Prophets, are "slaves of Allah" (40:31). Here, the meaning of the word *slave* has changed. This meaning has nothing to do with human trafficking or forced labor. Instead, the word *slave* means that all humans can act only by the will of Allah, because He maintains total control of the entire universe in every aspect. In other words, all humanity has 100 percent puppet-like dependence on Allah for every physical movement. In that sense, all of us continuously follow the commands of Allah. (The role of free will is discussed later.) We cannot independently act on our own. Therefore all humanity is slave to Allah.

The Quran points out another limitation of the Prophets: "**The Prophets who We [Allah] sent before you, [O Muhammad[PBUH]], *were also human* to whom We sent revelation. … We did not give them bodies which could survive without food, nor were they immortal**" (21:7–8). Please note that the verse places all Prophets at the same level as the rest of mortal humans, including their dependency on food to survive.

There are incidents in the Quran where Allah guided the Prophets, answered their questions, and encouraged them during calamities. Humans have limited knowledge and at times, we all make wrong choices. The

Quran relates some incidents in which the Prophets too made mistakes in judgment; and after they repented, Allah forgave them. On the Day of Judgment, Allah will judge every Prophet, along with the rest of humanity.

In summary, throughout the Quran, the relationship between the Supreme God and His slaves remains unchanged, and the roles of God and Prophets are never reversed or overlapped.

Even though the Prophets were human, this did not reduce their significance, because they brought Allah's guidance to the people. Allah sent Prophet Muhammad[PBUH] with two important purposes—to give humanity the Quran and the *hadith*. The term *hadith* (plural: *ahadith*) is defined as: "the traditions relating to the deeds and utterances of the Prophet as recounted by the companions [Muslims who saw Prophet Muhammad[PBUH] during his life]."[8] This included the tacit approval or disapproval of Prophet Muhammad[PBUH]. The Quran says to Prophet Muhammad[PBUH]: **"Allah has revealed to you the *Book* and *wisdom*, and taught you what you did not know"** (4:113). So, Prophet Muhammad[PBUH] not only conveyed to us the Quran, but also explained its meaning and other details in the form of ahadith.

It is interesting to note that no single Prophet hogs the attention of the entire Quran. That could have encouraged believers to promote the overtly discussed Prophet as believer-projected-god. Instead, the Quran conveys stories of several Prophets. For example, as many as 98 verses in chapter 12 relate the story of Prophet Joseph[PBUH]. The Quran also contains chapters named after the Prophets Joseph, Noah, Jonah, Hud, Abraham and Muhammad (PBUT).

All Prophets had exactly the same mission—to teach Islam: **"to every Prophet whom We sent before you [O Muhammad[PBUH]], We [Allah] revealed the same Message: '*there is no god but Me [Allah], so worship Me Alone.*'"** (21:25). This includes Prophet Jesus[PBUH], who preached Islam and said: **"I am indeed a *slave* of Allah"** (19:30). His followers were also Muslim. **"When Jesus[PBUH] found out that people had no faith, he asked: 'Who will help me in the cause of Allah?' The disciples replied: 'We will help you in the cause of Allah. We believe in Allah. Be our witness that *we are Muslims*'** [we submit to Allah]" (3:52).

Allah has praised some Prophets, however. Again, all praise is not directed toward just one Prophet. And the praise is never exaggerated; it does not project any Prophet into the human-god-overlap zone. For example: **"The**

7

slave of Allah **Prophet Job … was full of patience. He was an excellent devotee"** (38:41–44). In verse (33:56), Allah praised Prophet Muhammad[PBUH].

The Quran says: **"among the Prophets We [Allah] have exalted some above others"** (2:253). Instead of paying full attention only to the personalities of the Prophets, Muslims should focus on the *messages* of the Prophets. **"Say (Oh Muslims): 'We believe in Allah and that which is revealed to us; and what was revealed to Abraham, Ishmael, Isaac, Jacob, and their descendants and that which was given to Moses, Jesus, and other Prophets (PBUT) from their Rabb (Allah). We do not make distinction between them"** (2:136).

Over-emphasis on the idea that all Prophets are human should be adequate to prevent any human from trying to become a self-proclaimed-god.

NO INDIRECT ANTHROPOMORPHISM IN ISLAM

ISLAM STANDS OUT 3: ALL PRAYERS ARE MADE TO ALLAH ONLY

The Quran contains dozens of prayers. Every single prayer calls on Allah, and only Allah, and no one but Allah. For example, Prophet Moses[PBUH] called for help directly from Allah. **"O Lord! Surely I am in desperate need of whatever good that You may send down to me"** (28:24).

No prayer in the Quran is made to a controlling-intercessor. In the above prayer, Prophet Moses[PBUH] did not ask the deceased Prophet Abraham[PBUH] for help, nor his soul to pray to Allah on his behalf. Unlike the verses of Tanakh, discussed above, not a single prayer in the Quran is made to an angel or mysterious stranger or divine being other than Allah.

However, a believer can pray for others: **"O Allah! Guide *us* to the right way"** (1:6). Islam also allows a believer to request a living person to pray for a justified cause. When it comes to worldly affairs (like passing the salt or opening a door), Muslims are allowed to seek help from any suitable person. Here, the helping person must be alive, listening, and capable of helping. Why? So that the helper is perceived only as human and not as a divine being. Of course, a person can and should seek help from Allah for worldly affairs as well, but s/he must still have to give their full effort to achieve the worldly goal.

ISLAM STANDS OUT 4: ONLY ALLAH HAS THE AUTHORITY TO REWARD HEAVEN OR HELL

One question remains unanswered. All over the world, why are so many people converting to Islam, even if Islam does not rely on the popularity of idol worship and anthropomorphism?

The following incident gives a hint. In the early years of Islam, Prophet Muhammad[PBUH] and a few hundred Muslims migrated to the city of Medina. There they were constantly harassed and attacked by the majority of Mecca's pagans. One of the major pagan attacks resulted in the Battle of Uhud. In this battle, Muslims suffered heavy casualties, and Prophet Muhammad[PBUH] was seriously injured. His face was covered with blood and he lost a tooth. At this difficult moment, Prophet Muhammad[PBUH] commented that the pagans injured their Prophet who preached to them about monotheism. *How can such people succeed on the Day of Judgment?*[9] Immediately, the following verse from the Quran was revealed: **"O Prophet, it is not for you to decide; it is up to Allah whether He pardons or punishes them since they are wrongdoers"** (3:128).

You do not have to be a psychologist to realize that any human at such a desperate moment would easily be consumed by self-pity, anger, fear and revenge. At such moments, a human could not think of a verse like the one above. Only Allah, who controls every reward and punishment, could reveal such words.

In Islam, Allah and only Allah, and no one else but Allah, is the ultimate judge who can punish or reward. No human can bless others or accept prayers. As much as humans may desire to do so, they cannot take over this authority from Allah. Allah may forgive a person and inform a Prophet to convey information to believers. But no pious man, not even a Prophet, can independently forgive sins. On the Day of Judgment, Allah will judge every human, *including the Prophets*. People are converting to Islam because it is God's religion, not a man-made religion.

ISLAM STANDS OUT 5: NO HUMAN CAN OVERPOWER ALLAH OR HIS ANGELS

At times, a person may outsmart or fool other people. In some Xenophanic religions (based on Xenophanes' model discussed above), this human behavior is also present among gods. For example, in Greek mythology, an ordinary woman, Arachne, challenged Athena, the goddess of wisdom and crafts, to a weaving contest and she defeated the goddess.

Allah is not like a human in anyway. The Quran contains not a single incident in which a human outsmarts, overpowers or even competes with Allah. The Quran says **"you [humans] cannot challenge God in the heavens or in the earth"** (29:22). Allah is the Creator of all humans, and angels.

Muslims do not worship or consider angels as divine beings. Allah is the creator of the angels. Similar to Prophet Jacob's[PBUH] incident mentioned above, the Quran does not describe any incident in which a human has overpowered an angel, because that would be overpowering the command of Allah.

ISLAM STANDS OUT 6: ISLAM DOES NOT PERMIT WORSHIPING HEAVENLY BODIES OR *ANY* ENTITY FROM HUMAN IMAGINATION

When humans imagine or alter a religion, they may add an impressive or frightening entity as a deity. For example, the Egyptian Pharaoh Akhenaten (1364–1347 BCE) worshipped the sun god. Many religions have worshiped stars, the moon or the sun, because they are impressive and appear eternal. However, Islam explicitly prohibits their worship. **"Do not prostrate yourself before the Sun or the moon;** *rather prostrate yourself before Allah"* (41:37).

That is not all; the Quran strictly prohibits adding anything out of human imagination as a deity (e.g. a combination of human and animal): **"There is *nothing* similar to Him [Allah]"** (42:11). When humans imagine an entity, it is bound to be inspired by something we already know. Since Allah is not similar to anything we know, *we cannot even imagine what Allah is like.*

How should Muslims perceive Allah? Following chapter has the answer.

CHAPTER 2

SELF-REVELATIONS OF ALLAH

THE UNIQUE CONCEPT OF GOD IN ISLAM

HOW TO LEARN ABOUT ALLAH

The Quran makes a very general statement: **"there is nothing like Him [Allah]"** (42:11). It means Allah is not similar to *any* object. In addition, Allah is entirely beyond human imagination. Therefore, we cannot learn about Allah by guesswork. The Quran tells us that every piece of knowledge, worldly or spiritual, is also controlled by Allah. **"They [humans] cannot gain access to anything out of His [Allah's] knowledge except what He pleases"** (2:255). The verse states that He allows humans only limited access to knowledge. In other words, knowledge and human access to knowledge are both in the continuous and total control of Allah. Acquiring knowledge about Allah is possible only through His self-revelations.

The Quran talks about different ways by which a human can acquire knowledge about Islam. For example, knowledge about Allah is given to us as innate nature (*fitra*) (30:30), ethics of right and wrong (91:7–8), and knowledge in the form of personal spiritual experience (41:53). These ways of learning are essentially gifts of Allah to an individual. However, personal experiences are unlikely to influence society as a whole.

11

Knowledge about Allah and Islam that can guide human society is available only from the Quran (the word of Allah) and the ahadith.

WHO CREATED GOD?

In the early years of Islam, some pagans asked Prophet Muhammad[PBUH], "What is the ancestry of your God?"[10] The question is a typical example of trying to explain God in human terms. At that time, the following four verses of the Quran were revealed to the Prophet. These verses constitute chapter 112 of the Quran, called *Al Ikhlaas*.

> **Say: Allah is God the One and Only**; [1]
> **God is the Self-Sufficient** (independent of all, while everything else depends on Him); [2]
> **He begets not, nor is He begotten;** [3]
> **And there is none comparable to Him.**[4]

Here is a verse by verse explanation.

Verse 1: Another meaning of the Arabic word *ahad* (used in verse 1) is "alone." English orientalist E. H. Palmer translated this verse as: **"Say: God is alone."** In verse (4:82), the Quran says that it does not have any contradiction *anywhere*! This means that if the Quran says that "God is one and only," then the Quran will never say, 'Such a saint is also God,' or, 'Include certain pious men into divinity and God will still remain one.' Then, does Prophet Muhammad[PBUH] share the authority, power or control of Allah? According to both the Quran and the ahadith, the answer is an *emphatic* no. Allah does not share power or authority with anyone. The Quran even specifies **"Muhammad[PBUH] is** [a human and] **no more than a messenger of Allah, like the messengers that passed away before him"** (3:144). Muslims respect and love Prophet Muhammad[PBUH] as a role model and Prophet, but they are supposed to regard him as human and not worship him. In Islam, all Prophets were human. All Prophets worshiped Allah, and they prayed for forgiveness.

Verse 2: One may interpret Allah being 'alone' in terms of the human weakness of loneliness, but verse 2 clears this doubt away by telling us that Allah is completely self-sufficient in every way. In contrast to humans, Allah does not have physical dependency on air, water, food or sleep. He does not possess the emotional weaknesses of exhaustion, boredom, depression or loneliness. Allah is not only the Creator but also the Sustainer of the universe. All matter and energy are entirely dependent on Allah.

The following hadith gives an idea of Allah's infinite capability and majesty. Allah says that if all humanity becomes as pious as the best human (say, like Prophet Muhammad[PBUH]), it will still not increase Allah's kingdom in any way. Similarly, if humanity becomes as wicked as the worst person (for example, like the pharaoh), Allah's kingdom will not decrease in any way. If Allah fulfills every single wish of all humanity, the kingdom of Allah will not decrease even as much as a sea decreases when a needle is dipped and raised.[11] With this in mind, when the above verse says that Allah is self-sufficient, *believe it*!

It is interesting to note that the example from the above hadith does not say if a 'spoon' is dipped into the sea, because a spoon has a concave cavity to hold water. Similarly, Allah does not say a 'thread' is dipped into the sea, because a thread can soak up some water. Instead, the example uses a needle, which neither has any cavity or capability to absorb water.

Verse 3: This verse explains that Allah does not have any offspring, nor is He the offspring of anyone. However, reproduction is a basic characteristic of animals. All animals have a limited lifespan. Therefore, reproduction is the only way to perpetuate species. Except for species like bacteria, most animals require a father and a mother to produce a child. Parents influence many characteristics of their offspring, like race, height, weight and DNA. Reproduction continues across generations, as long as the species lasts. It must be noted that the father and mother are not the creators of the baby, but their bodies make the baby.

Canadian Professor of Logic and Mathematics Dr. Gary Miller has argued that it is impossible for God to have a son, because the son of any being must possess two qualities: (i) The son should owe his life to his father. (ii) The son must be just like his father, because *"son is the same kind of being as his father. Son of a horse is a horse and a son of a man is a man."*[12] However, God does not have a father. Therefore, how can a son of God have a father? Besides, God does not owe His life to anyone. By definition, God exists of Himself.

The Quran presents another argument: **"Praise be to Allah, the One Who has begotten no son and Who has no partner in His Kingdom; nor *He is helpless to need a protector* [unlike a human who needs son/daughter as supporter and protector in old age]"** (17:111). In other words, why does the everlasting, all-knowing, almighty, fully-contented God need a son? Did God lack anything that the son could provide? Don't forget, reproduction is an animal-level dependency. How could the Supreme God be dependent like His creation? Further, if you accept that there are offspring of God, then the offspring will share God's divinity. This means God can no longer be one and alone, as in verse 1.

The verse also says that Allah is not begotten by anyone. Allah created all lifeforms and gave them the ability to reproduce. But this rule does not apply to Allah. This should not come as a surprise because the Quran says, **"there is nothing like Him** [Allah]**"** (42:11).

Verse 4: This verse unequivocally rules out the possibility that anyone or anything can be *similar* to Allah. He is without any competition, challenge or partnership of any kind. No human can compete with Allah. Again, **"there is nothing like Him"** (42:11). It is prohibited to worship anything that claims similarity to Allah. Therefore, a Muslim[13] cannot imagine Allah in the symbolic form of a statue, idol, picture, Prophet or holy man. This leaves the Muslim with only one option—to *directly* worship Allah and none other.

Verse 4 rules out the possibility of all *indirect* ways of acquiring knowledge about God through a God-like being. For example, a student pilot can learn to fly a plane from a flight simulator, but to worship Allah, a similar approach cannot work.

Let us pause for a moment, to relish the simplicity and clarity of the four verses of Al Ikhlaas (Surah 112). According to scholars, every verse individually answers the pagan's question about the ancestry of God. Note the *order* in which each line appears and how every verse builds upon and adds to the message of the previous one. These four lines define the monotheism of Islam. At the same time, their logic is simple enough even for an illiterate desert-dweller to understand.

Muslim philosopher and theologian Abu Hamid al-Ghazali (d: 1111) said about Allah: "He is not a body with a form, or a limitary, quantitative substance, not resembling bodies in quantifiability or divisibility, or in being a substance or qualified by a substance....He does not resemble anything that exists, nor anything that exists resembles Him. There is nothing whatsoever like unto Him, nor is He like unto anything. He is not delimited by magnitude, contained in places, encompassed by directions, or bounded by Heavens or Earth...."[14]

THE KINGDOM OF ALLAH INCLUDES ALL LANDS AND RACES

Matthew Tindal (d: 1733) was an eminent deist, a free-thinker. He argued that it is unjust for the universal God to reveal the true religion to only a select few and hide it from the rest of humanity. If a religion rewards heaven only to believers and punishes unbelievers, then the choice to follow or reject religion should be available to all humankind, not just a few. Why deprive people who died before the Prophet/god-incarnation?[15] How about remote settlements and lost civilizations where people were probably never exposed to the true faith? These are sensible but tough requirements for a true faith. What does Islam say about this subject?

Anthropomorphic religions have an inherent weakness. When a god takes the form of a human, the incarnate human-god belongs to a specific race, lives in a specific country. This means that, out of so many choices around the world, god preferred a specific country and race combination, making them superior to the rest of the world. According to Xenophanes' example, Ethiopians and Thracians would both think of themselves as god's *chosen people*.

In contrast, Islam is free from anthropomorphism, and therefore does not have any inherently superior race or geographical region. The Quran tells us that Allah is the Supreme God of the entire universe. Beginning with Prophet Adam until Prophet Muhammad[PBUH], Allah's messengers covered different geographical locations over time. **"No doubt We [Allah] sent in every nation a messenger, saying: 'Serve Allah and keep away from false gods'"** (16:36). The Prophets used to preach in a central city and send their disciples to remote areas to preach Islam. All messengers worked as a perfect team. They never competed with, contradicted the basic teachings, ignored or rejected one another. They even acknowledged the earlier books brought by previous Prophets: **"He [Allah] has revealed to you this Book [the Quran] with the Truth, confirming the scripture which preceded it, as He revealed the *Torah and Gospel*"** (3:3) and Allah **"gave the *Psalms* to David[PBUH]"** (17:55). No messenger claimed personal glory, heroism or credit. No Prophet ever competed with or challenged Allah or claimed divinity for himself. They always gave full credit for all miracles to Allah.

The rules of superseding a previous messenger by a more recent messenger were simple and logical. If a new messenger brought a new book, then the believers were supposed to leave their old ways and switch to the latest book. That is because, over time, old books were fully or partially lost. The methodology (*seerat*) of subsequent messengers (who came with a new book) changed only slightly. The Quran, however, has been fully preserved both in text and in language; therefore, after Prophet Muhammad[PBUH], there was no need for any new Prophet.

It is interesting to note that, before Islam, Arabs were sharply divided by tribal, racial and cultural boundaries. Social customs, along with the law and order of that period, were based on tribal prejudice. An alternative social order was far beyond their imagination. Yet the Quran never calls Allah the *Lord of the Arabs* or labels other races or people as inferior. Islam places the entire human race on the same level: **"He is the One [Allah], Who has created you [all humans] from a *single soul*"** (6:98). This means that all humans had the same beginning. There are no preferred races or tribes.

Islam has entirely different criteria for superiority. Prophet Muhammad[PBUH] said in his famous last sermon: "All humankind is from Adam and Eve, an Arab has no superiority over a non-Arab nor a non-Arab has any superiority over an Arab; also a white has no superiority over a black, nor does a black have any superiority over a white *except by piety and good action.*" Allah judges all humans based on their piety and good deeds. Piety has nothing to do with any race or national origin. In Islam, there is no room for racial prejudice.

What about remote people who never received the message of Allah? According to the Quran, they are exempt from the wrath of Allah! Why? Because Allah always does justice: **"We [Allah] have never punished anyone *without sending them Our Messenger first* (to give them the message)"** (17:15). According to Muslim theologian Ibn Taymiyyah (d: 1328), "Those who have not received the message of Truth or received a distorted or incomplete version of the message will not be punished."[16]

Isn't it surprising that the subtle but valid point made by Tindal in the 18th century is fully answered by the holy book revealed to Prophet Muhammad[PBUH] more than 1000 years earlier?

The domain of the kingdom of Allah extends beyond the Arabian deserts, even beyond the Earth. Instead, Allah is the Creator and Sustainer of the entire universe and other universes beyond our comprehension: **"Your Rabb [Allah] is the Lord of the [seven] skies and the Earth"** (21:56).

NATURAL HUMAN INCLINATION TO ISLAM

The Quran tells us that, before any human was put on Earth, Allah created the souls of every human and made a covenant: **"Allah asked them [all** human souls]: '*Am I not your Lord [Supreme God]?*' They all replied: '*Yes! We bear witness that You are.*' This We [Allah] did, lest you humankind should say on the Day of Resurrection: 'We were not aware of this fact that You are our Lord and that there will be a Day of Judgment' "(7:172).

Why do we not consciously remember this promise to Allah? Because the choices between right and wrong we make in this life are tests from Allah. To make the tests valid, some knowledge is kept hidden from us. However, true believers are those **"who believe in the Unseen"** (2:3).

Nonetheless, this covenant remains hidden somewhere in our subconscious. There are occasions when we hear an inner voice that keeps reminding us that God is One. The tests of Allah last throughout our lifetime. While alive, we are free to choose between monotheism and polytheism. The last sentence of above verse (7:172) tells us that, on the Day of Judgment, we will all acknowledge that we had an adequate recollection of the covenant in our lifetimes, and we are therefore accountable for our choices.

Because of this natural inclination, even today, Islam is still the fastest-growing religion on earth.[17] This also explains the spread of Islam among Australian aboriginals[18] and among Latin Americans.[19]

Q: Can you think of another logical explanation as to why Islam is the fastest-growing religion?

RELATING TO ALLAH WHO IS BEYOND IMAGINATION

THE SIGNS OF ALLAH

Unlike Xenophanic religions, Allah does not have any symbol, statue, or idol. Allah is entirely beyond our imagination. Therefore, human vocabulary does not contain words to describe Him. It seems that relating to Allah is an impossible goal.

Since the Quran is a book of guidance, it provides several different solutions. Most of the solutions are simple enough for even an uneducated person to understand. The best part is that all the solutions are *entirely free of anthropomorphism.*

The Quran encourages readers to ponder and explore the *creation* of Allah and look for the signs (*ayaat*) that prove the infinite capability and power of the Creator. After all, a subset of Allah's creation is within reach of our observation and scientific exploration. What a beautiful solution, to feel the closeness of Allah! The Quran presents several *varieties* and *categories* of signs. Only a few examples from the Quran are quoted below.

SIGNS IN PLANTS AND TREES

The Quran says: **"In the Earth there are [different types of] tracts [of land] side by side: gardens of grapes, cornfields, and palm trees with single and double trunks - *they are all watered with the same water,* yet We make some of them excel others in taste. Surely in this, *there are signs for people who reflect"* (**13:4). This verse points out that even when the *input* is identical, the *output* can be very different. All vegetation feeds on the same water. Still Allah created not only numerous varieties of crops, but also different tastes within the same types of fruit. For example, all varieties of grapes do not taste the same. This verse not only inspires us to notice this fact, but also encourages us to ponder how only Allah can create so many varieties of food for us to survive on and enjoy. We should be thankful to Allah. Look at it this way; it is Allah who made the grapes a nourishing food for humans. He did not make grapes capable of raising and consuming humans as food.

SIGNS IN THE ANIMAL KINGDOM

The Quran says: **"Do they not see the birds, that wing their flight in the air towards the sky? Who holds them up but Allah? Surely in this, *there are signs* for the true believers"** (16:79). This verse points out that Allah made it possible for a solid, dense being or object (like a bird or airplane) to fly through the air. Also, the verse says that we should not only appreciate the wonders of nature, but accredit these wonders to Allah.

SIGNS IN HUMAN RELATIONSHIPS

The signs of Allah are not limited to the three-dimensional world. The Quran also tells us to listen to our hearts and pay attention to our emotions: **"another sign is that He created for you mates from among yourselves that you may *find comfort with them,* and He planted *love and kindness in your hearts*; surely there are signs in this for those who *think about it"** (30:21). This means that the love between spouses is not a coincidence; it is a blessing from Allah. The goal of marriage is that spouses should be able to seek comfort from each other. This includes both sexual and emotional comfort.

When a marriage does not contain these blessings, both spouses should pray and make a serious effort to create a peaceful and satisfactory relationship. In extreme cases of duress, Islam authorizes either husband or wife to file for divorce. However, marriage is a serious commitment, and spouses are expected, according to the above verse, to make full effort to achieve mutual comfort.

The second half of the verse refers to the general bond of compassion, empathy and love among humans as another beautiful blessing and sign from Allah. He makes humans capable of living peacefully in a group or society. The verse concludes that the reader should notice these *signs* and give credit to Allah.

DID YOU NOTICE THAT?

Another beauty of the Quran is that it tells us some obvious blessings of Allah that we usually do not notice. It becomes clear to an observant reader that only the Creator would point out such blessings. For example, some religions say that God created light. The Quran gives an entirely new perspective by saying, **"Praise be to Allah ... [who] made the *darkness* and the light"** (6:1). This verse tells us that Allah created not only the light, but also *darkness*. Even cave-dwellers knew that in the darkness of night, during a lightning storm, they could momentarily see their surroundings, but as soon as the lightning stopped, darkness resumed. We assume that in the absence of light, darkness is a natural consequence. According to the above verse, even darkness did not exist of itself. Allah created darkness, along with the light.

Here is another example. In almost all vertebrate animals, Allah created loving relationships between mothers and their offspring. He gave most animals, including humans, love and care during the tender childhood phase, fulfilling both the physical and emotional needs of the child. In addition to blood relations, Allah blessed humans with additional types of close relationships that no other animals have: relationships created by *marriage*. He **"made for him [human] *blood relationships* and that of *marriage relationships* [with spouse and with other in-laws]"** (25:54). This means relationships with fathers-in-law, mothers-in-law, brothers-in-law, sisters-in-law, and even cousins-in-law are all gifts of Allah, which he bestowed upon us. If we handle this opportunity tactfully, we can also sustain meaningful relationships created by marriage. Did you ever notice this as a blessing from Allah? Only the Creator of humans would point to this blessing.

And the Quran provides another example, in which Allah gives humans advantage over other animals; only humans have the capability to earn a living! To survive, before every meal, most of us do not have to directly hunt for food. Instead, humans have another option, earning a living: **"We [Allah] are the One Who established you on Earth and provided you *means of earning livelihood"*** (7:10). Most of us can earn money from a job or business. With that money we can buy necessities and other items. Only the Creator of humans would talk about this blessing.

SCIENTIFIC EXPLORATIONS AND SPIRITUAL EXPERIENCE AS SIGNS OF ALLAH

The Quran talks about our era and also the future: **"Soon We [Allah] will show them [the humans] <u>Our signs in the *Universe* and in *their own souls*</u>, until it becomes clear to them that this [Quran] is indeed the truth"** (41:53). About 1400 years ago, the Quran promised that humans would continue to find the wonders of the universe, which would keep providing new signs as proof of the existence of Allah. This verse encourages us to scientifically explore the universe and look for new signs. We should also look for signs of Allah in our hearts.

With the advancement of science, particularly in the last 200 years, people started noticing that the centuries-old Quran points to newly discovered scientific facts. For example, the Quran says: **"does man think that We [Allah] shall not be able to put his bones together [on the Day of Judgment Allah will bring all humans back to life]? Why not? We are able to put together, in perfect order, the very tips of his fingers"** (75:3-4).

To emphasize Allah's ability to recreate, the verse especially mentions the tips of the fingers. Modern research finds that no two humans who ever lived or who are now alive have had identical fingerprints (nail-to-nail). Even identical twins have different fingerprints. English anthropologist Sir Francis Golt discovered the uniqueness of fingerprints in 1880. However, in 1999, Belgian forensic consultant Andre Moenssens discovered the degree of this uniqueness. He claimed in an article that, "In all human experience with fingerprints world-wide, no two fingerprints from different digits have ever been found to match exactly." And, "fingerprint identification has been found to be even more discriminating than vaunted DNA."[20]

Please note that the purpose of the Quran is not to teach science. But the Quran contains signs to prove that Allah exists. Verse 41:53 predicted that

Allah would show us His signs in the future. Verses (75:3–4) not only give us the sign of Allah that human fingerprints are unique, but also fulfilled the prediction of verse (41:53)!

Verse 41:53 also tells us to keep looking within our hearts. No scientific instrument can prove our spiritual experience to others; only you can feel your own spiritual experience.

Let us combine the messages of the two verses discussed above.

1. Every human promised to Allah: **"Yes! We bear witness that You [Allah] is [the Lord]"** (7:172).
2. **"Soon We [Allah] will show them [the humans] Our signs in the Universe and in their [every human's] own <u>souls</u>"** (41:53).

Now here is a question for you:

Q: Have you ever heard an inner voice that says *God is One?*

ATTRIBUTES OF ALLAH – WITHOUT ANTHROPOMORPHISM

The Quran provides another way for believers to relate to Allah, who is absolute in the true sense. Again, this method is also without a trace of anthropomorphism.

The Quran describes Allah by His *attributes*. All attributes are easily understandable, even by an illiterate person. For example, one of the attributes or names of Allah is *the All-Seeing*.

However, it is important that attributes of Allah should be interpreted in the light of the verse **"*there is nothing like Him*"** (42:11). Therefore, the attribute *the All-Seeing* should never be interpreted in human terms or in terms of anything that we can imagine. Otherwise, two interpretations of the Quran (*All-Seeing* and 'there is nothing like Him') would contradict one another, which is not allowed, because the verse (4:82), tells us that the Quran does not have any contradiction anywhere. In addition, our interpretation of *the All-Seeing* should suit the majesty of the Creator of the universe and it should be in line with other attributes of Allah.

That is not all. The Quran says: **"No eye can see Allah, But He sees all visions (of all eyes). He is the *Subtle*, the *Aware*"** (6:103). This verse refers to Allah's attribute: *the Subtle.* He can see through our eyes, without our awareness. In addition to watching everything, He is fully aware of what is going on because, as the verse says, He is *the Aware*. For example, if a person looks at somebody with lust, anger, or hate, Allah is aware. When analyzing the above verse (6:103), we should not fall into the Xenophanes trap. It does not say that Allah sees only *human* visions. His vision includes, but is not limited to, all eyes of all creatures in the universe throughout time. Further, it is beyond human comprehension to discern what Allah can see or how Allah sees.

CAREFUL, IT'S ONLY A SIMILE

Sometimes, the Quran uses human-understandable similes. What if a reader misinterprets the simile in human terms? The verse **"*there is nothing like Him*"** (42:11) is an adequate warning against such anthropomorphism. The Quran also takes one additional step. The following verse *explicitly* (1) informs the reader that the Quran contains similes, and (2) warns against their misinterpretation. It is a very informative verse. To properly explain its meaning, I have divided it into three segments: beginning, middle and end.

> **He is the One Who has revealed to you the Book. Some of its verses are decisive [Arabic word *muhkamat* used here] - they are the *foundation* of the Book - while others are symbolic or allegorical [*mutashabihat*]** [beginning of the verse].

> **Those whose hearts are infected with disbelief, follow the allegorical part to mislead others and to give it their own interpretation, seeking for its hidden meanings. But no one knows its hidden meanings except Allah** [middle of the verse].

> **Those who are *well grounded in knowledge* say: "We believe in it; it is all from our Lord" None will take heed except the people of understanding"** (3:7)[21] [end of the verse].

The beginning segment of 3:7 divides Quranic verses into two groups: **decisive** (*muhkamat*) and **symbolic/allegorical** (*mutashabihat*). The decisive verses (*muhkamat*) clearly have one meaning. They constitute the foundation of understanding of Islam, for example, the four verses of the Quran's chapter Al Ikhlaas, discussed earlier in this chapter. Still, some of these verses also have symbolic meaning (*mutashabihat*), like the name of Allah *the All-Seeing*. Such symbolism allows us to gain knowledge about Allah.

The middle segment of the above verse warns that some people misguide others using symbolic verses, for example, misinterpreting the attribute of Allah, *the All-Seeing*, in human terms. When this happens, human limitations are imposed on the Supreme God. The middle segment prohibits any guesswork about Allah by speculating on hidden meanings.

The final segment of this verse offers three important concepts.

1. **A Muslim should understand the foundation of Islam**. Decisive verses are unambiguous. Words contained in such verses clearly convey their message; there is no confusion or room for guesswork. For example, **"God is alone"** (112:1). Such verses are the foundation of Islam, and the Quran credits the people who know the difference between decisive and allegorical verses, calling them well-grounded in knowledge.

2. **The middle and final segments imply that a Muslim has the authority to reject any scholar's interpretation that conflicts with the foundation of Islam**. Once you know the foundation of Islam, then you are in a position to evaluate the claim made by any scholar as to what the Quran says between the lines or about its hidden meanings. The full verse also implies that ordinary Muslims have the authority to detect and discard misinterpretations proposed by anyone, including scholars. This limits the control of Islamic religious scholars over society. The authority to judge, along with the responsibility of judgement, is passed on to each individual Muslim. For example, a scholar's encouragement to worship another god other than Allah or along with Allah can be rejected because it contradicts monotheistic belief. The last segment of this verse encourages us to reflect and ponder so we can make right decisions. Islam is not just a bunch of do's and don'ts. It is a lifelong spiritual journey of self-improvement, which includes introspection and pondering that leads to right choices.

3. **While rejecting the human interpretation of hidden meanings, continue to believe what is written in the Quran as is**. The symbolic verse of the Quran *itself* should not be rejected. Instead, accept what the Quran says *as is*. A Muslim does not have to know the hidden meaning. For example, do not reject the attribute, *the All-Seeing*; only reject interpretations that suggest that this attribute of Allah is similar to a human or any other creature. Ibn Taymiyyah advised how to interpret simile in the Quran: *"without misinterpreting [the text], without divesting [God of His attributes], without asking how and without comparing [God to His Creation]."*[22]

Allah is never similar to any part of His creation. In addition, He is unlike any human *concept*, because Allah is far beyond human intellect as **"they [humans] do not encompass any knowledge about Allah"** (20:110).

Therefore, making wild guesses about Allah can be very misleading. The Quran has a question for anyone who does so: **"Has Allah indeed permitted you or do you invent [false ideas] to attribute to Allah?"** (10:59).

Isn't it amazing how the Quran solves the impossible problem of limitations of human vocabulary by describing unimaginable Allah using similes? At the same time, it is a test for us, because we are responsible for rejecting scholars who try to convert Islam into a Xenophanic religion, or who make other mistakes.

HOW TO DISTINGUISH THE MUHKAMAT AND MUTASHABIHAT VERSES?

Let us evaluate the following three verses:

All the bounty is in the Hand of Allah (3:73)
Patient men, desirous of the Face of their Lord, who perform the prayer … (13:22)
Construct the ship under Our [Allah's] Eyes (23:27).

If we interpret that the above verses are referring to similarity between a human and Allah, and interpret that these are decisive (*muhkamat)* verses, then our interpretation will contradict the verse **"There is *nothing* similar to Him [Allah]"** (42:11). Such interpretation cannot be accepted because the Quran does not contain any contradictions. Therefore, the verses cannot be *muhkamat.*

So the only other option is to interpret that the above three verses are *mutashabihat,* and therefore face, eyes and hand are just similes. So how do Allah's face, eyes and hand look? As suggested by the above verse (3:7), this question has only one answer, *"we do not know."* Our knowledge is limited. For sure, they are not like those of humans or any known object, in any way. But if we believe the verses are true then, just like idioms, the messages the verses convey are also true. We do not have to know the full details.

Here is a summary of the above discussion:

1. In principle, a Muslim should try to distinguish between the two types of verses: *muhkamat* and *mutashabihat.*
2. Accept the *mutashabihat* verses for their apparent meaning. Do not reject verses.
3. Do not try to figure out the 'real meaning' of *mutashabihat* verses.

4. *Think* and take responsibility for your decisions. Do not follow scholars blindly.
5. Humans can *only* learn about Allah as revealed in the Quran and ahadith. Do not make wild guesses about Allah. Do not ask *how* and *why* about the attributes of Allah.
6. Do not forget that human knowledge is limited.

ALLAH, THE OMNISCIENT

Loosely speaking, humans divide knowledge into two groups: interesting and irrelevant. But in the case of Allah, there is no such distinction. Humans do not care if, three years ago, somewhere in the rainforest, a leaf fell from a tree. But all information is relevant to Allah, because He is the Creator of the leaf and only He can make it fall and decompose, cell by cell: **"… not a leaf falls, but He [Allah] knows it."** (6:59).

The following hadith tells about the extent of the knowledge of Allah: *The first thing which Allah created was the Pen. He commanded it to write. It asked: What should I write? He said: Write the Decree (Al-Qadr). So it wrote what had happened and what was going to happen up to eternity.*[23] This means Allah knew exactly what would occur in the universe, even before the universe was created. This knowledge has already been written down. Allah knows what we have done in the past and everything we will do in the future. For example, **"No human knows what he will earn the next day; and no one knows in what land he will die. Surely, Allah knows all this and is aware of everything"** (31:34). This means all events are predestined [*al-qadr*]. This controversial subject is discussed at greater length later in this book.

In contrast, human knowledge is very limited. **"Allah knows and *you do not know*"** (16:74).

Every bit of knowledge humans have is a gift from Allah. **"They [humans] cannot gain access to anything out of His [Allah's] knowledge except what He pleases"** (2:255).

That is not all. **"No one in the Heavens or the Earth has *the knowledge of the unseen* except Allah"** (27:65).

According to the Quran, **"Are they [humans] not aware that Allah knows their secret thoughts and their secret counsels and that Allah knows what is *beyond human perception*?"** (9:78). This verse says that Allah knows exactly: (1) what we reveal; (2) what we hide from others; and

(3) what we do not even know about ourselves. This means that no human can ever hide a secret from Allah.

In verses 6:27–28, Allah tells the people in hellfire that even *if* they were given a second chance, they would again return to their old sinful ways. This means that the knowledge of Allah is so exhaustive that He knows the outcome of every choice we can make. Suppose a woman receives marriage proposals from two men. She marries one of them. She will know the outcome of only one marriage. However, Allah knows exactly what would have happened if she had chosen the other man. Such ideas are beyond human comprehension.

ALLAH, THE CREATOR

One of the names of Allah is *the Creator (Al-Khaliq)*. Normally, the word *creator* is used to describe a human who makes something. For example, a factory creates hammers. However, it is Allah who created all raw materials, like iron ore, and fuels, like coal or petroleum.

In relation to Allah, the word *creator* has special meaning: **"He [Allah] is the *Originator* of the [seven] Heavens and the Earth"** (6:101). This means that Allah is not only the Creator, but also the Originator of the entire universe.

From a human perspective, when manufacturing (or creation) of an item is complete, control as exercised by the maker ends. For example, after the hammer leaves the factory, the manufacturer no longer controls the hammer. In contrast, Allah's control over Creation is continuous and perpetual.

One of the names of Allah is *Al-Musawwir* (59:24), the Ultimate Designer and Shaper of *every single thing*. As suggested in verse (41:53) above, let us look at the signs of Allah. What does science say about creation and changing matter? Subatomic particles spin, vibrate, and/or revolve, changing the internal and external shape of an atom. Astronomically, all stars are continuously changing shape due to gaseous motion and nuclear fusion. All planets and moons are moving, aging and changing. None of these changes are happening by coincidence. Allah is the one who changes the *shapes* of all matter, at every instant.

How does Allah create matter and make events occur? Feel the infinite power of Allah, as the Quran describes: **"Allah creates whatever *He* wants …. He only says 'EXIST' and it is (created)!"** (3:47). This means that everything in the universe (all nebulae, black holes, quasars, dark matter, quasi-stellar sources, supernovas, suns, planets, moons, asteroids, dust, gasses and all possible life forms) were created because Allah said: EXIST. Creation began and is going through continuous transformations, just as He planned and under His total and continuous control.

Allah is also the one and only Administrator, Provider, and Sustainer of all creation. For Allah, there is no effort, no learning curve, no fatigue, no remorse, no surprises and, of course, no failure. To perform any task, Allah is not dependent on angels, or anyone or anything else. **"Allah is the Self-Sufficient [independent of all, while all are dependent on Him]"** (112:2).

ALLAH IS THE MOST FORGIVING (AL-GHAFOOR) AND DOES JUSTICE (AL-ADL)

Allah's justice and forgiveness are amazingly fair and rational, yet not the same as humans think. The fundamental principle is: **"No bearer shall bear the burden [sin] of another"** (17:15). In other words, you are not responsible for the mistakes of others. At the same time, you will be fully accountable for your own mistakes and sins. One who misguides others is also a sinner, even if s/he does not commit an act of sin.

That is why, in Islam, humanity is not responsible for the sin committed by Adam and Eve. As German Scholar Annemarie Schimmel humorously states, in Islam, the original sin of Adam and Eve is not contagious.[24] In addition, *both* Adam and Eve sinned. Therefore, Allah blamed both of them, not just Eve. Allah asked them, **"Did I not forbid *both of you* to approach that tree"** (7:22). The Quran never singles out Eve as the only sinner. Unlike human justice, Islamic justice is free from gender discrimination.

Human justice is often swayed by emotional attachments to loved ones. In contrast, the verdict of Allah is always just; it is not influenced by misleading emotions. For example, if someone is a close relative of a Prophet, the relative has no special privilege over others. At the time of Prophet Muhammad[PBUH], unconditional tribal loyalties were an essential part of the culture. But Prophet Muhammad[PBUH] explicitly warned the people of his *own tribe,* the Quraish, and seven other tribes, to protect themselves from hellfire, because on the Day of Judgment he would have no power to protect or harm them. He ended this sermon by telling his own daughter Fatima, "I cannot protect you from [the wrath of] Allah."[25] Instead of intercession or blood relationship to the Prophet, Allah's reward/punishment will be based on an individual's belief and deeds.

Interestingly, this approach is in clear contradiction to the Xenophanic theory of a "chosen people." Which states that if gods belong to your race and homeland, then obviously there are some perks; you can expect inherited superiority over the rest of humanity! In contrast, Allah is the Supreme God of the entire universe, therefore, every human is entitled to a fair trial.

What about a person who is compelled by others to sin? Such a person would not be held responsible for his/her actions. For example, Islam strictly prohibits prostitution. However, during the early years of Islam some pagans forced their girl slaves into prostitution. Regarding such victims, the Quran says: **"If anyone forces girls into prostitution, then surely after such a *compulsion* Allah will be forgiving and be merciful to the girls"** (24:33).

Also, Islam does not hold those accountable who do not have the intelligence or maturity to use their free will to commit or avoid a sin. Prophet Muhammad[PBUH] said that *every* child is born completely sinless.[26] This means that, at the time of birth, we are completely innocent and free of guilt. If a child dies before 12 years of age, that child will go to Paradise, regardless of the religion of his/her parents.[27] That is because a young child is not mature enough to choose between right and wrong.

The judgment of Allah is so fair that on the Day of Judgment, every one of us will agree that Allah's verdict is fully justified. The Quran says: **"We [Allah] have fastened the fate of every man to his own neck and on the Day of Judgment We shall bring out for him a book spread wide open, [every human will be told]: 'Here is your book of deeds: read it. *Today you yourself are sufficient to take your own account'*** (17:14).

Allah is overwhelmingly forgiving. All humans, including the Prophets, are required to seek forgiveness from Allah. Toward the end of his life, Prophet Muhammad[PBUH] received the verse: **"Seek His [Allah's] forgiveness: indeed, He repeatedly accepts repentance"** (110:3). This instruction was not just for Prophet Muhammad[PBUH], but for all of us. Every Muslim should hope to receive Allah's forgiveness. If a person sincerely seeks forgiveness, then Allah will forgive over and over and over again. The Quran has many examples of Allah's forgiveness. Adam and Eve both asked for forgiveness of Allah. He not only forgave them both, but also made Adam the first Prophet of humankind. Adam and Eve were put on Earth because it was Allah's prior plan that humankind would inhabit the earth. **"Verily, I am going to place (humankind)**

generations after generations on *earth*" (2:30). They were not sent as punishment for their sin.

Here is another example of Allah's forgiveness. In the Battle of Uhud, Prophet Muhammad^{PBUH} assigned 70 Muslim archers to protect against a pagan attack from behind the Muslim army. He gave strict orders to the archers not to leave their posts under any circumstances.

Early in the battle, the Muslims started winning, and the pagan army fled. After that, the Muslim army followed the centuries-old Arab tradition of looting the war booty (later on, this practice was prohibited). At that time, many archers ignored the Prophet's instruction and left their posts to join the looters. Pagans used this opportunity to attack the Muslims from behind their lines. Consequently, many Muslims died. Several Muslims were injured, including Prophet Muhammad^{PBUH}. Even by today's military standards, such gross disobedience of a commanding officer would warrant severe punishment. Instead, Allah not only forgave the archers, but also commanded other Muslims to forgive them for their negligent and reckless behavior. Further, Allah told the Prophet to pray for their *forgiveness* and to *consult* the guilty archers on various matters, just like the rest of the Muslims. **"*Pardon* them [the disobedient archers] and *ask Allah's forgiveness* for them. Consult them in the conduct of affairs"** (3:159). Honestly, can a human be so generous?

Seeking forgiveness from Allah involves the following steps:
1. One should acknowledge that s/he has sinned. There is no room for denial or false rationalization.
2. *Sincerely* repent of sin and seek forgiveness from Allah.
3. When relevant, fully compensate those against whom damage was done. For example, if you stole someone's money, return it to the rightful owner. If you physically or verbally wronged someone, seek his/her forgiveness. The victim has a choice to forgive or take equal (but not more) revenge.
4. Stop committing the same sin; never repeat the sin in the future. Some bad habits (like drinking alcohol) are hard to quit and, in weakness, a person may repeat this sin. In that case, go back to step 1, because Allah forgives repeatedly. One word of caution: Omniscient Allah knows even our thoughts. So the entire process must be 100 percent sincere.
5. Obey Allah and sincerely worship Him.

Allah says: "Son of Adam, as long as you worship Me and hope in Me I will pardon you in spite of what you have done and I do not care. Son of Adam, if your sins were so numerous as to reach the lofty regions of the sky, then you asked my forgiveness, I would forgive you and I do not care. Son of Adam, if you were to meet me with enough sins to fill the Earth, then meet me, not associating anything with me, I should bring you as much pardon as would fill the Earth."[28]

In Islam, the punishment matches the sin. No one other than Allah can forgive a sin. He is most merciful, most benevolent. If Allah forgives a sin, then there is no punishment for the forgiven sin. But even the smallest sin will be accounted for. Since Allah is most merciful, His rewards for good deeds are much more than what we would expect.

However, there is one sin that Allah will not forgive—if a person *dies* while holding a polytheistic belief. In Islam, the 'sin of polytheism' is called *shirk*. The only way out is, during one's lifetime, a person must seek forgiveness for *shirk* and start believing in Islamic monotheism. This belief should then remain intact throughout one's remaining life. Therefore, *shirk is the greatest sin of all*. Likewise, sincere belief in Islamic monotheism is the greatest virtue.

ALLAH, THE OMNIPOTENT

When it comes to power and authority, once again, Allah is the only God. The Quran spells it out: **"*All power* belong to Allah"** (2:165). This means, nothing happens randomly, naturally on its own or by sheer coincidence. Natural and scientific laws exist because Allah created and enforced them. Allah also gave us the ability to *discover* some of the laws of science.

In the Quran, Allah showed a miracle to a pious scholar, Ezra, by bringing him back to life 100 years after his death (2:259). Allah told Ezra to notice that his food and drink stayed fresh for 100 years, but Ezra's donkey died and was reduced to a skeleton. Then Allah said, **"Look at the bones of your donkey how We bring them together then clothe them with flesh and bring him back to life!"** (2:259). In this example, time was suspended for the scholar's food and drink, while the donkey was brought back to life. When Allah chooses, He can even change the laws of science. This point is illustrated by the following example.

Allah created fire and gave it the property to generate heat. Humans did not independently invent the use of fire by themselves. Instead, it was Allah who taught humans to use fire for cooking, protection against cold and for other purposes. Because, the Quran says: **"no human can grasp anything from Allah's knowledge except what Allah has permitted them to grasp"** (2:255).

However, if omnipotent Allah wants, He can also change fire's exothermic property and make the fire cool and comforting. That happened when pagans tried to punish Prophet Abraham[PBUH] and threw him into a hot inferno of flames. But Allah commanded **"O fire, be coolness and safety upon Abraham"** (21:69). As a result, the law of nature changed and Prophet Abraham[PBUH] remained unharmed.

In conclusion, (1) Allah has total knowledge of everything, (2) Allah makes the laws of nature/science, (3) Allah teaches some of those laws to humans and teaches them how to benefit from them, and (4) these laws will continue to work as long as Allah permits.

ALLAH IS IN TOTAL CONTROL IN ALL AREAS

Allah controls everything in every way: **"He is the One who sends down the rain and He knows what is in the wombs"** (31:34). Islam does not have separate gods to give life and death. Instead, **"He [Allah] gives life and causes death"** (57:2). He makes us rich or poor. **"He gives abundantly to whom He pleases and sparingly to whom He wills"** (42:12). Similarly, we do not age by coincidence or as part of nature. Allah makes this happen. **"He [Allah] delivers you from the womb of your mother as a child, then He makes you grow to reach the age of full strength, then He makes you grow to reach an old age"** (40:67). This verse also tells us that Allah selects our parents and controls our creation and birth.

When it comes to human effort and perception, again Allah is in total control. Suppose you are walking through some bushes. Suddenly you spot a hissing snake, moving fast toward your hand. Your eyes will convey the information, via optic nerves, to your brain. Simultaneously, your auditory system will detect the hissing sound and inform the brain through neural impulses. Next, the brain will combine these two inputs and perceive the snake as a threat; it will order your hand to move away. In this example, and all others, Allah alone controls every event. He gave us our eyes and other sensory organs. He also gave us our brain and the ability to think: **"It is He [Allah] … gave you the faculties of hearing, seeing, feeling and** *understanding*** (67:23).

The question is: who controls human senses? Again, Allah controls all our incoming sensory information. The Quran describes a night when several pagans surrounded the house of Prophet Muhammad^PBUH. Their plan was to assassinate him in his sleep. But under Allah's control, without any fight or resistance, Prophet Muhammad^PBUH simply walked past the pagan encirclement, and none of the pagans even saw him. That was because: **"We [Allah] have covered them [pagans] over so they cannot see"** (36:9). In other words, Allah controls our senses.

How about mental perception and consequent emotions like fear, happiness and sadness? Again, Allah controls human perception, including the emotion of fear. Prophet Moses^PBUH was afraid to go to the oppressive pharaoh to preach to him about Islam, so Allah gave Prophet Moses^PBUH a special blessing to prevent fear: **"draw your hand towards yourself to ward off fear"** (28:32). Allah controls our happiness and sadness as well: **"He *alone* causes us to laugh and to cry"** (53:43). Allah controls the results of our efforts: **"He will cause your deeds to be virtuous"** (33:71).

Allah makes us remember or forget (87:6). Our approval or disapproval of others is based on how we perceive them. Since Allah controls our perceptions, it's no wonder He also controls our inter-personal relationships. Allah told Prophet Muhammad^PBUH that **"[Allah] increased your fame"** (94:4). Only Allah gives us higher or lower social status. A prayer in the Quran, praises Allah: **"You [Allah] give honor to whom You please"** (3:26). What about our desires? It turns out that Allah controls even our desires! **"You cannot will, except by the will of Allah"** (76:30).

Since Allah has total control, there is no point in comparing the plan of Allah to human effort. If human effort conflicts with the will of Allah, then human plans and subsequent efforts are useless. The Quran describes Prophet Jacob's^PBUH plan to protect his sons. But no human plan can override the will of Allah: **"it [the plan] did not avail them [sons of Prophet Jacob^PBUH] against the will of Allah"** (12:68).

The power of Allah is so exhaustive that human actions can occur only if He permits them. **"Allah has created you and all that you do"** (37:96). That is why the Quran advises: **"Never say of anything 'I will certainly do it tomorrow' without adding: 'If Allah wills!'"** (18:23–24). Allah also gives humans the ability to choose between right and wrong.

Similar to other Abrahamic faiths, Islam teaches belief in satan. In Islam, satan has the ability to tempt us or lure us into believing that sin is attractive. But satan cannot take any action or compel us in any way. On the Day of Judgment, satan will also be sent into hellfire and punished along with the rest of the sinners. The Quran records satan's statement on the Day of Judgment. **Satan will say [to humans in hell]: "*I had no power over you.* I just invited you and [without thinking] you accepted my invitation"** (14:22). To avoid the temptations of satan, one must use the guidance of Allah and one's intellect and reasoning.

Satan has the ability to tempt us with evil thoughts. How can humans stop wrongful *thoughts*? For sure our will power cannot stop our thoughts. This seems like an impossible goal. But, the Quran provides a solution: **"If Satan will try to seduce you, seek refuge in Allah"** (7:200).

Only Allah can award a person with entry into Paradise! Even the most committed and pious worshipper cannot enter Paradise on the grounds of good deeds alone. Only after Allah showers a monotheistic believer with His mercy will that believer qualify for Paradise. The mere act of worship does not give a believer sovereign control, power or authority. **"He whomever You [Allah] have saved from evil on the Day of Judgment has certainly been granted Your mercy"** (40:9). As a rule of thumb, Allah was, is and will always be in complete and total control of everything in every way.

Then what causes bad luck? Just like a Muslim is supposed to believe in Allah, in His Prophets, in angels and the Day of Judgement; a Muslim should also believe that all good luck and all bad luck is given by Allah. He is the only One who controls all our pleasant and unpleasant endings. For example, Prophet Joseph[PBUH] conveyed the message of Allah that predicted the destiny of an inmate that he "**will be crucified**" (12.41).

You have to admit that if the Quran says **"*all power* belong to Allah"** (2:165), there is no contradiction. Since Allah is the only God, it is no wonder, that He is the only Controller. How can we expect anything else?

CONTROL OF ALLAH VS. HUMAN EFFORT

What is the maximum extent of human effort? What is beyond human control and exclusively under God's command? For centuries, philosophers and illiterate people alike have been trying to figure out the answer to these crucial questions. Islam answers them by insisting that Allah is omnipotent in every aspect. Allah exclusively controls not only destiny but all human *actions, experiences and even perceptions*. Does this mean that humans are only puppets without free will? Then what is the justification of divine punishment?

FREE WILL AND THE PREDESTINATION PARADOX

EXPLANATION OF THE PARADOX

Ted Bundy was a serial killer. A Florida court found him guilty of murdering more than 30 women. He was executed in 1989. His case is referenced here only to elucidate the ever controversial 'free will and predestination' paradox.

Bundy was born out of wedlock and had an unhappy childhood. His birth and upbringing were out of his control. The question is: given his background, was Bundy predestined to commit these murders, or did he have a choice to avoid them? Many children are born out of wedlock, yet they do not grow up to become serial killers. Did Genetic factors compel Bundy to commit murders (biological determinism)? If so, would he still face divine punishment?

Every one of us faces similar albeit generally less extreme questions in our own daily lives when we try to make sense out of uncontrollable and deeply disturbing threats around us. Fear of an unpredictable future drives the popularity of astrology and superstition (like a broken mirror that causes bad luck). Which calamities are meant to be, and what can we change by our efforts? Throughout history, these questions have attracted both theist and atheist scholars and philosophers, as well as ordinary people. Theists have offered a broad spectrum of explanations, from stoic causal determinism to dialogues between Zeus and Odysseus. Elaborate rationalizations have been provided that God's knowledge of our future does not interfere with human free will. The only definite conclusion to this continuously controversial subject has been that it cannot be satisfactorily concluded. In the profound words of Albert Einstein: "If this being is omnipotent, then every occurrence, including every human action, every human thought and every human feeling and aspiration is also His work; how is it possible to think of holding a man responsible for their deeds and thoughts before such an almighty Being? In giving out punishments and rewards, He would to a certain extent be passing judgment on Himself. How can this be combined with the goodness and righteousness ascribed to Him?"[29]

WHAT DOES THE QURAN SAY ABOUT FREE WILL AND PREDESTINATION?

We have already discussed that Allah is in total and continuous control of every action or movement of all entities. Allah also controls every single scientific law. The domain of Allah's kingdom is the entire universe and six other skies. Allah even controls our thoughts.

Support of Predestination in the Quran: The following verses support predestination because it says that Allah fully controls human fate: **"God leads astray or guides to the right path whomever He wants"** (6:39). And **"You cannot will, except by the will of Allah"** (76:30).

Support of Free will in the Quran: The following verse says that humans have free will to choose between good and evil: **"O Prophet, proclaim: 'The truth is from your Lord.' Then whosoever wills, let him believe and whosoever wills, let him disbelieve"** (18:29).

Another verse says that the Quran does not have a contradiction: **"Will they not ponder on the Quran? Had it not come from someone other than God, they would have certainly found therein many contradictions"** (4:82).

In the context of predestination and free will, verses (76:30) and (18:29) seem to contradict. *How to reconcile?* The following section discusses this issue.

HUMAN INTENTION AND THE WILL OF ALLAH

Islam makes the following distinction:

Difference between Intention *and Action*

Suppose you intend to make a fist with your right hand, and you successfully do this. This means Allah allowed you to fulfill your intention. A person with a disabled right hand would be unable to act upon the same intention. In that case, Allah did not permit the action. So, *human intentions play an important role*, but Allah is *always* the Doer behind the scenes. According to Muslim philosopher and thinker Abu-l-Hasan al-Ash`ari (d:936 CE) "Actions of human beings are created (makhluq) by God, the creatures are not capable of creating any action."[30] This means that if a person has a serious sinful intent and plans to act on it, that person becomes a sinner the moment s/he takes their very first step toward that action. Prophet Muhammad[PBUH] said that, "if two Muslims take out their swords to fight each other, then both of them will be from amongst the people of the Hell-Fire." It was asked of the Prophet, 'It is alright for the killer but what about the killed one?' He replied, "The killed one had the *intention* to kill his opponent."[31] Here the Prophet is describing that the judgment of Allah is primarily based on our intentions. It must be noted that humans do not think in this fashion.

What about good intentions? Allah is most generous. He may reward us for good intentions, even for non-religious acts or, at times, without doing any action at all. The Prophet said, "If a man spends on his family sincerely for Allah's sake, then it is an alms-giving reward for him."[32] In summary, according to Prophet Muhammad[PBUH], "The reward of deeds depends on the intention."[33]

Act of worship performed with improper intention

A human judge declares a suspect guilty based on his/her illegal actions. In contrast, Allah has an entirely different set of criteria for judgment. Allah has total knowledge of both our intentions and our actions. So the judgment of Allah is primarily based on our intentions. The following hadith explains the significant role of intentions.

On the Day of Judgment, Allah would judge a man who would claim, "I fought for you [O Allah] until I died as a martyr." Allah would say, "You have told a lie. You fought so that people call you a brave warrior, and you were called so."

Similarly, another person would claim he acquired knowledge, taught others, and recited the Quran. Again, Allah would reject the claim because the man's goal was to get worldly recognition as a scholar, and Allah gave him recognition in the world itself.

A third person may claim that he generously donated wealth to charity. Again, Allah would judge that person as a liar because his real goal was to gain worldly recognition as a generous donor and he was recognized as a donor in this world. Allah would order hellfire for these three sinners.[34]

It must be noted that martyrdom, scholarship and charity are recognized as acts of Islamic worship. In the above three cases, even if the acts of worship were performed, the intentions behind them were to obtain the approval of other humans. So Allah rewarded those people with what they sought, *worldly recognition.*

Islam expects pristine monotheistic belief, in which both the intention and the act of worship are performed to please Allah alone and none other. Islam even defines a term for the scenario in which worship of Allah is performed with the intention of worldly recognition. Prophet Muhammad[PBUH] called it *riyaa* or 'hidden shirk.' Here is an example of riyaa: "A man will stand and pray and lengthen his prayer because he sees someone looking at him [so that he gets approval as a pious person]."[35]

The approval of other humans has no significance because Allah says: **"Who can protect you from Allah if He intends to harm you or who can prevent Him if He intends to show you mercy"** (33:17)? If a believer tries to impress onlookers with his/her worship, this simply means that s/he does not possess the correct concept of Allah. Because only Allah gives respect or humiliation.

Polytheism is usually defined as worshipping more than one god. Islam adds another characteristic to its definition. In Islam, polytheism can also exist if a believer has *wrong intentions.* In such a case, even the act of worship itself becomes an act of sin. This means that merely a verbal commitment to monotheism is inadequate. *A Muslim should honestly believe in monotheism, not just by the tongue but also by heart; this includes the correct intentions to please and worship Allah alone.*

What happens first? Identifying the cause and its effect

Let us analyze the order of events in the following verse: **"Allah has never changed the blessings which He has bestowed on a people until they changed the condition of their souls"** (8:53). The first step is that people must change their thinking and intentions. After that, if Allah decides, He changes their external environment. In other words, Allah allows the intentions of those people to influence events. So intentions are the triggers. Based on this, if Allah sees fit, He then causes the events to occur.

Allah is the only Doer. Therefore only Allah can open our hearts and minds to see His guidance. Humans cannot do this on their own. This applies to all our actions: **"Allah has created you and all that you do"** (37:96), along with the input from our senses and our perception: **"As for those who reject Faith; it is the same, whether you (O Prophet) warn them or you don't, they will not believe [Allah judged that their determination to reject faith is final]. Allah has sealed their hearts and their hearing, their eyes are covered, and there is a grievous punishment for them"** (2:6-7). This subtle point reveals the beauty of Islam. If you believe that a human is an independent doer, then God can no longer be the Almighty! Why? Because God no longer has control over the independent doers. In Islam, Allah, the Almighty, is the only Doer.

However, Allah has also given us the *free will* to choose between right and wrong: **"O Prophet, proclaim: 'The truth is from your Lord.' Then whosoever wills, let him believe, and whosoever wills, let him disbelieve"** (18:29).

Why does Allah seal the hearts?

The verse (2:6–7), quoted above, says that if a person holds an unwavering *intention* to reject all invitations to Islamic guidance [Allah will know when the intention is final], then Allah seals the heart of such a person from further guidance.

Why does Allah seal the heart? That is because there is only one Allah and *no event* in the universe can occur unless Allah allows it: **"all power belongs to Allah"** (2:165). Therefore *only* Allah can seal the hearts. However, the *person is responsible for choosing the wrong intention.* That is why the Quran categorically states this principle: **"The fact is that Allah does not do injustice to humankind in any way: but men are unjust to their own souls"** (10:44). In other words, we are responsible for rejecting guidance by our choice. Allah is not responsible. Similarly, the above discussed verse **"God leads astray or guides to the right path whomever He wants"** (6:39). should be interpreted without contradicting the above verse (10:44). The verse says when humans have bad intentions, then Allah would lead them astray. On the other hand, when people have right intentions Allah would guide them to the right path.

When Allah has total control, how can Humans be responsible for their good or bad intentions?

We cannot act independently on our own. All our actions occur only if Allah wills them. The question is, if Allah controls everything, then which part is within human control? Why did the verse 18:29, quoted above, say that Allah gave us the freedom to choose between right and wrong?

This point needs explanation. If Allah alone is responsible for every movement of every subatomic particle in the entire universe, including every neuron in the brain, then how can a human be accountable for what s/he chooses or intends? As Einstein's preceding quote puts it, "Every human action, every human thought, and every human feeling, and aspiration are also His [God's] work."[36] Though Einstein's statement is logical, but do not forget it is based on *human logic*, originating from a human mind. His conclusion carries an unspoken assumption: *since Almighty God has total control, therefore humans cannot be responsible for their intentions.* In other words, logically, it is impossible for God to create a human who is fully responsible for his/her intentions.

But is this a valid assumption? For all religions based on the Xenophanic model, this assumption makes perfect sense. When a religion claims that a god became human, this statement inherently enforces human limitations on god. It means that, just like an ordinary human, the god also has skeletal, circulatory, nervous, muscular, respiratory, endocrine, immune, urinary, integumentary, reproductive, and digestive systems. Just like a human, that god's DNA is also made from nucleotides. Otherwise, do not say God is a man. Once you accept that a god is bound by the physical limitations of a human, then it makes sense to assume that the god is also constrained by humans' *logical* limitations! To prove otherwise, particularly in the context of the free will-predestination paradox, would require a great deal of linguistic artistry.

Can we justify imposing human limitations on Allah?

Let us refer to the Quran to see if Allah is analogous to a human in any way. If we fail to find *even a single* item of proof of such resemblance, *it makes no sense to extend human limitation onto Allah*. Here is the evidence.

1. Islam is not a Xenophanic religion at all. In the entire Quran, there is not a single incident of anthropomorphism.

2. Allah is beyond human imagination. Muslims are prohibited from even imagining anything similar to Allah: "**There is nothing like Him [Allah]**" (42:11).

3. The Quran orders: "**Compare none with Allah. Surely Allah knows and you do not know**" (16:74). When a human compares Allah to any entity, s/he has no choice but to use human logic, which does not apply to Allah. That is why the first part of the above verse prohibits comparing any entity to Allah. The second half of the verse tells the reason why. Because of our limited human knowledge, there will always be ideas and circumstances that humans will be unable to solve or understand.

4. That is not all. The Quran strictly prohibits anyone from making wild guesses about Allah: "**Has Allah indeed permitted you or do you invent (ideas) to attribute to Allah**" (10:59)? Even if the Quran encourages us to ponder creation, the same Quran instructs us not to analyze Allah or draw conclusions about Allah based on human logic.

5. Since humans have limited knowledge, and Allah is beyond human imagination; human rules, ethics, and logic are not applicable to Allah. It therefore makes no sense for a created being even to question Allah: "**He [Allah] is accountable to none about what He does, but they [entire humanity] are accountable to Him**" (21:23).

Based on the above evidence, it makes *no sense to claim that human logic and limitations are applicable to Allah.* He is not created by human imagination; instead, Allah is the Creator of the entire universe, including the human mind. Here is just one example of the uniqueness of Allah. In Xenophanes' quote above, gods are begotten, just like humans. However, in the case of Allah, there is no similarity to humans: "**He [Allah] begets not, nor is He begotten**" (112:3).

Reconciliation Proposal # 1

Let us consider following two seemingly contradictory statements:

1. <u>Humans are responsible because they have free will</u>: "**O Prophet, proclaim: 'The truth is from your Lord.' Then whosoever**

wills, let him believe, and whosoever wills, let him disbelieve"
(18:29). And

2. <u>Humans are powerless to act on their own</u>: "**Allah has created
   you and all that you do**" (37:96).

Since Allah is not bound by human limitations, *Allah can give humans ability
to 'intend' in such a way where humans can fully exercise their own 'free will.'* Therefore
following two statements simultaneously remain true:

(1) Allah gave humans free will such that humans remain entirely
    responsible for what they intend.
(2) Throughout, Allah remains in total control of everything, in every
    way. Based in intentions, only Allah can seal the hearts or guide a
    person.

Reconciliation proposal # 2

Let us consider following two statements:

1. <u>Support of predestination</u>: "**You cannot will, except by the will
   of Allah**" (76:30).
2. <u>Support of free wills:</u> "**O Prophet, proclaim: 'The truth is from
   your Lord.' Then whosoever wills, let him believe, and
   whosoever wills, let him disbelieve**" (18:29).

We discussed in chapter 1 that there is nothing similar to Allah. He has
ability to say 'EXIST' and events occur. Allah is not bound by human logic.
Therefore, even if it is beyond human imagination, *Allah can make the
predestination and free will coexist.* It will be a mistake to claim that just because
humans can't do something then *Allah cannot do it* either. Unless supported
by the Quran and hadith, no human should make a *wild guess* about Allah
what Allah can or cannot do. The Quran prohibits that "**Has Allah
indeed permitted you, or do you invent (ideas) to attribute to Allah**"
(10:59)?

We do not understand how 'predestination and free can coexist.' That is
because we do not have adequate knowledge or the ability to understand
(see verse 16:74 above). And again "**There is nothing like Him [Allah]**"
(42:11).

Please note that this argument is not a rationalization forced to fit the
explanation. The concept of anthropomorphism-free Islamic monotheism

and above-quoted verses (42:11) and (16:74) are from the Quran itself. They are not the author's own arguments.

Here is a challenge to all readers who believe that human logic should be applicable to Allah. In the Quran, find just one instance in which Allah is precisely the same as a human. Please do not use hidden meanings or similes, as prohibited in verse 3:7 (chapter 1 of this dissertation). Also, your interpretation should not contradict any verse of the Quran.

Divine reward/punishment will be based on choices we make with our free will

Throughout this life, our knowledge is limited. Still, we have the freedom to accept the guidance of Allah or reject it. We have the ability to choose between good and bad. We have the limited capability to ponder and plan for our future. We have the freedom to act (in some areas) or to change the course of our lives. Some of us turn to Islam, while others turn away.

However, the moment a person dies, it is a different scenario. We no longer have free will and the ability to act. On the Day of Judgment, we will be given full memory of our good and bad deeds along with some necessary new knowledge so we will be able to fairly evaluate ourselves. Nothing relevant will be ignored. We will be unable to change or falsely defend anything. We will be surprised to see our book of deeds, which overlooks nothing. On the Day of Judgment, every one of us will agree that Allah's verdict is fair and just, "**On the Day of Judgment, We will bring forth the record of his [every human's] actions in the form of a wide-open book. We will tell him, "Read it and judge for yourself"**" (17:14). Even the people in hell will accept full responsibility for their sins, "**had we listened (to the Prophets) or used our minds, we would not have become the dwellers of hell**" (67:10).

On the Day of Judgment, no one would blame predestination for their mistakes.

Is "I do not know" a valid answer?

Point #3 and verse 16:74 mentioned above use the phrase, 'do not know.' Is this a valid answer? Suppose a high school student gives this answer in an examination; the student will get no credit for that question. In school exams, 'I do not know' is the same as a wrong answer.

But what if you are discussing Allah and you face a challenging question? Suppose its answer cannot be found in the Quran and ahadith. Then 'I do not know' is not only valid but also the only correct answer. Because wrong answers or wild guesses can mislead others. On the Day of Judgment, the person providing wrong information will be held accountable. We humans have been given only limited knowledge about Allah and many other subjects. Making wild guesses about Allah is strictly prohibited. Allah told the Prophet Noah, "**Do not ask me about that which you have no knowledge**" (11:46). Even Prophets did not have all knowledge. In this context, 'do not know' is not a weak or wrong answer. Instead, in some situations, it is the only correct answer.

Wait for the Full Explanation

Given that human limitations are not applicable to Allah, how does Islam explain the free will and predestination question? After all, the curiosity of the human mind does not rest. At some point, we would like to have a comprehensible answer, particularly if that answer involves divine punishment.

Islam only *postpones the explanation* to this question, it does not ignore it. The Creator of the universe takes it upon Himself to explain all paradoxes and questions. Allah advises believers to tell non-believers regarding their arguments and doubts: "**Be patient until Allah judges between us [on the Day of Judgment], for He is the best of all judges**" (7:87). On the Day of Judgment, Allah will settle all of our arguments. This includes every philosophical question we can imagine. It includes the free will-predestination paradox and the responsibility for horrific actions committed by humans like Ted Bundy.

During this life, a Muslim is supposed to believe in the unseen Allah, ponder the signs of Allah for spiritual support, and obey Allah. When in doubt, the best advice comes from an Urdu couplet:

> Tu dil mein to aata hi, samajh mein nahi aata
> Main jaan gaya bas teri pehchan yahi hai.

> *Allah, I can feel You in my heart, but fail to understand You*
> *Finally, I figured out how to recognize You!*

Lack of knowledge does not mean lack of guidance

Once a companion of the Prophet asked him, "Can a person give up good deeds and rely on predestination?" Prophet Muhammad[PBUH] instructed him to continue doing the good deeds and recited this verse: "**Who gives in charity, fears Allah and testifies to goodness, We [Allah] shall facilitate for him the easy way**" (92:5-7).[37]

Predestination does not mean that we give up our efforts. Once Prophet Muhammad[PBUH] noticed a Bedouin (nomadic Arab) had left his camel untied. Prophet Muhammad[PBUH] asked the Bedouin: "Why don't you tie down your camel?" The Bedouin responded, "I put my trust in Allah." The Prophet said, "Tie your camel first, then put your trust in Allah."[38] In other words, we should always put forth the best effort within our means first, and only then rely on Allah's predestination.

ISLAM RESPONDS TO ATHEISM

Verses "**there is nothing like Him**" (42:11). and "**Allah knows and you do not know**" (16:74) not only refute atheism but also challenge the foundation of atheistic ideology. Atheism is based on following logic:

Atheist assume just because a human cannot imagine how free will and predestination can coexist, therefore it is impossible for God as well.

For example, Einstein said, "If this being is omnipotent, then every occurrence, including every human action, every human thought and every human feeling and aspiration is also His work; *how is it possible to think of holding a man responsible for their deeds and thoughts before such an almighty Being?*"

In the last sentence of the above quote, Einstein assumed that God is constrained by human logic and limitations. As a result, 'free will and predestination' cannot coexist.

General atheist ideology is based on similar logic:

A. God exists.
B. God is a man and God is constrained by human logic.
C. Next, the atheists prove that a God constrained by human limitations cannot exist. This is an oxymoron.

The above assumptions imply that the initial stage of atheism is to believe that God exists and God is a human. Then they claim that a human-God cannot exist.

This approach is certainly applicable in context of all Xenophanic religions because they encompass the concept of human-god. However, the atheist has no explanation for Islam, a non-Xenophanic religion. When Allah is *not* bound by human logic, how can they use the same human logic to prove that Allah does not exist?

Need further proof? *In the entire Quran, find just one incident of anthropomorphism in which Allah is the same as a human*. Please do not use *hidden meanings* or *similes* as discussed in (3:7), and do not contradict the Quran, as in verse (4:82).

The subject of 'Anthropology of Religion' confirms that throughout history people have been strongly attracted to the Xenophanes' versions of the divine. Why has Islamic monotheism stayed so pristine? Something to think about.

CHAPTER 3

QURAN: THE WORD OF ALLAH

PERSONAL PERSPECTIVE: A SUSPICIOUS START

I was born into a prominent Muslim family, but during the first thirty years of my life, I did not give much importance to the religion. Luckily, my parents kept encouraging me to improve my understanding of Islam, and transform myself into a good practicing Muslim. Sometime in mid-30s, I had an unforgettable spiritual experience. Narrating the experience would be out of context here, but the message it conveyed was loud and clear: *God is One.* I knew right away that, undoubtedly, God was an eternal reality, more real than the existence of the universe. This spiraled into my earnest quest for an in-depth study of the religion of Islam.

Until that point in time, the only important thing I knew was that Islam is a monotheistic religion and that Prophet Muhammad[PBUH] was a Prophet. Still, this one small bit of knowledge of Islam was enough to raise a big question in my mind: Did Prophet Muhammad[PBUH] share divinity with Allah, *even once*? I was hesitant to seek the answer to this question, since in my heart of hearts I feared what might happen if the answer was yes, then what?

For me, worshiping a human-god overlap was no longer an option, because it would directly conflict with my "one God" experience. But eventually, I pushed myself to ask my mother, "Prophet Muhammad[PBUH] was, er…a human, right?" Without hesitation, she recited a line from the Muslim ritual supplication. *"Ashhdu anna Muhammadan abduhu wa Rasooluhu."* She explained its meaning as, "I bear witness that Prophet Muhammad[PBUH] is a *slave* of Allah and a messenger." Here, the word slave means that Prophet Muhammad[PBUH] was a creation of Allah and only human. (The word *slave* as defined in chapter 2).

This meant that there exists a real religion that matches my internal experience. The relief I felt was overwhelming. The above line from the ritual supplication opened my eyes, because it gave so much significance to being a slave of Allah. I noticed that the word *slave* came *before* the word *Prophet*, so the understanding is done with correct perspective. In Islam, this line is highly emphasized, because a believer repeats it daily, a total of nine times in five obligatory ritual supplications. With this encouragement, my next step was to read the Quran more intimately and more ardently.

At that time I was still suspicious if the Quran was a book from God, and a shade too proud of my modern education. So, before starting to read the Quran, I made up my mind that if I discovered even a trace of polytheism or found a single instance in which a human becomes God, I would immediately stop reading then and there. My attention was therefore focused on finding any instance in which a human takes over control from Allah, such as when a pious human becomes so powerful even God cannot harm that person, or when s/he tricks God into promising or doing something God did not intend.

Besides this main point of debate, there were other minor expectations I had in mind. For example, the book of God should not contain any scientific absurdities. Additionally, I wanted to ensure that the book of God was written for all humanity, not just the people who influenced the *personal* life of Prophet Muhammad[PBUH], like his wife, parents, children, close friends and enemies. I hoped that the Quran answered some serious philosophical questions that have baffled the human mind for centuries. These were very high expectations from a book that originated about 1400 years ago in a remote desert.

Surprisingly, I found that reading just a few pages of the Quran was sufficient to eradicate my false pride. I was convinced it is no ordinary book. As discussed in chapter 1, on the pattern of the lion and the horse, a human will think like a human. If a human writes a book, you do not have to be a genius to see human footprints in the writing. But in the entire Quran, human footprints are missing. Instead, you notice only the signs of Allah. The Quran is a miracle of Allah in countless ways.

PRESERVATION OF THE TEXT OF THE QURAN

The Quran makes an unusual but conclusive promise: **"We [Allah] have without doubt sent down the Message [the Quran]; and *We will assuredly guard it* [from corruption]"** (15:9). No human can guarantee that even a single concrete building will remain unchanged or undamaged over a decade. A book is far more fragile than a concrete structure! The contents of a book can easily be edited to change their meaning with a single comma; sentences and even chapters can be removed, or new text can be added. Every single copy of a book can be destroyed, its text can become illegible, and its language can become extinct over time. Against such great odds, after 1400 years, how did the Quran survive in its original form? Next let us examine this uniqueness of the Book a bit more closely.

In 610 CE, Allah revealed five verses of the Quran to Prophet Muhammad[PBUH] through Archangel Gabriel. The revelations of the Quran then continued to be revealed in small segments for approximately the next 22 years. As each new segment was revealed, Prophet Muhammad[PBUH] was the first person to memorize it. He also instructed several of his companions to do the same. Those who memorized the entire Quran were recognized as *Huffaz*, or protectors or guardians of the Quran.

From the beginning of the revelations, Prophet Muhammad[PBUH] ordered that the Quran would be written down. Before the death of the Prophet in 632 CE, the entire Quran was completed and compiled in a preset, divine order. The divine revelations were painstakingly preserved in written form (though it was still inscribed in segments on different kinds of writing materials available then), and were also memorized by several hundred Huffaz. After the death of Prophet Muhammad[PBUH], the first caliph Abu Bakr ordered the entire Quran to be compiled into one complete volume. This was saved as the master copy. When the Islamic Empire expanded to places like Iran, Syria, and Egypt, the third caliph, Usman (reign 644–656), ordered several duplicates of the master copy to be scribed and sent to different parts of the Muslim kingdom.[39] One early copy of the original Quran of that era is still preserved in the Museum of Istanbul. Every letter and every word of the Quran is from Allah. It does not contain any word of the companions or scribes, or even Prophet Muhammad's[PBUH] own words. The Quran only contains the revelations given to Prophet Muhammad[PBUH]. It is the literal word of God.

The Quran presents an interesting challenge: **"Produce one chapter like this [the Quran], you may even call to your aid anyone you want other than Allah"** (10:38). This was a humiliating challenge to Mecca's pagans, who took great pride in being Arabic poets. Throughout history, many efforts were made to meet this challenge. But every time someone composed some poetry, it looked ridiculously inferior to the verses of the Quran.

Like other religions, Islam also has sects with sharp differences. But no sect could support its beliefs by manually altering the Quran. No sect could add to the Quran, even the name of their favorite saint. For this reason, even today, all the main sects of Islam follow exactly the same Quran—a fact one can easily verify.

PRESERVATION OF THE INTERPRETATION OF THE QURAN

In addition to the Quran, Prophet Muhammad[PBUH] also gave us the ahadith, the second most important source of Islamic teaching. Both came from Allah. However, there is one important difference between the Quran and hadith: as far as the Quran is concerned, it is beyond human capability to alter it; no one can add or subtract its text. However, even though the bulk of the hadith was carefully collected by various scholars, it is not preserved with the same degree of purity and accuracy as the Quran. Hence, scholars classify some ahadith as authentic and other ahadith as unauthentic, or from unverified sources.

TRANSMISSION OF HADITH

In the early phase of Islam, most of the ahadith were memorized. However, some people began to write some ahadith even during the life time of the Prophet. Early Muslims meticulously followed, shared, and passed on this guidance. After Prophet Muhammad[PBUH], the community of companions was relatively small, and they knew the ahadith without confusion. However, after a few generations, Islam spread to distant lands and the community grew in size. As a result, mere informal verbal communication of ahadith was no longer adequate.

To preserve knowledge, dedicated Muslims of early generations therefore made commendable efforts to find and collect the original ahadith. Scholars traveled hundreds of miles and spent a great many resources just to verify from the original narrator if a particular hadith was true.[40] To avoid confusion, the Umayyad Caliph Umar ibn Abdul Aziz (reign: 717–719 C.E.) encouraged scholars to compile and write the ahadith.[41]

IMPORTANT ROLE OF HADITH

The hadith is an essential part of Islam. For example, the Quran does not provide a step-by-step procedure on how to pray the ritual supplication or perform the *Hajj* pilgrimage. Only the ahadith provide these and other important details. Also, the hadith plays a key role in preventing misrepresentation of the Quran.

The exegesis and explanations of the Quran, presented by Prophet Muhammad[PBUH], are preserved only in the hadith. This means that, throughout history, scholars did not have the freedom to interpret the Quran to suit their liking. Instead, every exegesis of the Quran must be in line with the interpretation of Prophet Muhammad[PBUH]. German diplomat and Islamic author Murad Hofmann concludes, "*…the Quran can only be properly understood if one is familiar with the historical context of individual revelations [available from* hadith] *and the coherent inner thread of text.*"[42] Thus, the hadith protects the Quran from any ill-intended exegesis.

Unfortunately, some Muslims believe that only the Quran is adequate and all ahadith can be ignored. This makes no sense. For example, names of caliphs Abu-Bakr, Umar, Usman, and Ali do not appear in the Quran. Still, no Muslim in their right mind would say that they were not real people. Similarly, the hadith tells us the location of the grave of Prophet Muhammad[PBUH]. Allah mandates that Muslims should consult the hadith to understand the Quran: **"We have revealed to you [Prophet Muhammad[PBUH]] the Book [The Quran] so that *you may explain* to them the reality of those things in which they differ"** (16:64).

PROTECTION OF THE INTERPRETATION OF THE QURAN

The Quran also protects the religion of Islam from *evolving with time,* or ending up as a polytheistic religion. Allah says: **"I have perfected your religion for you, completed my favor upon you and approved Al-Islam as a Deen [religion]"** (5:3). Because of this verse, no deviant sect emerging after Prophet Muhammad[PBUH] can argue that Islam can be perfected by including polytheism.

The Quran also says that Prophet Muhammad^{PBUH} was the very last Prophet and messenger: **"He [Muhammad^{PBUH}] is the Prophet of Allah and the Seal [last] of the Prophets"** (33:40). This means that, after Prophet Muhammad^{PBUH}, no Muslim saint can claim to be a new Prophet, apostle, or messenger of Allah, or add polytheism or introduce a self-proclaimed-god scenario.

However, verse 41:53 leaves the door open to include modern scientific miracles as signs of Allah (Chapter 2).

WHY DID ALLAH NOT PROTECT THE HADITH JUST LIKE THE QURAN?

Why are all verses of the Quran not as clear as the fundamental verses, and why are all ahadith not preserved like the Quran? It would have been a lot simpler for Muslims to understand precise instructions, instead of having to search for truth and face confusion.

As far as the fundamentals of the Quran are concerned, they are clear as daylight. Even an illiterate Muslim can understand that Allah is the one and only God. What about the *mutashabihat* verses? The answer is that Allah says: **"Do the people think that they will be left alone on saying 'We believe,' and that they will not be *tested*? We [Allah] did *test* those who have gone before them"** (29:2-3).

The Quran also tells us to ponder and reflect. It further guides us on *how to solve* issues by interpreting the allegorical verses in light of the fundamentals of the Quran. With this guidance to help us, our responsibility is to pray, study, learn from others, think, discuss and then, finally, using our intellect, make the right choices.

When it comes to a test from Allah, we normally only think of physical hardship and endurance. However, any confusion, and how we try to resolve a situation, is also a part of the divine test. For example, in the Battle of Uhud, it was rumored that Prophet Muhammad^{PBUH} had been martyred. Some Muslims became disheartened, while some remained firm in their faith. Here Allah tested the companions on how they reacted to confusion during an unexpected calamity.

PRESERVATION OF THE LANGUAGE OF THE QURAN

Language plays a pivotal role in communicating a message. As languages age, new words are added, unused words are discarded, and the meaning of some words get altered. Sociopolitical factors play a key role. For example, the amount of entertainment/literary/technical/news material available in a language affects its popularity. That is why in the last 200 years, the English language has become so popular. Over time, in a less used language, some words become undefined, or their meaning becomes ambiguous. Gradually, people may even stop using such language entirely. In our era of globalization, languages compete fiercely with one another for survival.

The language of the Quran is Arabic, which was also the mother tongue of Prophet Muhammad[PBUH]. In pre-Islamic days, the Arabian Desert was surrounded by the eastern wing of the Roman (Byzantine) and Persian Empires. Both of them had hundreds of years of rich cultural and linguistic heritage. In contrast, Arab lands were sparsely populated by farmers and traders who were more often than not divided into warring tribes. The majority of pre-Islamic Arabic literature did not have much depth, and only talked about desert-related subjects like *"camels, horses, women, tribal chiefs, tribal wars and tribal histories."*[43] All odds were against the Arabic language.

To preserve the meaning of the Quran, Allah protected not only its text, but also its language. After 1400 years, Arabic is one of the most thriving language. It is the mother tongue of 422 million people[44] and the official or co-official language in more than two dozen countries. Several schools and universities all over the world teach Arabic. Out of more than 6,000 languages of our era, the United Nations selected only six languages to record documents in. Arabic is one of them. And it is the only one that is also the original language of the holy book of a major religion.

Throughout these years, classic Arabic never phased out of usage, nor have its words lost their original definitions. People who speak different dialects of Arabic read and memorize the same Quran. As a result, the language of the Quran is still preserved. Is it possible to make the same claim about the original languages of the holy books of the other major religions? The answer is a glaring no.

VALIDITY OF THE INFORMATION DESCRIBED IN THE QURAN

The information contained in a genuine holy book *should* always remain true and relevant. That is a lot to expect from a book written hundreds of years ago. But why not? After all, Allah revealed the book, so this is a reasonable expectation. This is indeed a stringent expectation, because the

Quran covers many subjects, including astronomy, zoology, oceanography, geology, botany, physiology and embryology.

This section briefly covers a few scientific facts unknown at the time of the revelation of the Quran. For example, it was not known at that time that the moon does not shine a light of its own. It is interesting to note that the Quran mentions the lights from both the sun and the moon in three verses: 25:61, 10:5, and 71:16. Every time, the moon is referred to as bright or illuminating but *only* the sun is referred to as a *lamp*.

For example, in verse 10:5, the word *dia* is used to describe the sun. In verse 2:17, the Quran uses the Arabic root of the word *dia* to refer to the light originating from burning fire. Therefore, the sun as a lamp should be interpreted as resembling an old-fashioned oil-burning lamp, which is a simultaneous source of light, heat and fire. This is an astonishingly accurate description of our sun, which is powered by proton-proton nuclear chain reactions. In all three of these verses, the moon is referred to as a bright glow, but never as a lamp.

The Quran uses the term *sky* to describe the universe. The Quran says that Allah created seven skies, out of which He **"decorated the *sky of this world* with *lamps*"** (67:5). The Quran does not tell us much about the other six skies, but this verse tells us that the entire universe constitutes just one sky. At the time of Prophet Muhammad[PBUH], there was no way to know that the small, twinkling stars are, in reality, burning, hot, light-radiating suns. The Quran also hints that life exists on planets other than our Earth: **"Among His signs is the Creation of the Heavens and the Earth, and the living creatures that He has spread in both of them [Earth and skies]"** (42:29).

HUMAN WEAKNESS IN EXAGGERATING THE LOVE OF THE FAMILY OF PROPHET MUHAMMAD[PBUH]

In Islam, blood relation to a Prophet does not in itself grant a person entry into Paradise. Instead, the only criteria for entry into Paradise are one's Islamic belief and good deeds. For example, the Quran records that the father of Prophet Abraham[PBUH], wife of Prophet Lot[PBUH], and son of Prophet Noah[PBUH], refused to accept Islam and were condemned to hellfire.

Muslims dearly love Prophet Muhammad[PBUH]. Therefore, there is a risk that, after his death, some believers may assign divinity to him and his close family members. The question is: Does the Quran steer believers in this direction by focusing attention on the family and friends of Prophet Muhammad[PBUH]? This question also offers a stringent test of the undeniable human footprint. If a human had authored the Quran, we would have found detailed descriptions and praise of those who were close to the human writer of the Quran. Keep in mind that the Quran is a 1400-year-old book. At the time of its writing, praising one's tribe was a significant part of Arabic poetry and social customs.

In the Quran, Allah mentions the names of and praises some people. In this regard, there is an interesting observation: the Quran mentions the *names of* and *praises* Prophet Abraham, his son Prophet Isaac, his grandson Prophet Jacob, and his great-grandson Prophet Joseph (PBUT). The Quran also mentions the name of and praises Prophet Muhammad[PBUH]. But surprisingly, the names of Prophet Muhammad's[PBUH] grandfather, father, children and grandchildren are not in the Quran. This includes the grandchildren who were born during the lifetime of Prophet Muhammad[PBUH]. The names of the four-guided caliphs are not in the Quran either, even though the four caliphs unconditionally supported Prophet Muhammad[PBUH] under extreme conditions, and were the most respected among the companions.

Similarly, the Quran mentions the name of and praises Mary, mother of Prophet Jesus[PBUH]. There is even a chapter in the Quran titled Mary. However, the names of Prophet Muhammad's[PBUH] grandmothers, mother, wives, daughters and granddaughter are not in the Quran. In pre-Islamic days of tribal loyalties, such omissions would have been beyond comprehension. Only Allah knows the reason for these choices, because: **"You [Allah] give honor to whom You please"** (3:26). This situation speaks volumes about the truthfulness of the Quranic text. And it strongly discourages future Muslim generations from *exaggerating* the status of the Prophet's family by making them appear divine, as with believer-projected-gods.

HOW ABOUT THE PERSONAL TRAGEDIES?

Dr. Gary Miller points out that, "various books claim that the Quran was the product of the hallucinations of Prophet Muhammad[PBUH]."[45] Dr. Miller makes a good point that the Quran does not contain what must have been on the mind of Prophet Muhammad[PBUH] during the period of the revelation of the Quran, including his personal hardships. For example, Prophet Muhammad[PBUH] had seven children. Six of them died during his lifetime. Prophet Muhammad[PBUH] suffered all kinds of atrocities committed by Mecca's pagans. Once Mecca's pagans ostracized Prophet Muhammad[PBUH] and his tribe for three long years, during which they experienced austerity and long periods without food, at times eating tree leaves to survive. These hardships resulted in the death of the Prophet's beloved wife, Khadija. Miller writes: "The Quran does not mention these things—nor the death of his children, nor the death of his beloved companion wife—nothing; yet these topics must have hurt him, bothered him and caused him pain and grief … if the Quran were the product of his psychological reflections, then these subjects, as well as others, would be prevalent or at least mentioned throughout."[46] A valid observation by Miller, indeed!

ISLAM: A RELIGION FOR THE THINKING MIND

Knowledge is one of the gifts from Allah. Knowledge is not something humans can generate or discover on their own. The Quran teaches a prayer: **"O Lord! Increase my knowledge"** (20:114).

Allah gave humans another gift: **"[Allah] created man…and taught [the man] by *the Pen* – taught man what he did not know"** (96:2–5). These verses tell us that Allah also gave humans the ability to use the pen and thus *preserve the knowledge in some medium.* These verses specifically mention humans, because humans are the only species in the entire animal kingdom that can learn at such a rapid rate and then preserve the knowledge they learned. As a result, new generations do not have to reinvent the same knowledge. Instead, they benefit from knowledge preserved by their ancestors. Also, new generations keep adding new discoveries to the knowledge pool.

Preserving knowledge on a saved medium has another benefit. The medium in the form of books or a website can be communicated across geographical regions. Consequently, with the passage of time, humans became capable of making great progress.

Those who accuse Prophet Muhammad[PBUH] of authoring the Quran will have difficulty in explaining how about 1400 years ago he knew the value of knowledge and the significance of its preservation. Moreover, one should remember that Prophet Muhammad[PBUH] did not know how to read or write!

HOW TO ACQUIRE KNOWLEDGE

The Quran continues to guide us on *how to seek knowledge* in any field, including spiritual growth.

To start with, the Quran advises us to benefit from the stored knowledge in the saved medium: ***"Read!* In the name of your Lord Who created"** (96:1). Next, the Quran encourages our learning from one another. Verse 29:46 encourages us to hold *friendly* discussions with others. Verse 21:7 says, if you do not know about a subject, then ask those who know. Prophet Muhammad[PBUH] strongly encouraged scholars to teach others and spread knowledge. The Quran repeatedly asks us to think, analyze, and ponder: **"Why do you not reflect?** (6:50), **Do you not see…?** (31:31), **Will you not use your reason?** (2:44), **… so that you may reflect upon** (2:219), **see how they ignore the truth!** (5:75), and so on.

RESPONSIBILITY TO CHOOSE WHAT TO LEARN

Some types of knowledge can be harmful—such as the art of pickpocketing. Islam makes us responsible for doing our best, to evaluate the knowledge we learn, and to *verify* suspicious information from independent sources: **"O believers, if an evildoer comes to you with some news, verify it (investigate to ascertain the truth), lest you should harm others unwittingly and then regret what you have done"** (49:6).

What if, as suggested by the above verse, our verification confirms that someone is teaching us harmful or incorrect information? The Quran also authorizes the believers to reject such knowledge. **"You shall not follow anyone *blindly* in those matters of which you have no knowledge, surely the use of your ears and the eyes, and the heart - all of these, *shall be questioned* on the Day of Judgment"** (17:36).

The last part of the verse suggests that, we should use all our faculties to evaluate what we learn and we have full authority to reject non-beneficial knowledge, even if it comes from a scholar.

Once Caliph Umar announced a newly proposed law in a mosque; this law would place an upper limit on the amount of dowry paid by a man to his prospective bride. Right in the middle of his speech, an old woman spoke, "Allah gave the right to women, then, Umar, how dare you place such restriction?" Then she quoted verse 4:20. At that point, Caliph Umar publicly announced, "Umar is wrong and the woman is right!" and immediately withdrew the proposed law. At that time, the caliph was not only the head of state, but also the head of the Muslim clergy and judiciary. Nonetheless, based on right reasoning, an ordinary old woman successfully exercised the right to reject the caliph's opinion.[47] In Islam what is being said is more valuable and of greater importance than the status of the scholar making the statement.

THE QURAN TEACHES US HOW TO THINK AND ANALYZE

Verse 17:111 states that Allah does not have a son (Chapter 2). But it does more than convey this information. It also tells us the logical *reason*, explaining why there is no need for Allah to have a son. Similarly, chapter 5 of this book shows that the Quran not only tells us to believe in one God, it provides logical justification as to why there can be only one God. This encourages readers of the Quran to analyze this subject based on logic. That is not all; the following section shows that the Quran teaches us how to think, and to deduce the right conclusion.

THE QURAN POINTS TO THE ROADBLOCK TO LOGIC

Dr. Gary Miller observed that the Quran makes the fine distinction between *explanation* and *proof*. The Quran points out that explanation is neither proof nor logical justification.[48] At times, people avoid difficult questions by explaining and re-explaining rather than undertaking self-analysis and figuring out the reasons behind their actions. This behavior is a roadblock to one's thinking.

Here is an example. As a religious ritual, Mecca's pagans used to split the ears of their cattle. When Prophet Muhammad[PBUH] asked them the reason behind this practice, the pagans did not provide the *proof* of why their action was justified. Instead, they *explained*: **"Sufficient for us are the ways on which we found our forefathers"** (5:104). This incident was so important that not only did Allah record it in the Quran but He also responded to the pagans' explanation by asking if they would follow a tradition: **"even though their forefathers knew nothing and were not rightly guided?"** (5:104). The Prophet conveyed the Quran's question to the pagans. The Quran's question redirects responsibility back to Mecca's pagans and points out that their forefathers were not infallible. What if the forefathers made a mistake? Should the pagans follow their forefathers without checking the *reason* for their behavior? Islam is not a religion of ancestor veneration. Here, the Quran exposes the logical weakness in the pagans' claim. Further, the Quran identifies a general principle that *explaining* a wrong action is neither an acceptable justification nor a proof. An analytical mind should avoid this error by all means.

THE QURAN TEACHES THE SECRET OF EFFECTIVE COMMUNICATION

It should be noted that the previous verse (5:104) asks a question in order to communicate a message. When a question is based on fact and logic, the reader is forced to do more than just read information. S/he also thinks, analyzes, and tries to come up with a logical response. This opens the door to introspection. The Quran asks questions on more than a hundred occasions. Here is one example: **"Would you ask others to be righteous and forget to practice it yourselves? Even though you read your Holy Book? Have you no sense?"** (2:44).

Many scientific facts described here were discovered long after the revelation of the Quran. But Allah knew that a time would come when science would confirm the revelations. To people living in this age (like you and me), the Quran asks a direct question: **"If a sign [of Allah] comes to them they will still not believe?"** (6:109). Here, not only does the Quran predict that science will support the signs of Allah, but it forces readers to come up with a rational answer to this vital question.

While writing this book, I have also used the Quranic technique of asking questions. Such questions are preceded by a "**Q:.**" Here is one example.

Q: The Quran makes a distinction between *statement* and *proof*. Islam is based on logic and asks profound questions to stimulate introspection. Who do you think authored the Quran about 1400 years ago-- Allah, or a man without any formal education?

LOGICAL MIRACLE OF THE QURAN

Dr. Gary Miller has used his background in mathematics and logic to study the Quran. He states that, "when we *use* a word, we consider its *meaning*. When we *mention* a word we are discussing the word itself. If I said Toronto is a large city, I mean Toronto, that place, is a large city. If I say Toronto has seven letters, I am talking about the word 'Toronto'. In the first case I *used* the word and in the second I *mentioned* the word."[49]

The Quran states, **"The similitude of Jesus (Isa[PBUH]) before Allah is as that of Adam[PBUH]"** (3:59). Miller says, "It is very clear that what we have in the statement is an *equation*."[50] This verse can have two meanings.

1. The context of the verse explains that the birth of Adam was similar to the birth of Jesus[PBUH], because both were miracle births and both were devoid of a biological father.

2. Miller asks, "What about the *mention* of the words? Was the author aware of the fact that if we were considering the words as words themselves, this sentence also read that *'Jesus' is something like 'Adam'*. Well, they are not spelt with the same letters, how can they be alike in this revelation?"[51] The only alternative explanation was that both words should appear the same number of times in the Quran.

Dr. Miller used an index of the Quran "which lists every word in the Quran and where it can be found.[52] To his surprise, he found that both words were used 25 times.

To confirm, I also used an index of the Quran to find out how many times *Adam* and *Isa (Jesus)* appear in the Quran. Amazingly, the count turned out to be 25 times each.

You can verify that the word *Adam* is used in the following verses: 2.31, 2.33, 2.34, 2.35, 2.37, 3.33, 3.59, 5.27, 7.11, 7.19, 7.26, 7.27, 7.31, 7.35, 7.172, 17.61, 17.70, 18.50, 19.58, 20.115, 20.116, 20.117, 20.120, 20.121, 36.60.

Similarly, the word *Isa*[PBUH] (Jesus) also appears in 25 places: 2.87, 2.136, 2.253, 3.45 , 3.52, 3.55, 3.59, 3.84, 4.157, 4.163, 4.171, 5.46, 5.78, 5.110, 5.112, 5.114, 5.116, 6.85, 19.34, 33.7, 42.13, 43.63, 57.27, 61.6, 61.14.

Readers are welcome to verify that these words appear exactly 25 times – *not more and not less*. Please do not search the words using the English translation of the Quran, because translations may use a pronoun instead of the name. Use the word *Isa* in the Arabic text as in the verses above.

This proves that not only is the Quran the word of God, but it also authenticates that the Quran (as it appears today) is uncorrupted. Otherwise the above two counts would have been glaringly different.

CHAPTER   4

MUHAMMAD[PBUH 53]: A PROPHET FOR ALL HUMANITY

D r. Michael Hart authored the book *The 100: A Ranking of the Most Influential persons in History.* He studied the "world's greatest religious and political leaders, inventors, writers, philosophers, explorers, artists and innovators."[54] He concluded his study by giving the top ranking to Prophet Muhammad[PBUH] because his lifetime achievements exceeded accomplishments by any other human. Dr. Hart justified this ranking as "He (Muhammad[PBUH]) was the only man in history who was supremely successful on both the religious and secular levels."[55]

I BEAR WITNESS THAT MUHAMMAD[PBUH] WAS A *MAN*...

It is easy to verify Hart's claims, because Prophet Muhammad[PBUH] was not a mythological or fictitious character but a well-known historical personality. Historian Professor Philip Hitti says that the entire life of Prophet Muhammad[PBUH] is visible in the light of history.[56] In this chapter, let us take a glimpse of Muhammad's[PBUH] personality as a historical *man*, rather than as a religious figure.

REFUSED TO SELL THE DEAD BODY

In the Battle of the Trench (627 CE), Muhammad[PBUH] and his 3,000 allies were defending the city of Medina against an attacking army of Mecca's pagans, which was far better equipped, with more than 9,000 fighters. Muslims defended themselves by digging a trench around the city. The pagan army surrounded the city and cut off all incoming supplies. As a result, the entire city was pushed to the brink of starvation.

One famous pagan warrior tried to jump the trench separating the two armies and died. The pagans offered many camels and money just to retrieve his dead body. Muhammad^{PBUH} had the rare opportunity to accept the camels as desperately needed food for himself, the army and the city. At that time, no one knew how long the war would last or what would be its outcome. Surprisingly, Muhammad^{PBUH} said: "I don't sell dead bodies," and let the pagans retrieve the corpse for *free*.[57]

Even in the 21st century, all kinds of human rights violations exist. No one cares about the rights of the deceased. Yet Muhammad^{PBUH} enforced their rights in the 7th century.

Q: Who taught Muhammad^{PBUH}, *the man,* human dignity, even if it be a dead body not only of a powerful *attacking* enemy, but also of a non-Muslim?

NO RACIAL SUPERIORITY

Arabs used to look down upon blacks from neighboring Africa as an inferior race. Far ahead of his time, Muhammad^{PBUH} permanently prohibited racial prejudice in Islam.

Once, Abu Dharr referred to Bilal as a *son of a black woman*. This was considered an insult because Bilal was black. When Muhammad^{PBUH} learned about this incident, he told Abu Dharr that he still had the weaknesses of the pre-Islamic days of ignorance. In other words, he had not learned the Islamic teachings to avoid all racial prejudices. Muhammad^{PBUH} said, "I Muhammad^{PBUH} am equally the son of a black woman as I am of a white woman."[58] That made sense because, when an infant, Muhammad^{PBUH} was nursed by a black woman. Only a person who is completely free from racial prejudice can make such a public statement about his own self! Muhammad^{PBUH} also gave a beautiful message: *a woman's milk gives life to the baby, regardless of her skin color.* Muhammad^{PBUH} treated all people as equal, and he successfully changed the thinking of Muslims, even if the concept of racial equality was totally beyond the culture of his era. Compare this to racial prejudice as practiced in many countries, including the United States, today.

Q: Centuries ahead of his time, who taught Muhammad^{PBUH}, *the man,* that all humans have equal rights and status?

DIGNITY OF LABOR

Even when Muhammad[PBUH] was the head of state, he did all kinds of personal chores. For example, at times he stitched his clothes, mended his shoes, cooked his meals, and worked as a construction worker to build a mosque. While preparing for the Battle of the Trench, Muhammad[PBUH] dug trenches along with other Muslims. He could have easily let others do the manual labor, but he always insisted on doing his share. Does any other head of state behave this way?

Q: Who taught Muhammad[PBUH], *the man*, the dignity of labor?

RIGHTS OF CHILDREN: THEY DESERVE LOVE

Islam makes it a requirement that a believer should love everyone, including all humans and animals (Chapter 6). Once, Muhammad[PBUH] was with the companions and his grandson was playing on his lap. As Muhammad[PBUH] was talking, he was also affectionately kissing his grandson. One companion said that he had ten children, but he never kissed any one of them. Muhammad[PBUH] said, "Whoever is not merciful to *others* will not be treated mercifully [on the Day of Judgment]."[59]

Q: Who taught Muhammad[PBUH], *the man,* that it is all right for a man to express love to children?

RIGHTS OF CHILDREN: FOR BOTH GIRLS AND BOYS

In pre-Islamic days, some Arab parents used to hate their girl child and used to bury their baby girls—alive[60]. Muhammad[PBUH] prohibited the unjustified killing of anyone, including baby girls. He said that if a man has a sister or a daughter and treats her nicely, takes care of her basic needs, gives her a good education (including religious education) and marries her to the right person, then that man will enter Paradise. According to Muhammad[PBUH], all children are meant to be loved, irrespective of gender. According to his wife Aisha, throughout his life Muhammad[PBUH] never verbally or physically abused anyone. This included children, and even animals.[61]

Once Muhammad[PBUH] announced to his family that he would give an onyx necklace to "her whom I love best." This announcement got the attention of everyone in the household. It turned out that he gave the necklace to his granddaughter.[62] It must be noted that this was in an era when a boy child was regarded superior, and a protector of his parents in their old age.

Q: Who taught Muhammad[PBUH], *the man,* these revolutionary ideas about the rights of children, including infant girls? Keep in mind that even today, on a large scale, female fetuses are aborted and female infants abandoned in India and China[63].

RIGHTS OF PARENTS

Asma' bint Abu Bakr's mother, was a pagan, and came to visit her Muslim daughter. Asma' asked Muhammad's[PBUH] advice, if she should welcome her mother. Muhammad[PBUH] told her to keep good relations with her mother.[64] Regardless of the ideology or religion of the parents, Muslims are always required to treat their parents fairly and with love. Compare this to contemporary practice, in which so many people leave their elderly parents in nursing homes, even if they are not critically sick.

Q: Who told Muhammad[PBUH], *the man,* to respect parents, regardless of their religion?

DID MUSLIMS TORTURE THE POWS?

Across the globe, armies have been torturing prisoners of war since the dawn of humankind to the present day. Only relatively recently have the rights of POWs been codified in the Geneva Conventions of 1929 and 1949. Ensuring these laws are implemented has been a different story. What was Muhammad's[PBUH] attitude towards POWs 1400 years ago?

After Muslims migrated to the city of Medina, Mecca's pagans attacked them on several occasions. The first major pagan attack resulted in the Battle of Badr. Muslims won the battle, and captured many pagan prisoners. Amazingly, Muhammad[PBUH] not only instructed his army to treat the POWs humanely, he also successfully protected their rights.

Muslims gave POWs bread to eat while they themselves ate only dates, which was considered a far inferior food. Muhammad[PBUH] permitted all traditionally accepted means to free POWs expeditiously. For example, he allowed the Arab tradition of freeing any POW if someone paid a fine on prisoner's behalf.

These POWs were not only soldiers of an aggressive army; but some were directly responsible for oppressing and torturing Muslims. One prominent pagan public speaker, Suhail ibn Amar, was among these POWs. He had used his oratorical skills to instigate attacks against Muslims. In that era, poets and public orators used to sway the decisions of the crowd, and sometimes even their rulers, to go to war. A prominent companion of the Prophet who later became the second guided Caliph Umar asked

Muhammad's[PBUH] permission to remove Suhail ibn Amar's front teeth so he would never again use his oratorical skills against Muslims. Muhammad[PBUH] said: *"Were I to do this, Allah would disfigure me on the Day of Judgment, despite the fact that I am His messenger."*[65] And this was not an isolated incident. After the Battle of Hunayn, Muhammad[PBUH] also let POWs go free.[66]

The sad reality is that our modern world has discovered many methods of torture, including electric shock and waterboarding. In striking contrast, 1400 years ago, Muhammad[PBUH] not only prohibited torture, but also practiced incredible generosity toward prisoners of war. He said, if a mother and daughter are captured as POWs, do not separate them. Non-Muslim POWs were never forced to convert to Islam. Muhammad[PBUH] exchanged non-Muslim POWs for Muslim POWs.[67]

Q: Who taught Muhammad[PBUH], *the man,* about the rights of POWs?

EMPHASIS ON EDUCATION

In the preceding incident, some pagan POWs could not be freed because no one paid fine on their behalf. The tradition was to force the unclaimed POWs into slavery. However, Muhammad[PBUH] thought of a novel way to free more POWs. At that time, unlike the people in Medina, many of Mecca's pagans were literate. So, Muhammad[PBUH] announced that any POW who teaches ten children of Medina to read and write can earn his freedom without paying a fine.

In 7th century Arabia, no one could imagine the significance of knowledge and its future impact. Muhammad[PBUH] himself did not know how to read or write. Usually people without education try to compensate for their shortcoming by degrading the role of education.

Q: Who taught Muhammad[PBUH], *the man,* the value of education?

NOT GUILTY BY ASSOCIATION

In 631 CE, a Christian delegation from the city of Najran, visited Muhammad[PBUH] for religious debate. Pragmatically, this certainly was not the best occasion for a visit by a Christian delegation. By this time, the Muslims had conquered Mecca, and Muhammad[PBUH] was fully recognized as the head of state.

Just two years earlier, the Christian ruler Heraclius of the Eastern Roman Empire demonstrated open hostility toward the growing Islamic power. That resulted in the Battle of Mu'tah between the Christians and Muslims.

In 630, Muhammad^{PBUH} heard reports that Heraclius planned to attack Muslims in Medina. Consequently, Muhammad^{PBUH} had to ready the army to confront the Romans. At the time of the delegation's visit, the Christian Roman Empire was a clear threat to Muslims.

In spite of the possibility of an assassination attempt by the Christians from Najran, Muhammad^{PBUH} cordially welcomed the delegation with traditional Arab hospitality. He received them in the famous Mosque of Masjid Nabvi, which is regarded as the second holiest site in Islam. They had a friendly debate. Also, Muhammad^{PBUH} signed a treaty with the Christians for peaceful coexistence, and gave them the freedom to practice their religion in Najran. The treaty stated that, *"to the Christians of Najran and neighboring treaties, the security of Allah and pledge of His Prophet are extended for their lives, their religion, their property – to those present as well as those absent and other besides."*[68]

A paranoid king would have thought that *all* Christians were a threat and assumed that the visitors had some sinister motive. Kings normally try to increase their influence by humiliating and trampling the weak and unprotected. But Muhammad^{PBUH} did not make any false assumptions. Modern civilization generally recognizes that crimes committed by a few community members do not mean that the entire community is criminal.

Q: Who taught Muhammad^{PBUH}, *the man,* the wisdom to know that association alone is an inadequate reason to assume someone's guilt?

HUMANE TREATMENT OF ANIMALS

In the desert heat, meat rots at a faster rate. To prevent waste, Arabs had an age-old practice of cut off a piece of meat from live animal to be cooked and eaten. This way, the animal suffered for days before the final slaughter. Muhammad^{PBUH} immediately banned this practice.[69] He also banned cutting off the tails and splitting the ears of animals. He forbade that an animal be tied to a vehicle for too long, and prohibited animal fighting contests. Even today, some people eat animals *alive,* like Sannakji and Yin Yang fish, while the live animal is still writhing in agony.

Q: Who taught Muhammad^{PBUH}, *the man,* humane treatment of animals 14 centuries ago, while bullfighting is still legal in Spain and live raw oysters are considered a delicacy in the United States?

NO BODYGUARDS

After Muhammad^{PBUH} moved to Medina, several assassination attempts were made on his life. He used to have bodyguards. Later, a verse of the Quran was revealed that Allah would protect Muhammad^{PBUH} from assassination. From that moment onwards, Muhammad^{PBUH} did not bother about keeping any bodyguards. He went wherever he wanted, without a care.

Q: Even after several assassination attempts were made on his life, what convinced Muhammad^{PBUH} that he did not need to worry about his own safety?

Q: Are there any other heads of state who live without security and bodyguards?

RESPECT EVERY HUMAN, REGARDLESS OF RACE, RELIGION, OR NATIONAL ORIGIN

Once Muhammad^{PBUH} was sitting on the roadside with his companions when a funeral procession passed by them. Muhammad^{PBUH} stood up. Later, the companions informed him that the deceased was a Jew. Muhammad^{PBUH} asked, "Was he not a soul (human)?"[70] Even when Muhammad^{PBUH} was preaching Islam, he did not teach hatred toward non-Muslims.

Q: Who taught Muhammad^{PBUH}, *the man*, compassion for all humans?

NO VIOLENCE AGAINST THE WEAK

Muhammad^{PBUH} *never* hit any man, woman or child. That included his wives, slaves, orphans and prisoners. This behavior was consistent throughout his life and is confirmed by several ahadith. The only exception to this occurred when he was in battle field against an enemy. Also, Muhammad^{PBUH} never initiated any battle, only defended himself and his people. The only exception to this was when a certain group was preparing to attack Muslims; then he allowed preemptive strikes. One other exception was when a group violated a treaty that was crucial to Muslim survival.

Once Muhammad^{PBUH} ordered a slave woman to do some chores. She ignored him and continued to play with a sheep. Back then, tradition was to beat slaves for slacking. After calmly repeating the order a few times, Muhammad^{PBUH} pointed a *miswak* (a stick the size of a toothbrush that was used to clean the teeth) and said in a calm voice: "If I were not afraid of Allah, I would have beaten you with this" and he left the house which was the scene of conflict. Hitting anyone with even a small stick was not his style.

Q: Who taught Muhammad^{PBUH}, *the man*, to control his anger even when he had the upper hand?

66

LOOKING AFTER THE SLAVES

Muhammad[PBUH] was given a slave boy, Zaid bin Harithah, as a marriage gift. Muhammad[PBUH] looked after Zaid like a loving father. After some years, Zaid's biological father and uncle came to Muhammad[PBUH] and asked permission to take Zaid back to his family. Muhammad[PBUH] gave them permission, provided Zaid was willing to leave. Zaid recognized his father and uncle. However, Zaid had become so attached to Muhammad[PBUH] that he preferred to stay with him. Next, in presence of the father and uncle, Muhammad[PBUH] freed Zaid from slavery. When it comes to love, no one can fool a child, because a child recognizes sincere love.

Q: How did Muhammad[PBUH], *the man,* get such a loving personality that Zaid preferred Muhammad[PBUH] over his biological family?

RIGHTS OF THE DISABLED

When Muhammad[PBUH] was head of state in Medina, at times he had to leave the city. On such occasions, he would appoint someone to temporarily take charge of the affairs of the state. On several occasions, he gave this great responsibility to Abdullah ibn Umm Makhtoom.[71] This was quite a responsibility. Any decision made by him would have affected everyone.

Brace yourself for a surprise. Abdullah Ibn Umme Makhtoom was blind. Can you imagine the rights of the disabled awarded 1400 years ago? Even today, in some parts of the world, the disabled are treated worse than animals.

Q: Why did Muhammad[PBUH], *the man*, not only envision the rights of the disabled, but give them authority and responsibility, about 1400 years ago?

CHARITY AND COMMITMENT TO SERVE

Before Muhammad[PBUH] was assigned the duty of a Prophet, he and his wife were considered a wealthy couple. After becoming a Prophet, he devoted the rest of his life propagating Islam. He donated all his wealth to charity, often skipping meals for himself and his family. His overwhelming charity continued for the rest of his life, even after Muhammad[PBUH] became the ruler of the bulk of the Arabian Peninsula. His wife Aisha said that the family often had nothing to eat, and the fire to cook a meal was never lit for several consecutive days. They used to survive primarily on dates and water.[72]

Q: Today, is any other head of state generous to the point of skipping meals?

Q: Who taught Muhammad^{PBUH}, *the man*, so much sincerity and devotion?

DID NOT ESTABLISH DYNASTY

Kings or emperors of a state tend to hoard money, power, status and above all, they try to establish a dynasty. When he died, Muhammad^{PBUH} left no money to his family; he only left modest items like a mule and protective armor. He did not even name a successor caliph to replace him, even though he had many close friends and family members. The only goal of his life was to convey the message of Islam to humanity.

Q: Why did Muhammad^{PBUH}, *the man*, have no interest in dynasty, status, power or money?

NO SENSE OF SUPERIORITY OR ARROGANCE

Islam regards arrogance as a great sin. To avoid arrogance, a Muslim should give credit for all personal achievements to Allah. Once Muhammad^{PBUH} was traveling with some companions; they stopped to cook lunch. The companions allocated different tasks among themselves. Muhammad^{PBUH} offered to collect wood for the fire. The companions requested that he rest while they would take care of the cooking. Muhammad^{PBUH} replied that he was not superior to anyone, and insisted on doing his share of the teamwork. For some people, claiming superiority over their peers has high priority.

Q: Why did Muhammad^{PBUH}, *the man*, never claim superiority?

ART OF COMMUNICATING

Early on when Muhammad^{PBUH} started preaching Islam, Mecca's pagans tried different brutal techniques to stop him. They ridiculed, threatened and physically attacked Muslims, including Muhammad^{PBUH}. Some Muslims were tortured to death.

While Muhammad^{PBUH} and other Muslims were facing so much oppression, the pagan leaders also tried to bribe Muhammad^{PBUH} by making him unusual offers: if Muhammad^{PBUH} only agreed to stop preaching Islam, then the pagans would make him the chief leader of Mecca, or they would get him married to any girl of his choice or they would make him the richest man in Mecca. Still, Muhammad^{PBUH} refused every offer and said, "Even if they [the pagans] placed the sun in my right hand and the moon in my left hand [gave me all the wealth in the world] to cause me to renounce my task, verily I would not desist."⁷³ It is interesting to note that at the time this offer was made, his own life was under threat. Still, fearlessly, Muhammad[PBUH] spoke exactly what he believed.

One fundamental rule of effective communication is to say exactly what you want to say—clearly and without fear or hesitation. Trying to hide one's real motive with wordplay weakens a message. In the above incident, Muhammad[PBUH] had no trouble saying no. When a person depends on the approval of others, then saying no often creates a feeling of guilt.

Usually, Muhammad[PBUH] was silent. He did not talk unnecessarily. He spoke clearly and concisely, ensuring his listener understood. He used to pause while speaking. He spoke in a soft tone, without shouting or speaking in anger. He made sure to connect to his listener. If the listener was not intelligent, he would repeat his message patiently until s/he understood. When he assigned a task or duty to someone, he was polite; he made sure he did not overburden anyone.[74] He knew when to say something, what to say, and how to say it. Here is one example.

Muhammad[PBUH] was in a mosque when his wife Safiya visited him. When she was leaving, Muhammad[PBUH] accompanied her to the door of the mosque as they were talking to each other. It was night and dark. Two Muslim men passed them. They recognized Muhammad's[PBUH] voice, greeted him by saying salaam, then kept walking. In the darkness, a passerby *could* have thought that Muhammad[PBUH] was with some other woman.

Immediately, Muhammad[PBUH] told them in a loud voice that the lady with him was his wife.[75] Even a possibility of misunderstanding should be cleared up, and the best time to do that is right then and there, not afterwards. This demonstrated Muhammad[PBUH] had an alert, confident and guilt-free personality, who reacts appropriately to external situations.

Muhammad[PBUH] was an attentive listener. He used to turn his shoulders towards the speaker. People of all social status were equally important to him. He did not rush the speaker, and did not interrupt their speech. If someone whispered a private question to him, even then he did not cut the speaker short by moving his head away before s/he finished. When Muhammad[PBUH] was in the company of friends, he did not interrupt others while they were talking. Instead, he used to join them as a listener. If someone made a funny comment and the group laughed, he would also smile with them.[76] In summary, he made sure to listen, both with mind and with body language. Attentive listening gives a speaker the satisfaction that the message has been fully communicated.

Q: Who taught Muhammad[PBUH], *the man,* the fine art of modern communication?

OPENLY EXPRESSING EMOTIONS

Muhammad[PBUH] was very close to his Muslim uncle Hamza, who was martyred in a battle against the pagans from Mecca. When Muhammad[PBUH] saw the dead body of Hamza on the battlefield, Muhammad[PBUH] cried with tears. Some onlookers were surprised to see him cry, which was contrary to a domineering, controlling tough man image. Later, Muhammad[PBUH] explained that it is fine for anyone to cry, to express their true feelings.

Amazingly, modern psychology also promotes the expression of true feelings.[77]

Q: Who taught modern psychology to Muhammad[PBUH], *the man?*

ONLY MONOTHEISM: AN IDEOLOGY THAT DID NOT CHANGE

Muhammad[PBUH] performed the duty of a Prophet for 22 long, eventful years. Scholars point out that during all that time, he preached pure monotheism, *without changing his ideology, even for a moment.* This is unusual human behavior. Usually, people change their thinking over the years. Just recollect how much your thinking has changed in the last 22 years! Muhammad's[PBUH] preaching strongly clashed, not just with the existing religions, but also with the social and economic norms of pagan Arabs. For example, Islam prohibits usury and drinking. These were traditional means of doing business at the time, and played a crucial role in local economies. Islam also alienated pagan Arab tribes who kept their statues around Kaba. This practice provided prestige and revenue to Mecca's pagans.

Preaching Islam led to conflicts with much stronger adversaries, including the Roman and Persian Empires. As a result, Muhammad[PBUH] personally, and Muslims in general, paid a phenomenal price in the form of emotional and physical hardships. Muhammad[PBUH] could have easily avoided all that suffering by adapting little flexibility towards polytheism.

Once Mecca's pagans offered Muhammad[PBUH] a compromise: if he would just kiss the statue of any of their gods, they would pray to the God of Muhammad[PBUH]. He flatly refused.[78] His belief in monotheism was not to be compromised. When Muhammad[PBUH] was on his deathbed, he said, "As death is closing in, my message is that no other god exists besides Allah." Even at that time, his monotheistic belief did not waiver.

Q: Who gave Muhammad^{PBUH}, *the man,* such superhuman resolution to stick to his belief in pure monotheism throughout the prolonged period of 22 years?

THE ANSWER TO ALL THE ABOVE QUESTIONS IN THIS SECTION

Muhammad^{PBUH} *never* had a regular human teacher or mentor or spiritual guide throughout his life. He did not even know how to read and write. Can you guess why Muhammad^{PBUH} had such a versatile and refined personality so far ahead of his time? What was his source of ethical and spiritual guidance?

The explanation comes from the second *kalima* (declaration of Islamic belief). At the beginning of this chapter, only the first part of this kalima was written as a section title: *I bear witness that Muhammad^{PBUH} was a man ….*

Here is the full kalima:

"I bear witness that there is none worthy of worship except Allah, the One alone, without partner, and

I bear witness that Muhammad^{PBUH} was a slave [man] and a *Messenger [of Allah]."*

No wonder Prophet Muhammad^{PBUH} was an outstanding achiever. Peace be upon him, his wives, his family, his companions, and followers!

Now that you see the evidence presented in this chapter, what do you think? Did Dr. Michael Hart choose the right person as the greatest human achiever of all time?

Q: Disagree? In that case, the Quran has a challenge for you: **"produce proof to your claim, if you are truthful"** (2:111).

CHAPTER 5

BEAUTY AND SIMPLICITY OF ISLAMIC MONOTHEISM

TOP PRIORITY OF ISLAM: BELIEF IN ONE GOD

To come into the fold of Islam, a person must recite the following declaration of faith with full sincerity and understanding:

la ilaha il-Allah

Muhammadur Rasul Allah

Figuratively, this means: *there exists no god other than Allah*

Muhammad[PBUH] *is His messenger.*

These concise lines convey the following points.

1. **Monotheism of Islam**: Allah is the *only* deity there is.

2. **Negation of other deities**: Just saying that "God is one" is incomplete information. The first line of the Muslim declaration of belief explains why Islamic monotheism is different from the monotheism of other religions. *Islam also denies all deities other than Allah.* That too without contradiction! This leads to the following conclusions:

   a. Islamic denial of all other deities has absolutely no exception. Therefore, angels, gods, goddesses, Prophets, jinns (another intelligent creation of Allah), saintly humans or any other entities from human imagination are not allowed to share divinity with Allah in any manner whatsoever.

b.   This negation of other deities also rules out the possibility that several gods can merge or team up to create one Supreme God.

c.   Since Allah is the only God, it implies that Allah alone is the Creator, Sustainer and Provider. Therefore, only Allah deserves to be worshiped, and Muslims must therefore obey Allah.

This does not mean that Islam is intolerant of other religions. It is simply a matter of personal choice—whom to worship. In the same manner, Christians, Buddhists, Jews and Hindus have the right to refuse to worship the Maya goddess Ixchel.

3.   **Who is the God of Islam?**

The Arabic word "Allah" means God. That is why, just like the Quran, the Arabic Bible and Arabic Torah also call their God "Allah." This linguistic similarity leads to a question, "is the God of the Quran same as the God found in Bible or Torah?" The second line of the declaration, "Muhammad[PBUH] is His messenger" answers this question. The concept of the God of Islam should be in accordance with the teaching of Allah's messenger, Muhammad[PBUH].

4.   **Fulfilling a Contract:** Allah made an agreement with the souls of all humanity. **"Allah asked them [all human souls]: 'Am_I not your Lord?' They all replied: 'Yes! We bear witness that You are'"** (7:172) (chapter 2). When a Muslim recites the declaration of faith, s/he takes the first step toward fulfilling the covenant made with Allah.

Since monotheism is highlighted in first line of the declaration of faith itself, it makes monotheism the *most important message of Islam*. The Quran emphasizes monotheism in several different ways.

The most important virtue of a human: **"Who has a better faith than the one who submits himself *entirely to Allah* [and no other deity] and does good to others, and follows the faith of Abraham[PBUH]"** (4:125).

Different Prophets preached:

Prophet Noah[PBUH] said: **"Worship *none* except Allah"** (11:26).

Prophet Joseph[PBUH] said: **"It is not fitting that we *attribute any partners* with Allah (and become polytheists)"** (12:38).

A father's advice to his son: the Quran praises Luqman as a wise man. He told his son, **"*Do not ever commit shirk (associating anyone else with Allah)*; surely committing *shirk* is the *worst injustice*"** (31:13).

Seeking forgiveness only from Allah: In the Quran, one of the most important prayers seeking forgiveness includes the declaration of monotheism: **"There is no god but You [O Allah], glory be to You! Indeed I was the one who committed wrong"** (21:87).

Imaginary false gods are powerless: **"They worship other deities besides Allah, who can neither harm them nor benefit them"** (10:18).

Allah directly commands: **"No one else is *worthy of worship* except Me [Allah]"** (16:2).

Persistently worshiping only one non-Xenophanic God is no ordinary endeavor. Humans are strongly tempted to Xenophanes' style of faith. And a rational human mind demands answers to questions like, "Can an unseen God really exist?" and "Why does there have to be exactly one God instead of many gods and goddesses?" and "What is the harm in worshipping a pious man along with Allah?"

The Quran not only mandates Muslims to believe in "one God," but in so doing it also answers many basic questions about Islamic monotheism.

That is not all. Islam also meticulously identifies different forms of polytheism, including its most elusive morphs. Also, Islam continues to guide us in rooting out polytheism in its entirety. Without this information, it would be unfair to expect humans to follow Islamic Monotheism. Such teaching occurs with so much insight and thoroughness that by the end of this chapter, readers will wonder at the sheer beauty and grandeur of intelligence behind the 1400-year-old Quran.

DEFINITION OF *SHIRK*

Islam not only precisely defines what is prohibited to worship, but it also has a word for it—*shirk*. Loosely speaking, shirk is *associating a partner* with Allah or an *alternative* to Allah. Shirk encompasses more than the dictionary meaning of polytheism. It is amazing how shirk exhaustively describes every possible deviation so Muslims can identify and sustain pure monotheism. Here are some common categories of shirk.

WHY IS IT SHIRK TO HAVE A MONOTHEISTIC BELIEF IN GOD OTHER THAN ALLAH?

Suppose a person believes that the Egyptian god Ra is the only God, who is the Creator, Sustainer, Provider, Protector, Forgiver, and has all the attributes of Allah. Here the person believes only in Ra and does not believe in Allah. Islamic Scholars label such belief as shirk, even if there is no polytheism involved and the divinity in question is one, and not *shared.*

The Quran makes a subtle point: **"all that you worship instead of Allah is nothing but [merely] *names* which you and your forefathers have *invented*"** (12:40). The verse points out if someone worships a god other than Allah, then the worshipers imagine a name. For example, a person may call 'god of rain' by the name *Rainy*. Here the word *Rainy* is only a linguistic name. The Quran says that just because the name *Rainy* exists, it does not mean that god-of-rain also exists.

On the other hand, Allah exists, He is real, regardless of whether a person believes in Him or not. Suppose a believer assigns Allah's real attribute, *the Creator*, to a fictitious entity, Ra. In that case, the *real attribute* and the linguistic *false name* team up to create the belief. Therefore, it is a kind of *partnership*, which can be called sharing, or shirk.

IMAGINING NEW ATTRIBUTES AND ASSIGNING THEM TO ALLAH

This elusive trap can misguide even Muslims. Allah has given us the intellect to make scientific discoveries. But we do not have the ability to make laws or draw logical conclusions about Allah, or assign Him new and imaginary attributes. The human capacity for logical reasoning has its limitations. **"Surely Allah knows and you do not know"** (16:74). One such example of a man-invented attribute is *wahdatul-wajood* or 'unity of being,' from the extreme Sufi philosophy. One interpretation of *wahdatul-wajood* is that everything is Allah. This belief is the same as pantheism. This conclusion is based on guesswork and assumptions.

The Quran says Allah is *All-Knowing, All-Seeing, All-Hearing*, and has total control and power over everything. It means that Allah knows everything, sees everything, hears everything, and controls everything. But the Quran does not say that Allah is omnipresent or that matter and the Creator are the same. Since the Quran does not say so, therefore, we cannot assume that Allah is omnipresent. Such exaggeration changes one's perception of Allah because *the false attribute* is assigned to the *real* God. This too is shirk.

A subtle point also deserves an explanation. The Quran says, **"We [Allah] are nearer to him [a human] than his jugular vein"** (50:16). Even if Allah is near, it does not mean Allah is *present* everywhere. Why? In our three-dimensional universe, if a person is physically near you, then that person is also present near you. But such human limitation is not applicable to Allah, because He is the Creator of the three dimensions. Allah is not constrained by these three dimensions. Allah is beyond human imagination, and Allah resembles nothing and no one. We need to think beyond the Xenophanic trap.

Q: According to *wahdatul-wajood*, God is everything, including the stones. If you believe in this ideology, then can you explain why Islam prohibits worshipping a stone statue?

INSTRUCTIONS TO AVOID THE SUBTLE SHIRK OF FALSE ATTRIBUTES

While Prophet Muhammad[PBUH] was alive, he corrected mistakes made by Muslims and guided them to the right path. But, how can Muslims receive guidance after his death? The Quran provides guidance about issues that were likely to come *after* the Prophet was gone. Giving Allah imaginary attributes is one such mistake of indirect shirk, and the Quran guides the Muslims to avoid it: **"The Most Beautiful Names [present in the Quran and the ahadith] belong to Allah, so *call on Him by them*"** (7:180). In other words, Muslims should call Allah only by the names used in the Quran and hadith. Otherwise, in the absence of guidance, Muslims may unknowingly commit shirk. As subtle as this point may be, Muslims are guided to use *only* those names that are used in the Quran and ahadith.

ANY NON-ISLAMIC CONCEPT OF DIVINE IS SHIRK

Suppose a person believes in a God other than Allah (e.g., the Egyptian god Ra). In that case:

1. If a person believes that *only one* attribute of Allah belongs to Ra, while all other attributes still belong to Allah, even then that person is committing shirk.

2. If a person believes that all attributes belong to Allah, but Ra *shares* just one attribute with Allah (like both are *All Seeing*), even then the person is committing *shirk*.

3. What about a person who believes in Allah but also believes in supernatural power(s)? For example, belief in astrology or superstitions (like Friday the 13th as a bad omen). Here, the act of worship to any other deity is not involved. Still, the believer perceives that supernatural power is an independent doer that shares full or partial power with Allah. Therefore, according to Islam, this too would be *shirk*.

The above three cases violate the first line of the above "declaration of faith."

IMAGINING SIMILARITY BETWEEN ALLAH AND HIS CREATION

Imagining similarity between Allah and His Creation violates the verse: **"There is none comparable to Him [Allah]"** (112:4). This type of *shirk* includes anthropomorphism, such as believer-projected-god, self-proclaimed-god, incarnation or human manifestation of god.

ATHEISM

Chapter 2 discussed that atheists assume that God is constrained by human limitations. In Islam, any imposition of human limitations on Allah is *shirk*. The Quran says **"subhan-Allah"** (59:23), which figuratively means *Allah is pure from all human limitations or anthropomorphic associations*.

THE ONE AND ONLY UNFORGIVABLE SIN IN ISLAM

According to Islam, throughout one's lifetime, a believer can ask for forgiveness from all sins including the sin of *shirk*. If the believer is sincere and seeks forgiveness directly from Allah, then Allah has promised not only to forgive, but to forgive again and again, and over again. Before accepting Islam, many companions of the Prophet were polytheists. But after they accepted Islam and asked for forgiveness; Allah forgave them. But what happens if a person *dies* believing in shirk? **"Surely Allah will *never* forgive the one who commits the sin of shirk and may forgive anyone else if He so pleases"** (4:116).

It is interesting to note that shirk is the only sin in the entire Quran that is called unforgivable. This means that while monotheism is the greatest virtue, its violation, shirk, is the greatest sin. This is because Islamic monotheism and shirk are mutually exclusive. One more piece of evidence that, in Islam, monotheistic belief is the highest priority and has the greatest significance.

It must be noted that the above verse does not say that a monotheistic believer has the freedom to commit other sins. Later we will see that if a person who is sincere about monotheism, then s/he, by choice, will not commit any sin in the first place. This is because monotheistic belief is more than just a verbal commitment. It includes a total transformation of the heart and the mind.

ARGUMENTS AGAINST POLYTHEISM

FUNDAMENTAL WEAKNESS OF POLYTHEISM

The Quran makes a surprising statement that Allah did not make any rational ground for shirk: **"My Lord has forbidden…shirk with Allah for which He has revealed no logical ground"**[79] (7:33). Here is a subtle point: This verse supports verse 14:22 in chapter 2; this is why satan cannot find a logical argument in favor of shirk.

This is not all; the Quran even *proves* that shirk is illogical. Here is a subset of the arguments presented in the Quran.

ARGUMENT 1: WHY WE SHOULD BELIEVE IN ONE GOD

The Quran argues, if there were several gods, then their mutual conflict would have caused chaos in the universe. **"Never has Allah begotten a son, nor is there any god besides Him. Had it been so, *each god would govern his own Creation and each would have tried to overpower the others*"** (23:91). In this verse, the Quran is pointing to the primary flaw in the popular polytheistic approach that God must have several supporting gods and goddesses in a team to run the universe. This ideology envisions multiple gods, similar to human teams. For example, employees of an airline who cohesively pool their talents in different areas to fly a fleet of airplanes. It is a Xenophanic model of religion in which gods inherited the human trait of teamwork.

The above verse argues that the existence of several *different* gods would mean that they have to be independent of one another. Therefore, they would have individual godly opinions backed by matching egos. If gods work together like humans and look like humans (as per Xenophanes), then they would also fight like humans. Greek mythology contains many stories of inter-god conflicts. And when conflict peaks, then the team stops functioning, as can be seen during an airline employees' strike. Rival godly factions could even get violent. As the above verse points out, if several gods shared administration of the universe, then it would cause power struggles that lead to inter-god conflict.

ARGUMENT 2: GOD IS OMNIPOTENT—THEREFORE, DOES NOT NEED OTHER gods AND goddesses

Two attributes of Allah are *the Self-Sufficient* and *the All-Mighty*. This means Allah is fully capable of doing what He likes and when He likes, without any external help, because **"Allah is the Self-Sufficient"** (112:2). The entire universe is just a small segment of His vast creation, and Allah alone continuously causes, maintains, and sustains every single change in the universe. The Quran argues: **"Allah has not begotten a son. He has no partner in His Kingdom; nor is He helpless. *Therefore, He does not need any protector out of helplessness"*** (17:111). Here the Quran raises a subtle point. If God had partners, it would mean God lacks some ability, and has to depend on other partners to fill that void. This resembles a human who seeks help from others because s/he is incapable or unable of accomplishing a task. For example, an experienced tax accountant can easily do her own taxes, but she will still require the services of a car mechanic, heart surgeon, and hair stylist.

Q: If you believe God has a son, daughter or supporting gods or goddesses, then what are the shortcomings of God that compelled Him to create these divine partners?

Q: A man can manufacture a hammer from iron because God created iron ore. In contrast, the Supreme God makes everything out of nothing. This includes both matter and life forms, and would also include supporting gods and goddesses. If the Supreme God did not have the ability to make rain, then how did He manage to create from nothing a rain god capable of making rain?

One should not confuse gods in polytheism with angels in Islam. According to Islam, angels are just a part of creation. Angels obey, praise, and worship Allah all the time. In contrast, *Allah does not depend on angels* to do anything. **"Whenever He [Allah] intends a thing, He only says: 'Exist' and it is [the event occurs]"** (36:82). Humans and jinns have the ability to choose between right and wrong, so they are responsible for their choices. Whereas the angels do not have the power to choose and must literally obey Allah. Therefore, on the Day of Judgment, the angels will not be punished or rewarded like humans and jinns. Satan was not an angel; he was a jinn with the power to choose, and satan chose evil over good.

There are two significant differences between angels and polytheistic gods:

(1) In polytheistic mythologies, at times the gods disobey their highest God. But angels have to obey Allah.

(2) Muslims do not worship or pray to angels. In polytheistic religions, believers worship various gods and goddesses along with the highest God.

ARGUMENTS BY THE CREATOR OF THE UNIVERSE

The Quran asks us the following three questions. Each question builds on the previous question. The first two questions are about humans. We are good at relating to humans, so we can easily answer them. The third is about the entire universe, which consists of all life forms along with all lifeless objects.

"Were they [the humans] created without a Creator? Or were they their own creators? Did they create the Heavens and the Earth?" (52:35-36). Let us analyze one question at a time.

"Were they [the humans] created without a Creator?" A Muslim will answer no to this question because the Quran says that **"He [Allah] created man"** (16:4). Similarly, a non-Muslim theist will also answer no to this question, even if his/her definition of Creator differs from that of Muslims.

An atheist or one who believes in evolution might say that creation of humans was the consequence of a long evolutionary chain. *Homo sapien* was the last link, whereas the first link (or origin of life) was some bacteria-like micro-organisms. But how life originated either remains unknown or is credited to some reaction of a combination of chemicals. In other words, some mysterious event was the creator. Therefore, the answer to the Quranic question is still no.

"Or were they their own creators?" It is highly unlikely that any person, Muslim, non-Muslim theist or atheist, would claim that they gave birth to themselves. Again, the unanimous response to this question would be no.

"Did they create the Heavens and the Earth?" Again, no person is likely to argue that s/he is the creator of the universe. Do not forget that you are also part of the universe. If you were unable to create yourself, how could you create the universe? The unanimous answer to this question is also no.

These verses inspire the rational mind to reflect on the relationship between an object/life form to its creator. If some chemicals created life as bacteria-like micro-organisms in the ocean, then who created the chemicals? Who created scientific laws that allow chemical reactions to generate life? Who created the ocean? Who created earth? Who created the universe? Was the universe created without a Creator or was it created by itself? We agreed above that a man cannot create himself, a woman cannot create herself. Everything has a Creator. Then how could the universe exist without a Creator? This leads to the next obvious question: *Who created the universe?* The Quran answers: **"It is Allah, Who has created the Heavens and the Earth"** (14:32).

The above three questions are more relevant today than ever before. Science has already established that the universe did not exist since eternity. Instead, the universe began after the 'big bang.' But that couldn't have happened without a Creator. So, we can say with utmost certainty that Allah is the Creator of the universe.

ARGUMENT AGAINST ATHEISM: THE WATCHMAKER ANALOGY

This highly controversial subject has been discussed since the time of Aristotle and was made famous as the *watchmaker analogy* by the English clergyman William Paley (1743–1805). In plain English, the watchmaker analogy suggests that the *existence* of a perfectly functioning watch proves that the watch was not created by some random incident like an earthquake, hurricane, flood, tsunami or meteor shower. Instead, a watch that moves its hands precisely every second and accurately tracks every minute has to have been carefully designed, by a designer or watchmaker. The existence of the watch also proves that the watch was designed and created with a *purpose*, to calculate time. In other words, if the watch exists, its designer must also exist. Our universe is far more complex and precise than a watch; the planets and stars move and rotate at precise speeds. By the same logic, the existence of the universe proves that its ultimate designer (God) also exists.

Atheists may respond, "If the above argument is correct, then who designed the designer?" In other words, if the existence of the universe proves the existence of God, then by the same token, the existence of God proves that God also has a creator! Is this argument correct?

In all Xenophanic religions, the atheist's argument makes perfect sense. Since God is a man, that man must eat, or he will go hungry. He must drink water to quench his thirst. If he is wounded, he will bleed. If he has none of these limitations, how can anyone claim that God is man? In other words, human-god is *bound by human logic* and limitations, though a human-god may also possess some godly traits.

According to human logic, not just a watch but every object has a creator. Therefore human-god, who is compatible with human logic, should also have a Creator!

IS THE QUESTION "WHO DESIGNED THE DESIGNER" APPLICABLE TO ISLAM?

This is not a new question. Desert-dwellers asked Prophet Muhammad[PBUH] the same question and Allah *precisely* answered them (chapter 2): **"He [Allah] begets not, nor is He begotten"** (112:3). This unusual concept has no parallel among all earthly life. Throughout the Quran, Allah remains unique in every way. For example, today there are more than seven billion people on earth, while **"Allah is one (or alone)"** (112:1). Unlike a human, **"Allah is Self-Sufficient"** (112:2). With human beings, even the concept of self-sufficiency does not exist.

The atheist question, "Who designed the designer?" is based on human logic totally inapplicable to and incompatible with Allah. Why? Because, in Islam, the Creator never becomes any part of His creation and the creation never becomes part of the Creator. So there is no man and god overlap. The Creator never shared any trait or property with His creation. The Quran is very clear: ***"there is nothing like Him* [Allah]"** (42:11). Furthermore, the Arabic words **"Subhan-Allah"** (16:1) mean Allah is pure, free from all human limitations or anthropomorphic associations. Claiming that human logic is also applicable to Allah is like trying to impose human characteristics on the Creator of humanity. That is not possible in Islam. The following verse explains. **"He [Allah] is far above and beyond from the shirk they do"** (16:1). In Islam, even imagining similarity between Allah and humans is considered shirk.

Allah remains beyond our imagination. *In the absence of any similarity*, there is no justification that, just like in the human world, God would also have a Creator.

THE QURAN RESPONDS TO ANOTHER OBJECTION

The atheist may object, "What is the proof that God, as defined in the verse **"He [Allah] begets not, nor is He begotten"** (112:3) exists?" If we reject the message in verse 112:3, we must admit we are only guessing, just because there is no parallel to Allah in our worldly experience.

Next, the Quran responds to the atheist's objection by prohibiting people from making wild guesses. **"So far you have been arguing about things of which you had *some* knowledge! Must you now argue about that of which <u>you know nothing at all</u>?** *Allah knows while you do not"* (3:66).

It must be noted that the above arguments against the watchmaker analogy are drawn from different verses of the Quran, quoted earlier in this chapter. They are not the author's comments or opinion.

Q: Can you find any verse in the Quran that proves that human logic binds Allah? (Please do not use *hidden* meanings or similes, and do not contradict any verse of the Quran.) **"Produce proof to your claim, if you are truthful"** (2:111).

Q: The Quran asks you a question: **"Do you attribute to Allah something which you do not know?"** (2:80).

THE QURAN GUIDES THE ATHEIST

Atheism contains some major logical weaknesses. It cannot prove that God does not exist. Atheists have no explanation for how matter, time and energy *originated* out of nothing. How did the laws of science come into existence?

"All power belongs to Allah" (2:165). This verse includes all scientific laws and all forces of nature, including gravity and electricity. How was the darkness created? How was space created? The entire atheist ideology is based on the assumption that creation of the universe and the way it is sustained occurred by itself or by sheer coincidence. Therefore, the atheist concludes that God does not exist. The Quran points to the weakness in this approach: **"The fact is that most of them [the unbelievers] follow nothing but mere wild guesses and guess is in no way a substitute for the truth"** (10:36).

ARGUMENT AGAINST BELIEVER-PROJECTED-GOD AND SELF-PROCLAIMED-GOD

The Quran says: **"Do they associate with Him [Allah] those deities who can create nothing but are *themselves created*, they [deities]** have neither the ability to help them [their believers], nor can they help themselves?" (7:191–192). Here the Quran inspires us to ponder:

Q: Why does one person worship another human, when both humans are created by Allah and both depend on Allah?

Q: Why not worship Allah, who is the Creator, and also capable of helping every human?

MONOTHEISTIC ISLAM, POLYTHEISTIC MUSLIMS

Islam and Muslim are not synonymous. Scholars explain that Islam is a religion, while a Muslim is a person who claims to follow the religion of Islam. Just like the followers of other faiths, all Muslims do not share identical beliefs. A few years after Prophet Muhammad[PBUH], polytheism started making inroads among Muslims. Since then, under different pretexts, some (but not all) Muslims have been elevating their saints, Caliph Ali or Prophet Muhammad[PBUH] to the divine status via the believer-projected-god scenario. For example, an Urdu poet claims:

> *The one [Allah] who established Himself on the [Divine] throne as God*
> *Came down in Medina as Mustafa [Prophet Muhammad[PBUH]][80]*

One of the most popular songs of the Indian subcontinent says, "*Damadam must Qalandar… Ali dam de Ander.*" This means, "Sufi saint Mast Qalandar aka Lal Shahbaz Qalandar (1177 – 1274) is in every breath… Ali is in every breath." But according to Islam, Allah alone should be remembered with every breath, not any human (slave) of Allah. Surprisingly, this devotional song does not mention *Allah* even once.

Similarly, Rumi said about his contemporary, Sufi Shams:

"Let me inform you without mincing words, that my Shams is not only my guide, my disciple, my pain, my relief, but he is also my God."[81]

Is it possible for many Muslims to become polytheistic and yet Islam to remain monotheistic? Yes, it is possible! This is because the Quran is a 100 percent pure monotheistic book, and it is beyond human capability to alter the words of the Quran, to make it support the polytheistic belief of any sect (chapter 2). This has an interesting consequence—even if various major Islamic sects hold vastly different beliefs and a violent past going back 1400 years, they are forced to follow the exact same Quran, no matter what!

ISLAM STANDS OUT 8: *EVERY* MUSLIM WILL *NOT* GO TO HEAVEN

Since polytheism is an unforgivable sin, on the Day of Judgment, what will happen to polytheists who claim to be Muslims? While many other religions claim that *all* their followers will go to Paradise, Islam makes an unusual yet justified claim. The Quran gives a severe warning to polytheists who claim to be Muslims: **"*most* of them who believe in Allah *also commit shirk*"** (12:106). Prophet Muhammad[PBUH] said that after his death, eventually, the Muslims would be divided into 73 sects and, out of those, the members of only one sect will go to Paradise.[82] If a person verbally claims to follow Islam and performs Islamic worship rituals but privately believes in polytheism (as judged by Allah), then that person is still going to hellfire. Allah can do that because **"[Allah] knows exactly what you hide and what you reveal"** (27:25).

PRE-ANALYSIS DISCUSSIONS

Polytheism among Muslims is a complex, centuries-old problem. What makes this issue more complicated is that generally Muslims verbally deny committing shirk. According to Abd al-Wahab: "no Muslim will ever admit that he is falling into shirk." As a solution, he proposed: "what needs to be examined are a person's actions and beliefs and not any verbal denial of shirk."[83] Why do Muslims verbally deny shirk? Because the Quran, the holy book of all major Islamic sects, stands firmly against shirk, without any contradiction! So, members of all sects also have to deny that they are committing shirk, and profess that they are following the Quran!

Before addressing the problem itself, let us first analyze some relevant issues.

WHO IS THE SPEAKER?

Islam has several different sources of information and schools of scholarly interpretation. For example, while performing ritual supplication, is it a requirement for a man to wear a cap? Questions like this have conflicting answers, which can confuse a believer. The solution is to correctly prioritize information.

QURAN – THE LITERAL WORD OF GOD

The Quran is the unaltered, preserved word of Allah. It is the most important source of Islamic information. Problems arise when different schools of thought develop conflicting interpretations of the uniquely one Quran. Who is telling the truth? The Quran itself solves this problem. It says that *muhkamat* verses are unambiguous and decisive. They contain the fundamental knowledge about Islam (3:7 in chapter 2 of this book). Also, no interpretation can contradict the foundation of the Quran or *muhkamat* verses. For example, no interpretation can contradict the concept of monotheism. Based on the *muhkamat* verses, a Muslim is expected to discern which interpretation of the Quran is correct. The Quran mandates: **"Why do you not reflect?"** (6:50). Such confusion is part of Allah's test and forces a Muslim to ponder and carry out introspection.

HADITH: WORDS OF PROPHET MUHAMMAD[PBUH], BUT COMPILED BY MEN

Forging of the hadith literature

Scholars disagree about the earliest incident of hadith fabrication, but they all agree that an enormous amount of forgery has been committed, or has crept into the vast hadith literature.[84] Some anti-Islamic groups have tried to popularize fabricated hadith, primarily to corrupt the pure monotheism. Other motives were for political, theological or legal gain over rivals.[85]

How to evaluate a hadith

No doubt, the hadith is an essential part of Islam. At the same time, a false hadith can do all kinds of damage, particularly in regards to pure monotheism, and it can be used to gain political advantage. Therefore, it is important for every adult Muslim to learn how to verify if a proposed hadith is fabricated or true. Only the true hadith is from Allah and can therefore be part of Islamic belief.

Verification of a hadith is quite a challenge. Originally, ahadith were written in Arabic, but today only a small percentage of Muslims can understand classical Arabic. Confusion also arises because different sects of Islam have their own collections of ahadith books, some with vastly different contents. That is not all; the hadith books are so voluminous that it can take months just to read through them. (Arabic *Sahih Bukhari* has about 7,052 ahadith and *Sahih Muslim* has about 9,200 ahadith.)

Fortunately, the Quran itself addresses this difficult challenge in verse 3:7, wherein it states that no person should try to interpret the allegorical verses of the Quran so that their interpretation contradicts the *fundamental* ideas of the Quran. This condition is also applicable to ahadith. Every hadith should be in agreement with the essence of the Quran. Otherwise, the hadith itself should be rejected as a fabrication.

For example, if a hadith claims that a particular saint is a god, then it would violate the fundamental principle of monotheism. Such a hadith should be rejected, because Prophet Muhammad[PBUH] would never have said anything that contradicts the foundation of the Quran. It does not matter in which hadith book it is written. Of course, the people who collected the ahadith, years after Prophet Muhammad[PBUH], could have made mistakes, or someone else could have added false ahadith to the books.

Islamic scholars have been using this method of hadith evaluation for centuries. One of the most recognized biographies of Prophet Muhammad[PBUH], *Serat un-Nabi,* by Shibli Nomani (1857–1914), discussed this issue in detail. Nomani quoted the rules of hadith evaluation set by Muslim juris consult Ibn Jauzi (d: 1201). He rejected those ahadith that go *against the accepted principles.*[86] Thus the fundamentals of the Quran can be used to judge the authenticity of a hadith. Chapter 2 of this book explains that the hadith protects the interpretation of the Quran. Here we see that the fundamentals of the Quran can be used to judge the authenticity of a hadith, and thus the Quran helps in evaluating a hadith.

We can include one additional helpful tool of the information age. Many software and websites allow textual searches through the voluminous hadith literature. If we hear an unusual hadith, then the first step should be to do a text search just to ensure that the hadith exists in the recognized six books of authentic ahadith.[87] We may be surprised how many frequently quoted hadith are glaringly absent from the standard hadith books.

One word of caution: Suppose we find a hadith that contradicts a fundamental idea of the Quran, then we should reject *only* that specific hadith. We can say, "I do not understand this hadith." Also, we should keep looking for an explanation of the hadith, just in case we ourselves have been mistaken. We should, of course, avoid the extreme step of rejecting *all* ahadith and claiming only the Quran is adequate to learn Islam. Similarly, if we reject one hadith, then we should be careful *not* to reject the entire book that contained that particular false hadith.

ISLAMIC JURISPRUDENCE

Islamic Jurisprudence (*fiqh*) is defined as, "the science which deals with observance of rituals, principles of the five pillars, and social legislation."[88] Islamic Jurisprudence evolved more than a century after the death of Prophet Muhammad[PBUH] and it developed in different regions in different periods. Therefore, there are several different schools of Islamic Jurisprudence. As Muslim kingdoms expanded and the Muslim population increased, Muslim judges relied on Islamic Jurisprudence to resolve new situations which were not addressed in the Quran and hadith. To answer such questions, different schools of Islamic Jurisprudence used several permitted methodologies, including independent reasoning (*ijtihad*), consensus (*ijmah*) and deductive analogy (*qiyas*).[89]

At times, the schools have conflicting opinions. For example, according to the Shafai and Hambali Schools, women should be fully veiled, but according to the Hanafi and Maliki Schools, women need not cover their hands and faces.[90] When it comes to personal worship, such difference of opinion can be a blessing, because it permits flexibility. Based on necessity, Muslims can select a suitable school of jurisprudence for themselves, to avoid undue hardship in worship.

Is it binding upon Muslims to follow any particular school of Islamic Jurisprudence? Medieval Islamic jurisconsult and theologian Ibn Qayyum (1292–1350) argues that following a school of Islamic Jurisprudence is not necessary, because these schools came into existence about a century after the death of Prophet Muhammad[PBUH], and the first few generations after the Prophet never followed any school. Therefore, following schools is certainly optional.[91]

As discussed above, if any rule of Jurisprudence conflicts with monotheism, then the rule can be rejected. After all, many jurisprudential rules are man-made deductions, and therefore they cannot overrule the foundation of the Quran either.

RELIGIOUS RULING (*FATWA*) BY A SCHOLAR

At times, new situations occur that were not addressed in the Quran, hadith or Islamic Jurisprudence. In that case, contemporary Muslim scholars are allowed to issue a religious ruling or *fatwa*. Sometimes, Muslim scholars have conflicting opinions. How to choose the right opinion? The following verse (23:47) solves this problem by telling us to analyze "what is being said," instead of "what is the status of the speakers." When Prophets Moses and Haroon (PBUT) went with the message of Islam, the Pharaoh's courtesans said: **"Should we believe in two human beings like ourselves and *whose people are our slaves*?"** (23:47). The courtesans made the mistake of evaluating the message on the basis of the status of the speakers, instead of appraising the message itself.

In addition, fatwa should be in line with the Quran and hadith. For example, any *fatwa* that conflicts with monotheism should be outrightly rejected. That is why some of the opinions of extreme Sufis are debatable and can be rejected. There is a saying: *Kalame soofian dar shariat hujjat neest* (do not use the quotes of the Sufi as logical arguments for Islamic Jurisprudence).

SEEKING HELP FROM OTHER HUMANS AND DANGER OF SHIRK

The Quran clearly states this fundamental rule: **"[O'Allah] You Alone we worship and You *Alone* we call on for *help*"** (1:5). It should be noted that: (1) this verse uses the word *help* in the context of *worship*; and (2) in divine issues, seek help *only* from Allah. In other words, when it comes to *praying* (seeking help in a divine context), then one should pray only to Allah, not any intermediary or any human (dead or alive).

What about the kind of help that is not related to worship? Can humans seek such help from each other? The Quran explains that seeking help in our daily lives from other people is not only allowed, but in accordance with the divine plan: **"It is We [Allah] Who distribute the means of their livelihood in the life of this world, *raising some [humans] in rank above others, so that one may take others into his service*"** (43:32).

A restaurant cook serves hungry customers; at the same time she is dependent on her dentist and stockbroker. When it comes to seeking help from other people, there are some conditions, however. You can only ask for help from a person who is alive, present, and capable of helping you. Just because Prophet Muhammad[PBUH] asked for someone's help on a worldly issue, it does not mean that a Muslim today can ask for help from that same person, who died a long time ago.

There was a time when Prophet Muhammad[PBUH] was left without tribal support and he used Arab tradition and for a brief period asked for shelter from a pagan Al-Mut'im bin 'Adi against the atrocities of Mecca's pagans.[92] This does not in any way mean that today if a Muslim feels threatened, then s/he can also ask Al-Mut'im bin 'Adi for shelter. By the same token, many companions helped Prophet Muhammad[PBUH] in relation to worldly issues during his lifetime, but we cannot seek their help because they are no longer alive.

Suppose you were seriously ill and a competent doctor brought you back to health. In that case, who cured you, the doctor or Allah? The correct answer obviously is Allah, because He is the one who provided the capable doctor along with many supporting factors, like the prior discovery of a cure and availability of medicine. Therefore, only Allah should get full credit and gratitude. However, Islam expects the patient to pray for and thank the doctor as well. Humans need reassurance and encouragement to continue to perform good deeds. The problem starts when the patient thinks that, instead of Allah, it is the doctor who deserves more than a human share of the credit. This is a tempting thought, because Allah is unseen, but you can see and hear the doctor. It means that the patient does not believe that Allah as the only Doer and Sustainer. To such a patient, the doctor appears as a partner with Allah, as in a believer-projected-god scenario or shirk. Such shirk must be avoided at all costs.

THE INTERCESSION (*SHAFA'A*)

Loosely speaking, there is not much difference between a prayer and an intercession, *provided* the believer directly and exclusively calls on Allah, without any intermediary or intercessor. When a believer says, "Allah, forgive me" or "Allah, help me," the believer is acting as his/her own intercessor.

The beneficiary of the intercession can also be someone else. Islam allows group prayer, in which people jointly intercede for one righteous cause. For example, the prayer **"[O'Allah!] Guide *us* to The Right path"** (1:6) seeks guidance for the entire human race. Similarly, it is allowed to request a living person to pray for someone, for the right cause.

INTERCESSION BY PIOUS PEOPLE

Just like group prayers during our lifetime, on the Day of Judgment, restricted intercession will be allowed. For example, Allah will allow selected righteous people and Prophets to make different types of intercessions for others. This leads to an interesting point: it is difficult for human intercession to coexist with justice! For example, if a sinner is a blood relative of a saint or Prophet, then that person would be expected to be forgiven, while an unrelated sinner of the same degree would be punished. The Quran solves this problem by restricting intercession, thus ensuring justice will prevail and the Judgment of Allah will always remain fair and final.

1. On the Day of Judgment, Allah will choose the person *who can benefit* from intercession. If a sinner does not deserve this, then no pious person on his/her own can intercede for that sinner: **"They**

do not intercede except for the *one whom He [Allah] approves"* (21:28).

2. On the Day of Judgment, Allah also chooses the intercessor: **"Who can intercede with Him [Allah] without His permission?"** (2:255). This verse means that we will not be able to select and choose our own intercessor. According to Egyptian-Canadian Muslim scholar Dr. Jamal Badawi: this qualification for this intersession is that this can only be granted after God gives permission.[93]

3. Even after human intercession, on the Day of Judgment, it is up to Allah to approve or reject the proposed intercession: **"Their intercession *can avail none* unless Allah gives them permission in favor of whom He wants and *is pleased with*"** (53:26). Therefore, throughout this process, Allah remains the only and final judge. The Quran gives an example of such rejection of intercession. Abdullah bin Ubai converted to Islam, but he was leader of Medina's hypocrites. His intention was to harm Muslims and his belief in Islam was not sincere. He was responsible for causing tremendous suffering to Muslims and to Prophet Muhammad[PBUH]. Still, when he died, Prophet Muhammad[PBUH] asked Allah to forgive him. The following verse was then revealed: **"O Prophet! It is the same, whether you ask forgiveness for them [hypocrites] or not; even if you ask for their forgiveness seventy times, Allah is not going to forgive them"** (9:80).

4. No matter who intercedes, Allah remains in continuous and total control at all times. There is absolutely no concept of independent controlling-intercessor in Islam.

According to the Quran, the bottom line is: **"Say [Oh Muhammad[PBUH]]: 'Intercession is *wholly* in the hands of Allah'"** (39:44). With so many restrictions, what is the point of human intercession? Allah alone is the real Doer behind the scenes (chapter 2). For example, even if an angel kills a person, Allah is still the real Doer, because Allah orders it and makes it happen. Similarly, on the Day of Judgment, if a person is forgiven because of the intercessor, again Allah would be the real Doer. Pakistani-American Muslim scholar Yasir Qadhi explains that intercession on the Day of Judgment is just a form of honoring the intercessor.[94]

OTHER INTERCESSIONS

On the Day of Judgment, the good actions of a person will also serve as intercessions. Prophet Muhammad[PBUH] said, "On the Day of Resurrection it [the Quran] will come as an intercessor for those who recite it."[95] Similarly, ritual fast (*sawm*) will say, "O Lord, I prevented him from his food and desires during the day. Let me intercede for him."[96] In both these cases, a believer has to *earn* his/her intercession by right belief and good actions in this life.

Intercession is not something that a person hopes to receive because of his/her closeness to a saint or Prophet. The Quran says: **"As for those who believe and do good deeds, for them there will be prosperity and a beautiful place of final return"** (13:29). In this life, our intercession is based on whom we love. In contrast, on the Day of Judgment, intercession will be based on belief and good deeds alone, while Allah will be the ultimate Judge. The Quran describes many instances in which close relatives of different Prophets were sent to hellfire. For example, the son of the Prophet Noah[PBUH] was condemned to hellfire.

Prophet Muhammad[PBUH] said, "When a man dies, his acts come to an end, but three –recurring charity, knowledge [by which people] benefit, or a pious son, who prays for him [after a parent's death]."[97] The important point is that in all three of these cases, the deceased benefits from the long-term consequences of his/her own good deeds performed during his/her lifetime. For example, the deceased person gave the correct Islamic education to his/her children and, as a result, the children prayed for the parent. So the parent gets the benefit.

WASEELA AND TAWASSUL

The word *waseela* is a noun derived from the Arabic root wāw sīn lām, which means *to get close*. According to Ibn Manzur's Arabic Dictionary, the word *waseela* is a means to approach something to attain *nearness*.[98] The word *tawassul* is derived from the same root and means 'using waseela.'

That is why a status in Paradise is also called Waseela, which is closest to Allah, and only one person will be awarded this status. Allah promised this status to Prophet Muhammad[PBUH]. Muslims pray that Prophet Muhammad[PBUH] will be the one who is awarded this highest status of intercession. However, Prophet Muhammad[PBUH] explained in a hadith that on the Day of Judgment he would only be able to intercede for those who deserve it. For example, he would not intercede for a person who mistreated his animals.[99] Abu Huraira asked Prophet Muhammad[PBUH],

"Who will have the greatest chance to gain your intercession?" Prophet Muhammad[PBUH] said, "one who says *there exists no god but Allah* with a *sincere heart.*" Again, without contradiction, Islamic monotheism retains the highest priority.

The Quran says: **"O believers! Fear Allah and seek the means to be closer [Arabic word *waseela* used here] to Him [Allah]"** (5:35). The question is, how can one exercise tawassul, or "seek means to get closer to Allah?" Another verse of the Quran provides the answer: **"Whoever hopes to meet his Lord [get close to Him], let him do good deeds and join no other deity in the worship of his Lord [have correct belief by avoiding shirk]"** (18:110). In other words, the only way to get closer to Allah is by *personal* belief and righteous actions of each individual believer.

Just as we are not responsible for the actions of others, others cannot do the work for us. Pakistani Canadian Islamic scholar Dr. Farhat Hashmi described the following types of permissible waseela, along with evidence from the Quran and hadith: Belief in Islamic monotheism (*iman*), calling Allah using his attributes, ritual supplication (*salah*), fasting (*saum*), Hajj pilgrimage, *jihad*, recitation of the Quran, remembering Allah (*dhirk*), and reciting *Subhan-Allah*, and other short sentences to glorify Allah (*tasbih*), reciting the prayer of peace on Prophet Muhammad[PBUH] and his followers (*durood*), seeking forgiveness from Allah, prayer, praying for others, good deeds, and staying away from sins.[100] This interpretation of waseela is in line with the above discussion and the theme of the Quran: **"no soul shall bear the burden of another"** (53:38).

EXAMPLES OF CONTROVERSIAL TAWASSUL OR SHAFA'A

CATEGORY 1: PRAYER CALL TO DECEASED PIOUS MAN WITH OR WITHOUT ALLAH

1. Asking a deceased pious man to *intercede* in divine affairs: For example, instead of Allah, Tunisian historian Ibn Khaldun (d: 1406) asked Prophet Muhammad[PBUH]: "Grant me your intercession for which I hope, a beautiful page instead of ugly sins."[101]

2. Instead of Allah, directly asking for *help* from a deceased pious man: "Ya Ali madad" [O Ali help] or "Ali Mushkil-Kushā" [Ali is the solver of problems]. An Urdu poet, Shakeel Badayuni, calls *bekas pe karam keejiye sarkare Medina* [help the helpless oh master of Medina (Prophet Muhammad[PBUH])].

CATEGORY 2: CALLING ALLAH USING THE LEVERAGE OF RANK OR LOVE OF A PIOUS MAN

1. Saudi Islamic scholar Muhammad Alawi suggests a sample prayer that uses the leverage of *love*: "O Allah, indeed I love so and so and believe that he loves you, that he is sincere to You and that he strives in your path. I believe that You love him and are pleased with him; so *I use him as a means to You* by my love for him and my belief in him."[102]
2. Ask Allah while using the *rank* of a pious man as leverage. Alawi provides a sample prayer: "O Allah I ask you by the *rank* of the Prophet."[103]

ANALYZING CONTROVERSIAL PRAYERS

DOES THE QURAN SUPPORT CONTROVERSIAL PRAYER OF CATEGORY-1?

As discussed above, the verse **"O'Allah! You Alone we worship and You Alone we call on for help"** (1:5) proves that a Muslim can seek help in the divine context only from Allah. This means no prayer should use any intercessor or intermediary. Since the Quran does not contain any contradiction, therefore, out of dozens of prayers in the Quran, *every single prayer* should follow the rule set by verse 1:5. This is quite a challenge, since humans have a strong attraction to Xenophanic practice. When we search the Quran, it turns out that *every single prayer in the Quran calls on Allah only and never uses any intercessor or intermediary*. Thus, the Quran remains free from contradiction. One more proof that the Quran is the word of God, not man. No wonder all the controversial sample prayers (in categories 1 and 2 above) are man-made sample prayers. The reason is obvious. In the Quran, they could not find any prayer using an intercessor or intermediary!

Here are some examples of prayers from the Quran:

Prayers by Prophets prior to Prophet Muhammad[PBUH]: Prophet Jonah[PBUH] asked for forgiveness, directly from Allah: **"There is no god but You, glory be to You! Indeed I was the one who committed wrong"** (21:87). Here Prophet Jonah[PBUH] did not use the tawassul of Prophet Abraham[PBUH] or any other previously deceased Prophet.

Prayers used by Muslims during the lifetime of Prophet Muhammad[PBUH]: The Quran quotes the companions of Prophet Muhammad[PBUH] who were late to migrate to Medina as praying, **"Our Lord! Forgive us…"** (59:10). Here we must note that, in this prayer, the companions did not use tawassul or intercession of Prophet Muhammad[PBUH], even though he was alive.

<u>Prayer by Prophet Muhammad</u>[PBUH]: Allah teaches Prophet Muhammad[PBUH] a prayer, **"Say: 'O Lord, forgive, have Mercy'"** (23:118). This prayer is for all Muslims, to be used during and after the lifetime of Prophet Muhammad[PBUH]. This prayer does not use tawassul of Prophet Muhammad[PBUH] or Caliph Ali.

<u>Prayers taught by Allah</u>: When Prophet Muhammad[PBUH] went on the *meeraj* (nightly journey), he was given the following verse. This verse has eight different prayers. Every prayer addresses Allah *directly*. These prayers are meant for all Muslims. No prayer uses tawassul or shafa'a of Prophet Muhammad[PBUH] or Caliph Ali, even though both were alive at the time of the revelation. Here is the first line of the verse: **"Our Lord! Do not punish us if we forget or make a mistake …"** (2:286).

A man once said to Prophet Muhammad, "By the will of Allah and then by your will." To this, the Prophet seriously objected and asked the man, "Have you made me an associate with Allah?" and then suggested the correct prayer, "What Allah *alone* wills."[104]

Readers are encouraged to read the Quran and verify that it passes this crucial test of non-contradiction. Please do not confuse actual *prayer* with the *request for prayer*, because it is allowed to make a prayer request to a live person. Instead, try to look for a prayer in which the *words of the prayer* itself include the tawassul. For example, the prayer suggested by Shakeel Badayuni above. If you do manage to find a prayer that uses tawassul of any pious man (alive or dead) to pray to Allah, you would be the first person in 1400 years to find a contradiction in the Quran.

As a word of caution, in case anyone quotes a *translation* of a prayer from the Quran that uses controversial tawassul described above, then how is one to verify if it is *muhkamat* verse? A quick but less than thorough test would be to visit any website that shows the Quran in translation by several authors. All website translations should be the same as the suggested translation and support the controversial tawassul.

Challenge Q: When no prayer from the Quran contradicts the fundamental principle set by verse 1:5, does any human have the authority to suggest a sample prayer (similar to both categories above) that violates the fundamental principle of monotheism?

In the believer-projected-god scenario, the believer hopes to control the out-of-reach God through an intermediary. Such Muslims usually visit the graves of pious men. These believers may end up elevating the intermediary to the status of Allah, or even higher. *Nauzubillah* (it means "we seek refuge from Allah." In this book, this term is used when a statement is written to explain or describe something sacrilegious.) For example, an Urdu poet said: *Arshe Aala se A'ala meetha nabi ka roza* (the tomb of the sweet Prophet [Muhammad] is higher than the throne of Allah). Or *Ali naam hai Khuda ka, koi maane ya na maane* (Ali is the name of God, whether anyone believes it or not).

DOES THE QURAN SUPPORT THE CONTROVERSIAL PRAYERS OF CATEGORY-2?

Humans can be influenced by love and the rank of others. For example, a human judge, if persuaded by loved ones or higher officials, may deviate from justice. The category-2 prayers try to use the same persuasion on Allah. But this violates the principle of justice set forth in the Quran: **"Today [on the Day of Judgment] every soul shall be rewarded for whatever it has earned; today there shall be no *injustice*"** (40:17).

Category-2 prayers lower the status of Allah to human level. They assume that, just like a human, Allah can also be influenced by the love and rank of pious men to do injustice. This assumption is invalid because **"Allah is the Self-Sufficient"** (112:2). Also, **"*there is nothing like Him*"** (42:11) therefore, do not imagine that Allah has human limitations and can be influenced by the love and rank of pious men.

Q: Humans may commit injustice when influenced by love and rank of an intercessor. Can you offer proof from the Quran that Allah also does similar injustice (Nauzubillah)?

Pakistani-Canadian Islamic Scholar Tahir-ul-Qadri claims that the use of love and rank in prayer can make prayer more effective: *"The prayer is submitted only to Allah* and while appealing to Him to grant these needs and desires, the mediation of the holy Prophet, a saintly person or a pious deed is cited because they enjoy Allah's love and favor and, therefore, He has greater regard for them than for other creatures. So such form of intermediation not only makes the words of *prayer more effective but also raises its chance of acceptance by Allah."*[105] Is the above statement true?

The following questions can help us decide:

Q: The Quran records that Prophet Joseph[PBUH], in his most desperate moment, prayed: **"May Allah protect me"** (12:23). If seeking help from the deceased and using the leverage of love are more effective, then why did Prophet Joseph[PBUH] not say, "Allah, you love my father, Prophet Jacob, grandfather, Prophet Isaac, grand-uncle Prophet Ishmael, and great-grandfather, Prophet Abraham (PBUT). I use them as a means to You. So help me?"

Challenge Q: In the entire Quran there is not a single prayer that uses the leverage of love or rank. If the statement by Qadri: "The mediation of the holy Prophet, a saintly person…. makes the words of *prayer more effective,"* is correct, then it would mean that every prayer in the Quran is of inferior quality (Nauzubillah). Is this true? Definitely not!

Challenge Q: If love leverage makes a prayer more effective, then can you improve Prophet Joseph's[PBUH] above Quranic prayer in Arabic by adding love leverage (Nauzubillah)?

DOES THE HADITH SUPPORT CATEGORY-1 OR CATEGORY-2 PRAYERS?

In addition to the Quran, Prophet Muhammad[PBUH] also gave us hundreds of prayers through the hadith. One such prayer from the hadith says: "O Allah Our Lord! And all the praises are for You. *O Allah! Forgive me."*[106] This prayer does not say, "Allah, forgive me because You love Prophet Muhammad[PBUH]" or "Allah, I ask you by the rank of Prophet Muhammad[PBUH] to forgive me." In Qadri's book "Islamic Concept of Intermediation", you will find that the ideology to promote intercession is based primarily on very few ahadith, which support the case of tawassul of a deceased human. But the overwhelming majority of prayers found in the six hadith books[107] do not use the tawassul of any deceased human. Nor do they use the leverage of love and rank. Those ahadith prayers obey the rule: **"O'Allah! You Alone we worship and *You Alone we call on for help"*** (1:5).

Unlike the Quran, a hadith can be easily fabricated, or even a sincere compiler of hadith may make the mistake of including a false hadith to his collection. The Quran records some Prophets making mistakes (judgmental errors). No hadith compiler can be higher than the Prophets. This means, the hadith compilers can also make mistakes. However, the fact remains that about 99 percent of hadith prayers found in six hadith books[108] do not use four types of controversial tawassul. This means that the hadith prayers also obey the rule: **"O'Allah! You Alone we worship and *You Alone we call on for help"*** (1:5). Praying to Allah alone is the foundation of the Quran. Consequently, no hadith can contradict the foundation.

Just because a hadith exists, does not mean that Prophet Muhammad[PBUH] actually said so. All it means is that people of later generations *claimed* that

Prophet Muhammad[PBUH] made that statement. As suggested by the criteria set by Ibn Jauzi, any hadith supporting the four controversial types of tawassul should be ignored.

METHOD OF EVALUATING THE HADITH THAT SUPPORTS TAWASSUL

Next, let us analyze one sample hadith that supports the controversial tawassul. For example, Alawi quotes the following hadith: "When Adam committed his mistake he said, 'O my Lord! I am asking you to forgive me by *the right of Muhammad[PBUH].*' Allah said, 'O Adam! How do you know about Muhammad[PBUH] whom I have not yet created?' Adam replied 'O my Lord! After you created me with Your Hand and breathed into me of Your Spirit, I raised my head and saw on the heights of the Throne: 'there exists no god but Allah and Muhammad[PBUH] is His messenger'. I understood that you would not place next to your name any but the most beloved one of Your Creation.' Allah said, 'O Adam! I have forgiven you and if it were not for Muhammad[PBUH] I would not have created you."[109]

Whenever you hear an unusual hadith, as a rule of thumb, always do a text search in a hadith collection, just to ensure the hadith exists in the same form as claimed. Next, let us analyze this hadith:

1. The Quran already contains the prayer of Adam and Eve, which Allah accepted. They prayed: **"Lord, we have done injustice to our souls. If You will not forgive us and have mercy on us, we shall certainly have incurred a great loss"** (7:23). The prayer in this verse was the reason why Allah forgave Adam and Eve, and it is without tawassul of Prophet Muhammad[PBUH].

2. Which of the two prayers of Adam is better? If anyone believes that the hadith prayer using an intermediary is better, then it would mean that Allah quoted the inferior quality prayers in the Quran (Nauzubillah)!

3. The prayer quoted by Alawi above, contradicts the principle established by 100 percent of the prayers in the Quran and about 99 percent of the prayers in standard hadith books.

For sure, Prophet Muhammad[PBUH] would never make a statement that leads to shirk. Therefore, as suggested by Ibn Jauzi, such a hadith cannot be accepted as true. The same principle applies to the few other ahadith quoted to support an intercessor or intermediary or leverage of love and rank.

Does Islam allow seeking help from a *deceased* pious person?

Muslims believe that after death the souls of people remain behind a barrier or veil (*burzakh*). There martyrs are given higher status because: **"Do not say about those who are slain in the cause of Allah (martyrs), that they are dead. Nay, they are alive, but *you do not perceive it*"** (2:154). This verse tells us that martyrs who died in battle were not losers. Instead, they are alive to Allah, even though they are dead to us. In addition, Allah has rewarded them. Since Prophets hold the highest status compared to the rest of humanity, they should also have similar or better privileges.

Qadri concludes from the above verse (2:154): "*Just as it is valid to beseech the help of a person during his earthly life and during his life after death and to rely on his means, it is also an equally valid act to beseech his help and to rely on his means in his purgatorial life.*"[10]

Can the deceased hear and assist us? The above verse itself answers this question: **"*you do not perceive.*"** (2:154) It means that as far as we are concerned, the deceased are no longer with us. That is why Muslims bury their dead (instead of making mummies). The Quran not only specifically prohibits calling the deceased, but also explains the reason: **"Those whom they call on besides Allah have not created anything while they are *themselves created.* (They are) *dead, not living.* And they do not [even] know when they will be raised [on the Day of Judgment]"** (16:20-21). Another verse says: **"The fact is that you cannot make the dead hear you"** (27:80).

Since the deceased cannot hear us, therefore, not even a single prayer in the Quran calls the deceased to help or intercede. However, when it comes to the capability of the deceased listening to our words, there are a few exceptions.

Prophet Muhammad[PBUH] said: "*When any Muslim sends greetings to me, Allah returns my soul to me so that I may respond to his greetings.*"[11] But we are not aware of his response, just like the Quran says: **"*You do not perceive.*"** (2:154) Such communication is *limited* to only salutations and greetings sent to Prophet Muhammad[PBUH]. This hadith does not say anything about other subjects, like seeking his help or request to intercede in any divine affairs.

Similarly, another hadith tells of an incident after the victory of the Battle of Badr. When Muslims had finished burying the dead pagan warriors, Prophet Muhammad[PBUH] asked the deceased pagans, "*Surely, we found the promise of our Lord absolutely true. Did you also find the promise of your lord true?*"[12] He later explained to the companions that the slain pagans could still hear him. This too is an exceptional case in which only the newly buried continue to hear for a short period of time after their burial. Qadri's argument of assuming that the deceased can hear us leads to many absurd assumptions, which assign some attributes of Allah to a human (discussed later).

The following hadith proves that the deceased cannot hear. On the Day of Judgment, the Lake-Fount of Paradise called *Kauthar* will be awarded to Prophet Muhammad[PBUH]. Only the followers of Prophet Muhammad[PBUH] selected to enter Paradise will be able to reach that lake, where Prophet Muhammad[PBUH] will offer them a drink from Kauthar. Here again, Prophet Muhammad[PBUH] is honored. He said, "I will be at my Lake-Fount (*Kauthar*) waiting for whoever will come to me. Then some people will be taken away from me whereupon I will say, '(those are) my followers!' It will be said, 'You do not know they turned Apostates as renegades.'"[113] This hadith also tells us that: (1) after his death from this world, Prophet Muhammad[PBUH] had no knowledge about the status of his followers; and (2) no human, including the Prophets, can overrule the judgment of Allah.

Qadri's argument supporting tawassul

In exegesis of the Quran, a mistaken assumption can lead to wrong conclusions. For example, let us examine the following verse: **"If they [the non-believers] would have come to you [Prophet Muhammad[PBUH]] when they had wronged themselves to seek Allah's forgiveness and *if the Prophet had also asked Allah's forgiveness for them, they would have found Allah Forgiving, Merciful*"** (4:64). The correct explanation of this verse is: if non-believers and sinners had come to Prophet Muhammad[PBUH] in submission and requested him to perform a group prayer, and the Prophet had prayed for them, Allah would have forgiven them. In contrast, Qadri draws a different conclusion: "Through this verse, Allah is directing the believers…. among the many modes of repentance available to the believers, *the most effective mode is to seek Allah's forgiveness through the Holy Prophet.* His intercession will be a guarantee of its immediate acceptance. And this Qur'ānic injunction applied not only to his Earthly existence but shall *remain valid even after his death.*"[114]

Here, Qadri makes the following two assumptions:

1. Just like during the lifetime of Prophet Muhammad[PBUH], one can ask him to act as an intercessor even after his death.

2. A prayer seeking repentance using a deceased intercessor is of superior quality than a direct prayer to Allah.

Challenge Question: Do you agree with Qadri's statement that even after the death of Prophet Muhammad^{PBUH}, *"The most effective mode is to seek Allah's forgiveness through the Holy Prophet?"*

If your answer is yes:

> **Q:** Does that mean that every single prayer seeking forgiveness in the Quran and nearly all hadith prayers are inferior because they all pray directly to Allah and not through any intermediary (Nauzubillah)?

> **Q:** One such prayer in the Quran reads: **"grant us forgiveness"** (2:286). These are the words of Allah. Can you *improve* on this prayer by asking forgiveness through the Prophet (Nauzubillah)?

If your answer is that both types of prayers are equally effective:

> **Q:** If both types of prayers are equally good, then half the prayers in the Quran would use tawassul of a deceased intermediary. Why is there not a single prayer in the Quran that uses tawassul?

> **Q:** What is the point of using tawassul when it adds no value to prayer?

Tacit-belief in calling on a deceased intermediary

Let us study the following Urdu prayer that uses controversial tawassul: *"Jholey Lal khushiya de gham tal"* ("Sufi Lal Shahbaz Qalandar give me happiness and remove worries"). In this prayer what are the implicit beliefs of the supplicant? Here the callers believe that a saint can hear every caller, from all corners of the Earth, round the clock. The saint can understand even if multiple callers talk simultaneously in different languages. Therefore, tacit-belief is that the saint is all-hearing. Also, a call to a saint is different from the phone call you make to the passport office, where you identify yourself by providing personal information. In the case of a saint, the tacit-belief holds that the saint already knows the supplicant's full background, because the caller to the saint does not provide the first name, last name, email address, phone number, or details of their hardship. Just like prayers to Allah, sometimes people may call on a saint in their thoughts instead of out loud. So tacit-belief holds that the saint can read the mind of the supplicant, or the saint is also all-seeing and all-knowing, just like Allah (Nauzubillah).

The Quran says: **"He [Allah] is the All-Hearing and the All-Knowing** (2:244) and **Allah has full power and control"** (12:21). Assigning His attributes to a saint or any other human is shirk.

Q: Which verse of the Quran states that deceased pious saints can *hear everything* around the globe at all times?

Q: Which verse of the Quran states that deceased pious saints can *understand all languages and know everything*?

Q: If a saint is alive and listening, and has *power to change destiny*, then the same should be true for the Prophet (Nauzubillah). And if this is true, Prophet Muhammad[PBUH] should still be the ruler of Muslims, even after his death. Why did Abu-Bakr, Omar, Uthman and Ali become caliphs after the death of Prophet Muhammad[PBUH]?

When a person asks a saint for mercy, there is tacit-belief that the saint is more merciful than Allah (Nauzubillah*).* If one believes that Allah is more merciful, then why ask help from the saint? Is Caliph Ali a better helper than Allah? Did Allah lack something (Nauzubillah) so that you have to go to someone else? None of the Prophets in the Quran prayed to anyone other than Allah. The Quran says: **"The fact is that most of them follow nothing but mere assumptions and assumption is in no way a substitute for the truth. Surely Allah is well aware of all that they do"** (10:36).

Challenge Accepted

To support the prayers that use an intermediary, in his book *Notions That Must Be Corrected*, Alawi cites 17 eminent scholars with references.[115] Alawi says that, compared to opponents of tawassul, these "*luminaries… [are] more expansive in knowledge and expertise, of deeper understanding and greater in light, piety and sincerity."*[116] Similarly, Qadri lists more than 20 scholars who support controversial tawassul.[117]

Since I disagree with this concept entirely, it is obligatory for me to accept their challenge. Here is a list of scholars who have prayed directly to Allah, without using tawassul:

Prophet Noah[PBUH]: **"O my Lord! I seek refuge with You"** (11:47).

Prophet Abraham[PBUH]: **"O my Lord! grant me authority. Join me to the righteous ones"** (26:83).

Prophet Moses[PBUH]: **"O Lord! Open my heart, ease my task"** (20:25–26).

Prophet Jesus[PBUH]: **"O Allah…provide us our sustenance"** (5:114).

Allah gave this prayer to Prophet Muhammad[PBUH]: **"Our Lord! Put not on us a burden greater than we have strength to bear"** (2:286).

The above scholars were also Prophets, and their words are recorded in the Quran itself. Not a single prayer in the Quran uses love-rank leverage, tawassul *or* shafa'a of a deceased or any other intermediary to reach Allah. Compared to rest of humankind, Prophets hold the highest status. This means that any scholar quoted above, supporting intermediary prayer is mistaken.

Challenge Q: Which luminaries quoted by Alawi and Qadri surpass the Prophets Noah, Abraham, Moses, Jesus and Muhammad (PBUT)?

Why are Intermediaries So Popular Amongst Muslims?

Most of us are consciously or unconsciously terrified of our uncontrollable and unpredictable future. On a daily basis, television brings us, in vibrant color, various calamities happening around the world. Our imagination keeps tormenting us that we might be the next victim. Besides, we are also afraid of our own death and afraid of life after death. The Quran provides the solution that Muslims should rely only on the unseen Allah and not be afraid of anyone else except Him. This is because only Allah can protect or harm us. But some Muslims find it hard to practice. They desperately seek additional human protection in the form of believer-projected-gods.

Rituals that Create Polytheist Muslims

According to verse (9:24), loving Prophet Muhammad[PBUH] is an essential part of Islam. The problem arises when love and praise, for any human, are *exaggerated*, because this may lead to shirk, as proven by the prayers listed in categories 1 and 2.

It is human nature that when we repeatedly *exaggerate* love and praise of a saint, then s/he begins to appear more dependable than the invisible God. The reason for this is: (1) *love* creates a feeling of closeness and trust; and (2) excessive *praise* elevates a human to the status of believer-projected-god (chapter 1).

The praise-love cycle is presented in the form of ceremonies like *Mawlid* (*Milad*) or rituals related to the martyrdom of Hussain or death anniversaries (*urs*) of saints. These ceremonies and rituals are projected as an essential part of Islam and, under different pretexts, various rituals are repeated several times a year. As a rule of thumb, these rituals are designed to be highly emotional. Participants engage in repeated praise-love cycles in the form of passionate lectures, and the recitation of poetry, songs and slogans. Audiences participate in singing and other physical group activities. All along these activities are emphasized as highly religious Islamic rituals. In some cases, the emotion of *hate* toward a rival Muslim sect is also included. After an intense emotional roller-coaster, participants fail to notice that they have exaggerated their heroes to the level of God. Here poetry, rhythm, music, and group participation play key roles. If you say in prose that "Muslim Saint Khwaja is God," Muslims may object. But if you recite as poetry: *Haqeeqat main dekho to Khawaja Khuda hai* (In reality, Khwaja is god), people do not object.

Eventually, participants end up believing that deceased saints are listening to us; if we praise and love them enough, then both in this life and on the Day of Judgment they will be our controlling-intercessors. Instead of relying only on unseen Allah who does not have any statue or picture, such Muslims count on the saints as their backup plan. Please note similarities to the tradition of ancestor veneration practiced in many Asian countries like Cambodia and China.

Q: The Quran says that the greatest praise and love should be reserved only for Allah: **"All praise belongs to Allah"** (1:2) and **"have *maximum* love for Allah"** (2:165). Instead, why do some Muslims choose to have greatest praise and love for a slave of Allah (Prophet Muhammad[PBUH] should be loved but not more than Allah)?

HOW TO PRAISE AND LOVE PROPHET MUHAMMAD[PBUH] WITHOUT EXAGGERATION

The linguistic meaning of the word 'Muhammad' is the 'praised one'. In the Quran, Allah Himself blesses Prophet Muhammad[PBUH]: **God showers His blessings upon the Prophet and the angels seek forgiveness for him. Believers, pray for the Prophet and greet him with, "Peace be with you (i.e. As-Salamu 'Alaikum)** [33:56]. Similarly, when it comes to loving, the verse (9:24) says that Muslims should love Prophet Muhammad[PBUH] more than any worldly possession. Of course, *there is nothing wrong in loving and praising the Prophet*. The chapter 4 of this book itself praises the Prophet.

The problem starts only when the praise and love for the Prophet is *exaggerated*. Because excessive praise and love leads to veneration. These days this behavior is so prevalent that Annemarie Schimmel wrote a 377 page book named "And Muhammad is His Messenger: The Veneration of the Prophet in Islamic Piety" citing hundreds of samples, from many countries, where poets and writers have exaggerated the love of Prophet

Muhammad[PBUH]. This problem starts with Mawlid (Milad). According to Bengali scholar Enamul Haq, "the main theme of the *gazals* [which are sung after the milad proper] is to eulogize the Prophet in most exaggerated terms, after giving him identical place with God. *All the audience relish these songs enthusiastically without a murmur of dissent.*"[118]

Here are some ideas to prevent exaggeration:
1. If you wish to arrange a public event to study the life of the Prophet, please do not call the event Mawlid or Milad. Instead, name it something like 'Lessons from the life of the Prophet' or 'Tradition of our Prophet.' Of course, there is no need to sing *gazals* after the event.
2. The speaker should be told to avoid exaggeration. S/he should recite and explain the meaning of the second line of Kalima "I bear witness that Prophet Muhammad[PBUH] is a *slave* of Allah and a messenger."
3. Very politely, Muslims, in general, should be made aware about the consequence of exaggeration and how it leads to shirk.

SAY WHAT? ISLAM EXPECTS AN EVEN *PURER* MONOTHEISM?

Allah knows the words and deeds of every human, for which all of us will be held accountable on the Day of Judgment. Allah also knows our every single thought, throughout our lifetime (chapter 2). Therefore, in some cases, we are also accountable for our *thoughts*: **"Whether you reveal what is in your minds or conceal it, Allah will call you to account for it"** (2:284). This verse worried the companions, because it is nearly impossible to consciously control our thoughts. The companions expressed their concern to Prophet Muhammad[PBUH]. In response, the Prophet gave the good news that Allah forgives Muslims for their *involuntary* sinful thoughts, unless they speak those thoughts aloud or commit sins inspired by those thoughts.[119] This shows that the judgment of Allah is fair and we are not responsible for mistakes we make that are out of our control.

The Quran describes that the first time Prophet Moses[PBUH] saw the miracle of Allah, his staff changing into a snake, his initial involuntary reaction was fear. Such spontaneous emotional reactions are allowed. The fundamental principle will always remain true: **"Allah does not burden any human being with more than he can bear."** (2:286) And Allah assures that: **"No injustice will be done to anyone [on the Day of Judgment even] as much as a thread inside a date seed"** (4:49).

Voluntary sinful thoughts not only can be a sin, but also they can be *shirk*, which is the greatest sin there is: **"Have you considered the case of such an individual who has made his *own desires as his god*"** (45:23).

SHIRK IN THE ABSENCE OF AN EXTERNAL DEITY: EGO WORSHIP

The Quran describes a story of two friends. One of them was the rich owner of a garden. He bragged to his poor friend: **"I am richer than you and my clan is mightier than yours... I do not think that this garden will ever perish!"** (18:34–35). To analyze this verse, please keep in mind that Islam permits doing legitimate business, to become rich and have friends and supporters, and to fully enjoy them as blessings of Allah. The important condition is that a person must give full credit for all their achievements to Allah alone. Such an approach makes a person humble and polite. In the above case, however, wealth and clan support made the rich man arrogant.

The poor friend responded in the Islamic way. Instead of getting upset, he stayed calm and provided guidance with compassion. He told the rich man that 'Allah created you from dust, then from one sperm (when you were completely helpless and obviously at the mercy of Allah), and nurtured you all the way to adulthood. But you are denying His blessings?' The poor friend not only identified the rich friend's arrogance as shirk, but also provided him with a solution in the form of a prayer: **"As for myself, Allah is my Lord and *I do not do shirk with Him*. When you entered your garden why did you not say: '*It is as Allah willed* [or all achievements are blessings of Allah], *no one has power except Allah!*"** (18:38).

Nonetheless, the rich friend refused to acknowledge his arrogance and continued his boasting. He consciously and voluntarily chose to remain stubborn. Eventually, Allah punished him by destroying his garden. After that, the rich man repented. **"I wish I had not done *shirk*"** (18:42).

This story does not mention any deity besides Allah. In the above verses, why did both friends refer to shirk? Even in the absence of an external god, one's wrong attitude (or thoughts) can also act as a false deity. If an arrogant person consciously believes that, 'I am an outstanding success because of my plan, my effort, and my know-how,' then the credit goes to the self, or ego. Such a person refuses to acknowledge that Allah is the only Doer behind the scenes. According to Pakistani scholar A. A. Islahi, "such a person thinks of himself as one who shares the divinity with Allah."[120] This is shirk. As subtle as this point is, the Quran both identifies it and provides

106

its solution in the form of the above prayer, to help us handle the seemingly impossible domain of our own thoughts.

INTENTION THAT LEADS TO SHIRK: APPROVAL OF ONLOOKERS

What about a believer who performs a ritual supplication to worship Allah, but lengthens the supplication time to impress the onlookers with his/her piety? Prophet Muhammad[PBUH] called this hidden *shirk* or *riyaa* (chapter 2). Ritual supplication is essential part of worship, but if the believer has wrong desire to impress the onlookers, the same action becomes a *shirk*.

WHAT IS THE GOAL OF CONTROLLING THE DESIRES?

The *goal* of controlling desires is: *at any moment, we should be fully satisfied and content with ourselves and with our surroundings!* Let's recall that Allah is the only Doer there is. When we accept whatever Allah gives us (both good and bad luck), then we *emotionally* surrender to Allah. Only then can we be at total peace with Allah and with our own selves. Such a person can honestly and sincerely thank Allah. People who achieve this goal are given high honor, and Allah says that they have *nafse mutmainna*, or **"fully satisfied soul"** (89:27). On the Day of Judgment, they will enter Paradise: **"Return to your Lord, *[you are] well-pleased with Him and He [Allah] is also pleased with you"* (89:28).

What does it take to be fully satisfied with the world around us? It means, no matter which future threat may frighten us or which ugly memory may haunt us or which problem we are facing at this very moment, in all these cases we need to continuously believe that Allah is the only Doer. Whatever Allah does in our life, we *emotionally* accept it and surrender to His will or decree. That is the difference between satan and a true Muslim. Satan also believed in Allah, but satan did not surrender to the will of Allah and disobeyed Him.

As far as bad luck is concerned, it is a test of Allah, and we are supposed to be patient. **"Certainly We [Allah] shall test you with something of fear and hunger, and loss of wealth, and lives, and crops; but *give glad tidings to the steadfast"* (2:155). Muslims should always remember that Allah is **"the Most Gracious, Most Merciful"** (27:30) and emotionally accept all tests of Allah.

Emotional acceptance does not mean that we give up our efforts to make change. After this emotional acceptance, we still have full freedom to do the corrective effort (provided these are not sins). Even if we fail to make change, it will always be the will of Allah and we should accept that as well. Emotionally surrendering to Allah is always a win-win situation. In contrast, emotional resistance brings nothing but suffering. Rumi said, "The moment you accept what troubles you've been given, the door will open."[121]

Suppose you studied for several months in preparation for a qualifying exam for a job you desperately need. On the night before the exam, you would like to have a peaceful sleep so you are well-rested and relaxed during the exam. Otherwise, during the exam, you will be unable to use your full potential. You try to lull yourself to sleep, but some thoughts keep bothering you. "What will I do if I fail?" "What if I forget what I have studied?" "I have always failed in everything." The only way to block these thoughts and have a peaceful sleep is to emotionally accept whatever is going to happen. In other words, even if you fail, you will emotionally accept that as a decree of Allah and go on with your life. Such emotional acceptance will block all non-productive thoughts. Rumi said, "The hurt you embrace becomes joy."[122] Doubtful? Why don't you try surrendering to the will of Allah?

Just a few days before his death, Prophet Muhammad[PBUH] received an emotional shock that his only surviving son, Ibrahim, was fatally ill. The infant died in his mother's arms as Prophet Muhammad[PBUH] was watching and crying. In this moment of extreme grief, he prayed, *"The eyes send their tears and the heart is saddened, but we do not say anything except that which please our Lord. O Ibrahim, we are bereaved by your departure."*[123] This incident shows us that involuntary emotional reactions to calamity, including expressing emotions, like crying, are permitted in Islam. Still, we should not blame our fate on ourselves or, for that matter, anyone else. We should not blame Allah either. With such an attitude of surrender to the will of Allah, it is much easier to recover from emotional shock, because the negative thoughts such as why me? or, if only such and such incident had not happened, can no longer bother us.

The Quran teaches us a prayer to stop the memories/worries about past events, present incidents, and future uncertainties: **"Allah (Alone) is Sufficient for us and He is the Best Disposer of affairs"** (3:173). After this prayer, we fully surrender our past, present and future worries/fears to the will of Allah. Next, we must do full effort to change any unpleasant situation, so long as our actions are not sins. Here, let's recall the example of "tie your camel" (chapter 2). In summary, first stage is to *emotionally surrender* to Allah, then do *effort* to change any unpleasant situation we can and eventually put *trust* in Allah that He will do whatever is best in our interest.

Emotional surrender and unconditional love (explained in the next chapter) cut down the major part of suffering. Instead of feeling helpless in the face of painful external events, we can take charge to reduce or eliminate suffering. In the absence of suffering we can use all our capabilities to do the corrective effort. By so doing, we are bound to find peace and contentment, right here in this life. Emotional surrender to the will of Allah is so important that the word *Islam* itself includes this very concept! The figurative meaning of the word *Islam* is "voluntary submission to the will of Allah."

The Spiritual Journey of Islam

During my first serious reading of the Quran, as I was thoroughly enjoying the continuous emphasis on monotheism, there came an unexpected surprise. The Quran says that humans are supposed to get rid of shirk, even from their own desires: **"Have you ever seen the one who has taken his own desires as his god?"** (25:43).

I was in middle age. I was not overly enthusiastic about changing my habits of thinking. It seemed like a losing battle. At the same time, I knew that shirk is the biggest sin of all. So I came up with an excuse. "Changing my thinking is beyond my capability and Allah does not burden anyone with more than what s/he can bear. Therefore, I should not be held accountable." The idea worked—*almost*. Later, a question came to my mind. "In my effort to change my desires, did I seek help from Allah?" I could have ignored or ridiculed the question, but I could no longer justify my reluctance to purge wrong desires that lead to shirk. In this way, the Quran literally forced me to do self-analysis. Back then, I did not realize that it was the beginning of a beautiful journey to Islamic spirituality and inner peace. This journey not only purges sinful desires, but it also teaches us to surrender to the decree of Allah. As a result, we learn how to remove negative emotions like anger, malice, fear, hate, and depression.

In summary, Islam is more than verbally reciting the declaration of belief and performing religious rituals. Instead, a Muslim should make the best use of his/her intellect, be sincere, and persistently make an effort to *remove voluntary and conscious sinful thoughts*. A spiritual journey of this nature changes one's personality from within. It is highly unlikely thereafter that such a person would voluntarily commit sin.

WORST WAY TO PREACH ISLAMIC MONOTHEISM

Islamic monotheism is indeed a delicate intellectual experience. Its message can only be communicated by discussion in peaceful environments. The worst way to preach it is to use violence and threats. In a violent environment, people tend to focus only on defense and survival—not introspection. In the past, some radicals have used violence to promote monotheism. For example, ISIS blew up the tomb of Prophet Jonah[PBUH] [124], and hardliners have bombed crowds visiting the shrines of saints. This kind of violent behavior only generates hatred towards Islam; both Muslims and non-Muslims wrongly perceive Islam as a violent religion.

ISLAM: NOT JUST ANOTHER RELIGION, BUT ANOTHER *CATEGORY* OF RELIGION

The following conclusions are based on the Quran, ahadith and Islamic worship practices of the *majority* of Muslims. The practice of cults and minority Muslims are not discussed here.

Number of gods

Islam not only has one God, but also negates even the existence of any other deity. In the Quran, *God never changes into a man*. Similarly, *no man, no matter how pious, ever changes into God*.

The God of Islam Was Not Born like Created Life Forms

The life of Allah is not like the life of His Creation. Allah has no offspring, nor is He the offspring of anyone. Unlike humans, there is no need for the God of Islam to have been born.

Number of Roles of God

Human-god plays a dual role, that of a man, and that of a god. The role of a man includes human physical and emotional limitations. Islamic monotheism is unique because Allah never plays the role of a human, not even once.

Monotheism in worship

Every single prayer in the Quran calls only upon Allah. No prayer in the Quran calls upon any Prophet, angel or pious man, or makes them intercessors. Even the multipurpose worship of Allah, which also seeks the approval of the onlookers, is rejected.

Monotheism of Omnipotence

Allah is in perpetual control of everything in every way. Allah is the only Decision-maker, Judge on the Day of Judgement, Forgiver and Doer. Only Allah can award Paradise or Hell. No human, no matter how pious, can share power with Allah.

No statue, image, or picture of God

Mosques do not have a statue, image, or picture of Allah.

No statue, image or picture of the Prophet or Founder-of-the-Religion

Even statues, pictures or paintings of Prophets are not allowed, because that could encourage a believer-projected-god scenario.

Prophets Are Not Overtly Praised but Treated Like Humans

The Quran clearly states that all Prophets were human. The Quran even describes some of their mistakes (judgmental errors).

Spiritual Progress

By *mandating* the removal of shirk by desires, Islam forces capable Muslims to carry out introspection and acquire nafse mutmainna. This eventually removes not just sin, but even the desire to commit sin.

Q: Based on the above discussion, can you think of any major religion that has a belief identical to Islamic monotheism?

No doubt, Islamic monotheism is unique.

Isn't it surprising that even if polytheism has so many attractive features, there still exists a major world religion that is monotheistic not only in principle, but also in practice?

CHAPTER 6

ISLAM: PATH OF INFINITE LOVE

Wherever you are and whatever you do, be in love

~ Rumi

Something amazing happens when a person sincerely follows Islam with proper understanding: deep inside s/he feels peace and tranquility. Surprisingly, this feeling persists even if external circumstances turn unfavorable. Such inner contentment (*nafse mutmainna*) originates from loving Allah and feeling His love. The Quran praises such people because they have **"fully satisfied soul"** (89:27) and promises them the Paradise. Such person discovers is that Islam nurtures, grows, develops, flourishes, and prospers in love, and only love, and nothing else but pure and continuous unconditional love of Allah. Ibn Qayyum explains love as "the very spirit of Islam, the pivotal point of religion and the axis of [eternal] happiness and deliverance."[125] It is literally impossible to imagine spiritual Islam without love.

> Once Sufi Rabia Basaria was asked, "Do you love Allah?"
> She answered yes.
> "Do you hate the devil?"
> She answered, "My love for Allah leaves me no time to hate the devil."[126]

Rabia's love for Allah was uninterrupted, unconditional, beautiful and infinite. Love engulfed her every single moment and entire existence. Loving Allah takes a believer to the highest form of spiritual ecstasy. On the other hand, hating anyone causes suffering to one's own self. There was

112

no reason for Rabia to take time away from everlasting bliss just to hate the devil, was there?

WHAT IS LOVE: ACTION OR FEELING?

Love is only a *feeling*. That is it. Love is not an action. Sometimes love can inspire an action. In other words, love and action can exist simultaneously. Consider when a loving mother gives water to her thirsty baby. Here, the mother loves the child and the inspired act is giving the water. Conversely, an action alone does not necessarily prove that love exists. The same physical action may be performed without love. If a babysitter gives water to a baby, without emotion, then even though the action is identical, love is not involved. Rabia says:

> In love between heart and heart.
> Speech is born out of longing,
> True description from the real taste.
> The one who tastes, knows;
> the one who explains, lies.[127]

The Quran says: "**My Lord is indeed *Merciful, Loving*"** (11:90). This verse uses two names of Allah together: the Merciful and the Loving. Allah is loving, and His love is manifested by the action of mercy.

The Quran has hundreds of verses in which Allah reminds us of His infinite mercy, which as the above verse suggests, coexists with love. According to the Quran: **"Who sends down rainwater from the sky and therewith produces vegetation of all kinds: He [Allah] brings forth green crops … gardens of grapes, olives, and pomegranates…In these things *there are signs* for true believers"** (6:99). A true believer not only thanks Allah for His mercy but also feels the love of Allah. Love takes the believer closer to Allah.

WHO CREATED LOVE?

Allah is the only Creator there is. The Quran specifically mentions that the beautiful gift of love is also from Allah: **"He [Allah] *created love* and kindness in your hearts"** (30:21). This verse tells us that Allah created not only the *emotion* of love in the human heart, but also made us *capable* of doing *simultaneous* actions of kindness. Allah also gave humans the capability to choose. It is sad that some of us choose hatred over love.

113

WHO GAVE HUMANS THE CAPABILITY TO LIVE IN A SOCIETY?

Allah also gave humans the capability to form social groups. Before Prophet Muhammad[PBUH] migrated to Medina, two Medina tribes, Aus and Khazraj, were committed enemies. At that time Arab tribes took pride in taking revenge, and inter-tribal wars could last for generations. However, after Prophet Muhammad[PBUH] migrated, by the blessing of Allah, these tribes immediately made peace. **"Remember Allah's favors upon you when you were enemies; He brought your *hearts together*, you became, by His favor, brothers"** (3:103). Sure enough, the early Muslims had incredible love and compassion for each other.

IS LOVE IDENTICAL TO SEX?

Islam makes an amazingly subtle distinction between love and sex, even if the *emotion* of love and the *action* of sex can exist simultaneously. Fasting Muslims are not allowed to eat, drink or engage in sex from sunrise to sunset. While fasting, does Islam allow *love* between spouses? During the fast, even if sex and lust are prohibited, love is *allowed*.

A young man and an old man asked Prophet Muhammad[PBUH] if a fasting man is allowed to embrace his wife. Prophet Muhammad[PBUH] prohibited the young man. However, Prophet Muhammad's[PBUH] Prophetic judgment concluded that the old man would only embrace his wife out of love, not out of lust. So the Prophet permitted the old man to embrace his wife.[128] One word of caution: if the embrace leads to the emotion of lust, then Allah will know, and the fast will be broken.

WHOM TO LOVE?

When it comes to the question of whom to love, one school of thought teaches us to shun this world, because love and attachment to the world are hindrances to worship and spiritual growth.

But Islam provides an unusually balanced approach; it permits a Muslim to engage in the pursuits of this world, to get married and have family and friends. It is natural that we love the people, animals and even objects that please, help and benefit us. However, priority plays an essential role. According to the Quran, a Muslim should love Prophet Muhammad[PBUH] more than any worldly possession (9:24). After all, Prophet Muhammad[PBUH] brought us the message of Islam. As far as the first priority is concerned, **"those who have faith, have *maximum* love for Allah"** (2:165). Love of Allah is naturally embedded in our hearts, we just have to learn how to tune into it. This requirement closely binds Islamic spiritual growth to love.

A great deal of Sufi literature, accumulated over centuries, proves that it is not only possible for a person to love Allah, but it is the most satisfying human spiritual experience. Islamic spirituality opens the door to continuous, infinite and unconditional love. Rumi said, *the inspiration you seek is already within you. Be silent and listen.*

LOVE CANNOT BE MANIPULATED

The famous Urdu poet Ghalib said:

> Love is like an uncontrollable fire
> Which can neither be started nor extinguished by force.

Love happens naturally, as if all by itself, in an environment of total freedom. A mother is not paid or forced to love her child, yet she does. Coercion and compulsion can never create love. A robber can rob a bank at gunpoint, but no one can be forced to love at gunpoint. It just does not work that way.

You cannot create love by willpower, either. For example, you cannot say that I will love my spouse from 12:05 PM to 3:47 PM on alternate Thursdays. Since loving Allah and loving humankind are essential parts of Islam, it is impossible to impose Islam by force. The Quran clearly explains **"there is no compulsion in religion"** (2:256). The reason is, compulsion never creates love, whereas Islam cannot exist in a heart that lacks love. Why? Because the believers are required to **"have *maximum* love for Allah"** (2:165).

WHAT IS CONDITIONAL LOVE?

Conditional love is like a cold and impersonal business transaction. A person has to fulfill the conditions or expectations of the other person, and only then receives compensation in the form of conditional love. It is like when you deposit a coin in a vending machine, then expect the machine to dispense a can of soda. If expectations are not met, then conditional love is put on hold.

Suppose you spent lots of energy and money on your best friend's last birthday. In response, you were expecting your friend to return the favor. Instead, your friend even forgot your birthday. For sure, your expectations were not met and your feelings would be hurt. If your love is *unconditional*, then you do not need to hold back the natural flowing love; therefore, you do not have to hold onto the memory of the emotional pain. As a result, the suffering is greatly reduced. Also, in the absence of suffering, your wisdom is fully functional, allowing you to think of the most appropriate response. Close analysis of this behavior reveals that unconditional love is the consequence of emotional surrender to the decree of Allah.

But if your love is conditional, to *get even,* you may hold back your love. You hold onto painful memories to justify the restriction you have placed on your love. Therefore it is harder to get over the pain; this prolongs suffering. Your wisdom is clouded, and your response may be out of proportion.

Conditional love also influences our social lives. Every person around you has to qualify to earn your love. Precious personal relationships are reduced to haggling sales, like, 'I bought you a $50 jacket last year and you just sent me a cheap New Year's card!'

To some people, lasting love seems an impossible goal, with the risk of heartbreak. They do not like to hear or say, "I love you." Such preconditions complicate love beyond recognition. When two people interact over an extended period, it is natural to have disagreements and conflicts of interest. Such clashes can influence relationships. Even best friends, couples, siblings, and parents and children have arguments. If the love between them is merely conditional then, sooner or later, the relationship will be severed, hearts will be broken, and only bad memories will remain.

UNCONDITIONAL LOVE IN ISLAM

In contrast, the unconditional love of Islam has nothing to do with the behavior of others. A Muslim should continuously love others, regardless of what others do or what they believe.

A desert Arab came to meet Prophet Muhammad[PBUH] in the Al-Masjid an-Nabawi, which is regarded as the second-holiest Mosque in Islam. When the desert Arab felt the need, he started urinating in one corner of the mosque. Prophet's companions tried to stop him, but Prophet Muhammad[PBUH] told them to let the desert Arab finish.

Later, very lovingly, Prophet Muhammad[PBUH] said to him, "These mosques are not the places meant for urine and filth, but are only for the remembrance of Allah, prayer and the recitation of the Quran."[129] Later, the area was washed clean with water. This incident is one beautiful example of unconditional love. Prophet Muhammad[PBUH] did not order punishment, even if it may have been justified. He did not humiliate the desert Arab either.

At the same time, unconditional love does not mean that you grin and bear it all, or refrain from saying your side of the story. Prophet Muhammad[PBUH] tactfully and lovingly conveyed exactly what he wanted to say. Thereby unconditional love can be practiced in real life. Here we must note that Prophet Muhammad[PBUH] also explained the reason why the sanctity of the mosque must be preserved. His response was calm and logical.

Loving unconditionally does not mean living in a make-believe world. When we love unconditionally, we can still say no without guilt. If a child tries to stick a finger in an electric socket, the mother will say no and still love the child unconditionally.

What if someone crosses all reasonable limits of ethics, or without any justification physically attacks you? In such a case, Islam allows defensive measures. On rare occasions even Prophets prayed against their oppressors, as in case of Prophet Noah (26:117-118).

At the same time, do not make demands that are beyond the capability of others. Prophet Muhammad[PBUH] let the Arab finish urinating because, once started, the process cannot be immediately interrupted. The best part of unconditional love is that one's heart is always free from the hate and anger that only causes more suffering. Instead, we must love others continuously, regardless of how they behave toward us. Another good example is a mother's love for her newborn. This love does not diminish, even if the baby cries or keeps the mother awake at night. Rumi said, "whenever we manage to love without expectations, calculations, negotiations, we are indeed in heaven."[130] He describes unconditional love as,

The garden of love is green without limit
and yields many fruits other than sorrow or joy.
Love is beyond either condition:
without spring, without autumn, it is always fresh.[131]

Here is another example. At-Tufayl ibn Amr was the leader of the Daws tribe. The people of his tribe respected and obeyed him. He learned Islam from Prophet Muhammad[PBUH] and converted. He was very confident that, if he asked, the Daws would also convert to Islam. However, to his disappointment, the tribe refused.

Disheartened, At-Tufayl complained to Prophet Muhammad[PBUH] about his tribe. After hearing him, Prophet Muhammad[PBUH] raised his hand to pray. The onlookers thought that Prophet Muhammad[PBUH] would curse the tribe. Instead Prophet Muhammad[PBUH] prayed, "O Lord, guide Daws."[132] He prayed that members of the tribe of Daws would be successful in attaining a good afterlife, which is the greatest success any human can possibly achieve.

Unconditional love in Islam is not just the discipline of one's emotions. Instead, it is 100 percent sincere caring for everyone. This incident also shows that unconditional love in Islam is not limited to Muslims, but includes all humanity, regardless of their religion.

TRADING LOVE FOR ALLAH'S FAVOR

The Quran has many prayers that describe various reasons to seek help from Allah. For example, Prophet Moses[PBUH] used his helplessness. **"O Lord! Surely I am in desperate need of whatever good that You may send down to me"** (28:24). In another prayer, Prophet Zakariyah[PBUH] used the weakness of his old age. **"O Lord! Surely my bones have weakened and the hair of my head glistens with gray, …. grant me an heir by Your grace"** (19:4–5). But not a single prayer uses love as leverage. No prayer says, 'Allah, help me because I love you.' This is because Islam advocates *unconditional* love. You cannot trade unconditional love like a currency in exchange to buy favors.

LOVING ALLAH UNCONDITIONALLY

The Quran *directly* orders Muslims to perform various worship rituals. **"*Be steadfast* in prayer; *practice* regular charity"** (2:43). When it comes to love, the Quran only mentions the *characteristic* of believers that, **"those** who have faith, have *maximum* love for Allah" (2:165). It is interesting to note that, unlike the worship rituals, the Quran does not *directly order* believers to love Allah. Why? Because Allah created the emotion of love. Allah also gave love the limitation that love cannot be forced. Any specific command to love Allah would have violated the very nature of love! That would be an impossible instruction. This is yet another evidence that the Quran is the book of God.

Here we must note that to have maximum love for Allah (2:165), is a *requirement* of Islam. It is not an option. The word *maximum* encompasses two meanings. The first meaning is that believers should love Allah more than anyone else. It can also mean that believers should love Allah to their maximum capability. The verse does not say that believers should only love Allah and no one else. Instead, we are allowed to love others, though our utmost love should be for Allah alone. This does not mean that if a mother loves her child, she should set a fixed quota for the child's love and transfer remaining love to Allah.

A Muslim mother of a newborn realizes that her existence is not by coincidence. Allah is the one who gave her life. Her every heartbeat and breath is a gift from generous and loving Allah. She thanks and loves Allah when she appreciates the beauty of the bright, oversized rainbow on the horizon, or the happy movement of red flowers when washed clean by raindrops, or peaceful, aimless floating seagulls in a nippy ocean breeze. In her appreciation, she also appreciates Allah's mercy and love.

She also knows that Allah is the only One who created love and put love in the hearts of the humankind. Therefore, all the love she ever received from her parents, siblings, other relatives, spouse, children, friends and even pets is a manifestation of Allah's love for her. She prays: **"My Lord! Grant me the grace that *I may thank you* for the favors which You have bestowed on me and on my parents"** (46:15). Her precious child is not a coincidence either, but the most cherished gift of love from Allah. She thanks Allah for the gift of her child. With this understanding, she naturally ends up unconditionally loving Allah the *most*.

This does not mean that loving Allah is yet another burdensome responsibility. When we learn how to love Allah, we simply learn how to love more, in general! This is the most enlightening thing one can do for one's spiritual and emotional growth. When we love Allah unconditionally, we also end up unconditionally loving His creation, including the entirety of humankind. This love fills every moment of our life with beauty, peace and happiness. Persian Sufi Attar said:

The whole world is a marketplace for Love,
For naught that is, from Love remains remote.
The Eternal Wisdom made all things in Love.
On Love they all depend, to Love all turn.
The Earth, the Heavens, the sun, the moon, the stars
The center of their orbit find in Love.
By Love are all bewildered, stupefied,
Intoxicated by the Wine of Love.[133]

HOW TO EARN THE LOVE OF ALLAH

The Quran defines how a believer may earn Allah's love. Allah encourages continuous generous behavior toward humanity, by specifically saying that Allah *loves* those who give to charity (3:134), who are patient in adversity (3:146), who do good deeds (2:195), and who seek forgiveness from sins (2:222). Muslims should remain kind even when others mistreat them. Allah ordains a general principle: ***"Repel other's evil deeds with your good deeds.* You will see that he with whom you had enmity, will become your close friend"** (41:34).

THE ONE EXCEPTION

We discussed that even if you love someone unconditionally you still have right to say no. Is a human allowed to say no to Allah's commands as well? According to the Quran, a Muslim cannot refuse the commands of Allah. Since Prophet Muhammad[PBUH] gave us the message of Allah; therefore, a Muslim must obey both the Quran and the hadith: **"Tell the people O Muhammad[PBUH]: 'If you sincerely love Allah, then follow me'"** (3:31).

Obeying Allah without questioning is not an unfair requirement, because the Quran assures us that **"Allah does not burden any human being with more than he can bear"** (2:286). Verse 3:31 also recommends that obedience to Allah should be motivated by love instead of other minor motives, like discipline or habit.

ALLAH LOVES YOU

French novelist George Sand (1804-1876) said, "There is only one happiness in life, to love and be loved."[134] This is one of the undeniable realities of life. We like to be loved and at the same time we want to wholeheartedly love someone. The unconditional love between a mother and her newborn baby is a beautiful example. However, the most special moments are when both mother and child love each other simultaneously. Memories of such precious moments give lasting pleasure to both the mother and the child.

Similarly, love between a believer and Allah is a two-way communication. Allah not only tells believers to **"have *maximum* love for Allah"** (2:165), but also assures us that He **"is the *Forgiving*, the *Loving*"** (85:14). Again, two names of Allah, the Forgiving and the Loving, come together. This means that the love of Allah is manifested by His forgiveness. Allah says, **"O My servants [a very loving Arabic term used here] who have transgressed against their souls, *do not despair of Allah's mercy*, for Allah forgives all sins. It is He Who is the Forgiving, the Merciful"** (39:53).

There are numerous examples of Allah's forgiveness and mercy. One sinner was so concerned about his sins that, before his death, he directed his sons to cremate him and scatter his ashes into the sea. His plan was to escape Allah's punishment; he hoped that Allah would not be able to recreate his body. After he died, of course the omnipotent Allah did recreate his body, and He asked the man why he preferred cremation. The man admitted his plan to escape Allah's punishment. In response, Allah forgave him.[135]

Here we must note that the man was a sinner, but he did not ask any intermediary, Prophet, deceased saint, god, or goddess to save him. He was afraid of Allah only, and no other deity or human. The man firmly believed in *la ilaha il-Allah*, or, there *exists* no god other than Allah. The man also believed that the punishment of Allah is real. Though he was a sinner, yet he completely fulfilled the agreement he made with Allah alongside all human souls to worship Allah only, as described in the Quran (7:172). No wonder the Merciful, the Forgiving, the Loving Allah forgave this man. According to Sufi Poet Sultan Bahu:

> The river of oneness has surged,
> quenching the thirst of the deserts and wastelands.
> If you don't nurture God's love in your heart,
> you will be dry and parched like those deserts.[136]

LOVING HUMANKIND

The Quran never says that Allah is the God of Muslims only, or Arabs only. Instead, the Quran emphasizes: **"Say: I seek refuge in the Lord of** *humankind,* the King of *humankind,* the God of *humankind*" (114:1–3). Here the word *humankind* appears three times for emphasis. Those who love Allah are naturally compassionate to His creation. This love should manifest in the form of kindness (see verse 30:21 above) and charity: **"Spend [your] wealth out of *love for Him* [Allah] on relatives, orphans, the helpless, needy travelers, those who ask for money, and on the redemption of captives"** (2:177). The verse makes no distinction based on age, tribe, race, religion, nationality or sex. Also, the believer's family is notably at the top of this list for charity. In other words, charity should begin at home and continue beyond.

It must be noted that the instructions are generous, realistic and logical. This verse also describes a beautiful motive to carry out acts of charity: give charity for the *love of Allah.* According to Ibn-Qayyim, "The love of the beloved must be unconditionally returned. If you claim to love yet oppose the beloved, then your love is but a pretense."[137]

UNCONDITIONALLY LOVING YOURSELF

To reach the level of nafse mutmainna or **"*fully* satisfied soul"** (89:27), you must also learn to love yourself *unconditionally.* If you hold back from loving yourself then, as a rule of thumb, you can never become a fully satisfied person. Muslims are supposed to have maximum love for Allah. This can only be realized if a Muslim not only loves Allah but also *feels love from Allah,* because **"He [Allah] is the *Forgiving,* the *Loving*"** (85:14). This creates a two-way loving bond between Allah and a believer. This also results in loving yourself unconditionally. If you do not love yourself, then compulsively you will also deny feeling the love from Allah. Consequently, it is impossible to have the maximum love for Allah.

However, love should always be done in the Islamic way. When it comes to personal achievements and possessions, we should give full credit only to Allah and not to ourselves. Even our bodies are not our own. They belong to Allah. **"To Him belongs all that is in the Heavens and the Earth"** (2:255). A good Muslim constantly thanks Allah for His mercy, seeks His forgiveness, and generously gives to charity. Such a person is polite, humble and kind to others. Such love can never lead to arrogance, egotism or narcissism.

I AM UGLY, SO I DO NOT DESERVE LOVE

In conditional love, the physical appearance of a person plays a significant role. That is why, when searching for a spouse, we look for a beautiful person, because it is easier to love a beautiful person. Similarly, children are cute, so everyone loves them. But old people lose their good looks. Therefore, they are no longer popular.

What if a Muslim believes that I do not look good and concludes Allah does not love me or I do not deserve love? Or s/he thinks that Allah made me ugly, which means that Allah does not love me. For this line of thinking, the Quran has an important message. Allah made us the way we are at this time and *we are always beautiful to Allah.* The Quran says that, **"He [Allah] has given you shape and *made your shapes beautiful"*** (40:64). In this verse, Allah assures us that at any age and under any circumstances, we are beautiful. In other words, *we are good the way we are.* If Allah judges us beautiful, there is no reason for us to have low self-esteem or withhold love from ourselves.

Further, we all face different challenges as a test of Allah. Our looks are also a test. Always remember that Allah created you beautiful.

Sufi Malik Muhammad Jaisy (d- 1542) was blind in one eye. Once when he was passing through a village, some people made fun of his blind eye. Jaisy asked them a question: "Who are you laughing at, me or my Creator?" The onlookers were dumbfounded by this question.

Next time you look at your image in the mirror, tell yourself, "My Creator loves me the way I am right now." Try it. This statement is inspired by: **"He [Allah] is the *Forgiving,* the *Loving"*** (85:14) and (40:64).

I HAVE COMMITTED TOO MANY SINS, THEREFORE I DO NOT DESERVE LOVE

A Muslim may hold back self-love because s/he has already committed too many sins. Taking full responsibility for your sins is a requirement of Islam, but it is not an excuse to distance yourself from Allah. In hopelessness a person may even quit worshiping Allah. Such a person will also hold back self-love.

But the Quran says that Allah **"is the Forgiving, the Merciful"** (12:98). All a Muslim has to do is *sincerely* seek forgiveness. Chapter 2 has many examples Allah's forgiveness.

The Quran also prohibits hopelessness and despair. **"Never give up hope of Allah's mercy"** (12:87). If any Muslim gives up hope of forgiveness by Allah, then s/he has the wrong concept of Allah. Rumi said:

> You are more precious than both heaven and Earth;
> You know not your own worth.
> Sell not yourself at little price,
> Being so precious in Allah's eyes.[138]

THE ISLAMIC ART OF HANDLING HEARTBREAK

Our emotional well-being critically depends on love. We desperately desire to receive continuous unconditional love from others and, in return, we desire to love others (though usually with conditions). We strive hard throughout our lives to achieve both of these goals. However, sooner or later, conditionally loving other people is guaranteed to end up in heartbreak. Why? The way this life is designed, all loved ones are eventually separated. There can be several reasons for separation—losing interest, geographical separation, disagreements, meanness, rejection, exploitation, abuse, conflict of interest, and, inevitably, death.

When a person has the correct understanding that Allah is the only Doer there is, and every hardship s/he faces is a test from Allah, then it becomes easier to love Allah unconditionally. Such a person does not blame other people for personal difficulties. Instead, a good Muslim emotionally accepts whatever Allah sends his/her way and still keeps loving Allah unconditionally.

When Prophet Muhammad's[PBUH] infant son died, was deeply saddened but he did not blame anyone (chapter 5). Without blame, the scars of a broken heart heal faster. Even in our saddest moments, a continuous flow of unconditional love from our hearts will consistently support us and keep us from breaking down. All human love relationships eventually end in separation, but the continuous bond of unconditional love with Allah remains uninterrupted. As a result, the loss of second-priority human love relationships will no longer feel like the end of the world. We never lose by loving Allah most. We feel His love right in our hearts. Loving Him is necessary for us to find continuous peace and tranquility. It is an essential part of Islamic worship. Ibn-Taymiyyah said:

> Even if it [the heart] attains all that it can enjoy of created things,
> it will not feel at peace or find tranquility, because it has an
> inherent need for its Lord, for He is the focus of its worship,

love and seeking and this is the only way to attain joy, happiness, pleasure, peace and tranquility.[139]

SUMMARY: UNCONDITIONAL LOVE OF ISLAM

A Muslim is supposed to do his/her personal best to emotionally surrender to the will of Allah and accept His every decree in the past, present, and future. This is the true meaning of the word *Islam*. The highest level of satisfaction and contentment over a prolonged period of time is only possible when a Muslim unconditionally loves Allah the most and simultaneously feels Allah's love. This is in itself is a spiritually gratifying and truly pleasant process that drastically reduces all kinds of suffering. It is like an infant who stops crying the moment her mother picks her up. The baby knows without doubt that her mother loves her, and motivated by a love, the baby trusts that her mother will remove every type of discomfort. Love brings instant satisfaction and contentment to the baby. And Allah is more loving and more merciful than all the mothers in the world.

Emotional surrender, loving Allah unconditionally and feeling His love, is the only way to acquire the state of nafse mutmainna or a **"fully satisfied soul"** (89:27). This is a surprisingly realistic goal, because Allah also knows our individual circumstances and limitations. All we have to do is aim our efforts in the right direction and pray. We are not expected to outdo ourselves either, because **"Allah does not burden any human being with more than he can bear"** (2:286).

CHAPTER 7

ZULM: OPPRESSION AND INJUSTICE

The previous chapter explains that Islam requires spiritual growth through unconditional love, and further explains that love is a feeling, not an action. How about *actions* of a Muslim towards one's own self and others? Islam promotes the following two guidelines, leading to the same goal:

1. The Quran encourages *adl* (justice), along with its several synonyms *insaf* (fairness) and *qist* (righteousness).[140]

2. The same idea is reinforced by repeatedly discouraging/prohibiting *zulm* (oppression and injustice). The Quran also prohibits actions described by several close synonyms of *zulm*, like "*baghy* (encroachment, abuse), *djawr* (oppression), *fisk* (moral deficiency), *inhiraf* (deviation), *mayl* (inclination), and *tughyan* (tyranny)."[141]

The nearest translation of the Arabic word *zulm* would be *exceeding the appropriate limits of behavior in dealing with others, while violating their essential human rights*[142] or *putting a thing in a place not its own*.[143] Any harmful/senseless action or concept is *zulm*. So, the word *zulm* encompasses the meanings of the English words oppression, tyranny and injustice.[144]

It must be noted that the antonym of *zulm* is *adl*. By prohibiting *zulm* and simultaneously mandating *adl*, the Quran strongly prohibits human rights violations.

126

One way to evaluate the importance of a concept in the Quran is to do a word count. The Quran emphasizes justice by using the word *adl* 18 times (if the word *adl* is used in a different meaning, then it is not counted here), and condemns oppression by using the word *zulm* an extraordinary 291 times (not counting occurrences of the same root word *z-l-m*, which means "darkness"). Appendix A lists the verses numbers that use the words *adl* and *zulm*. Brill's Encyclopedia sums up the importance of emphasis on *zulm*: "It can be seen as one of the most important negative value-words in the sacred book."[145]

Zulm is man-made suffering inflicted on others. Allah says in Hadith Nawawi [# 24], "O My servants, I have made oppression unlawful for Me and unlawful for you, so do not commit oppression against one another." Allah does not do zulm on humans, **"God has not done injustice to them [humans], but they have wronged themselves"** (9:70).

In this chapter, we will consider the number of situations and the number of ways Islam expects Muslims to do justice and avoid *zulm*.

THE WORD *ZULM* IN THE QURAN

> **Those who misappropriate the property of orphans with *zulm* [unjustly], swallow but fire into their bellies** (4:10).
>
> **Allah does not love those who do *zulm*** (3:57).
>
> **Hellfire shall be their home; and evil is the home of those who do *zulm*** (3:151).

ISLAMIC PRINCIPLE OF 'LIVE AND LET LIVE'

Here is the Islamic version of the 'golden rule': **"do no *zulm* and you will not be subjected to *zulm*"** (2:279). If people follow this rule, they will avoid doing zulm on others and in turn make their own lives easier.

ZULM OF PREJUDICE

In pre-Islamic Arabia, the social and economic framework revolved around tribal and family loyalties. Tribes protected their members from fair and unfair external threats. Stronger tribes exploited weak tribes. Inter-tribal wars lasted for generations. In these prevalent conditions, Prophet Muhammad[PBUH] prohibited the practice of all kinds of racial, tribal, and regional prejudices or zulm (chapter 2). The only criteria for entry into Paradise are one's Islamic belief and good deeds.

ZULM AGAINST CHILDREN

Islam teaches parents to be fair to all children and not to mistreat or do zulm to less favored children. Once a man planned to give a gift from his wealth to his favorite child while ignoring the rest of his children. He requested Prophet Muhammad[PBUH] to witness the gift. Prophet Muhammad[PBUH] asked: "Did you offer the same to all of your children?" The man replied, "No!" Prophet refused to be the witness and said: "Fear Allah and be just in dealing with your children."[146]

ZULM AGAINST PARENTS

Elderly parents are often sick, frail, and irritable. They lose their good looks and disposition, and taking care of them involves effort and time. This makes aged parents vulnerable, particularly when they are dependent on their independent adult children. The Quran protects elderly parents from both physical and emotional abuse. **"You shall be kind to your parents; if one or both of them live to their old age in your lifetime, you shall not say to them any word of contempt nor repel them and you shall address them in kind words"** (17:23).

ZULM OF VIOLATING THE PRIVACY OF AN INDIVIDUAL

Islam protects privacy and other rights of an individual in several ways. Here are just three examples:
1. **Do not spy on one another** (49:12).
2. **Do not backbite about one another** (49:12).
3. **O believers! Do not enter houses other than your own until you have sought permission** (24:27).

ZULM ON THE DOWNTRODDEN

The Quran protects all those who are downtrodden, regardless of their religion or race. **"Feed the poor, the orphan and the prisoners *for the love of Allah*"** (76:8). This verse orders Muslims to manifest their love of Allah through charity. When Muslim General Khalid bin Waleed took over the Heerah in Iraq, where almost the entire population was non-Muslim, he declared the following laws:

> Any elderly person, disabled worker, terminally ill person or a rich person who went bankrupt and based on that deserves charity from the fellow religious people, will not be required to pay head-tax. Furthermore, each one will become entitled for suitable allowances from the Islamic Treasury for himself and his dependents.[147]

ZULM OF WASTING RESOURCES

All our resources and possessions are blessings of Allah and should be used to benefit ourselves and others. For example, if Allah blesses someone with wealth and that person does not use that wealth to meet essential needs, that would be zulm on self. Similarly, if a person wastes the excess wealth on unnecessary luxuries and does not donate the required percentage to charities, that would also be a zulm. According to the Quran, righteous people **"spend of that wherewith We [Allah] have provided them"** (28:54).

Prophet Muhammad[PBUH] said that if you are at the bank of a river using the water for drinking and ablution, even then do not waste the water.[148] The Quran teaches a prayer: **"Our Lord! Forgive our sins and our *excesses*"** (3:147).

ZULM IN BUSINESS TRANSACTIONS

All business transactions should be fair and just. The Quran condemns those who cheat in business by measuring improperly. **"Woe to those who defraud, [when] they take by measure from men, take the full measure, but when they give by measure to others, they give less than due"** (83:1–3). Fair dealing is not limited to selling merchandise. This verse states a general rule that in all business and social transactions, *give* and *take* should both be fair and just.

ZULM ON EMPLOYEES AND EVEN ON SLAVES

One of the latest management strategies is to treat employees with respect and avoid overburdening them. Prophet Muhammad[PBUH] gave the same message several centuries ago: "[workers] are your brothers and Allah has put them under your command. So, whoever has a brother under his command should *feed him of what he himself eats* and *dress him of what he himself wears*. Do not ask them to do things beyond their capacity and if you do so, then help them."[149]

ZULM BY THE EMPLOYEE

It is also zulm if an employee does not fulfill his/her duties, whether out of carelessness or laziness. Prophet Muhammad[PBUH] said: "Whoever wants to earn an honest living and is on my Sunnah and does not harm people [do zulm] will be admitted to Paradise."[150]

ZULM ON ANIMALS

Islamic fair treatment also protects animals, who cannot verbally complain. Owners are responsible for treating their pets humanely. Prophet Muhammad[PBUH] said: "A woman entered the (Hell) Fire because of a cat which she had tied, neither giving it food nor setting it free to eat from the pests of the Earth."[151]

Besides physical abuse, Prophet Muhammad[PBUH] also forbade the mental abuse of animals. He instructed that if you plan to slaughter an animal to eat its meat, then do not sharpen the knife where the animal can see it. Also, before the slaughter, to reduce the animal's suffering, make sure the knife is sharp.[152]

ZULM BY GIVING FALSE WITNESS

False testimony in a court of law, can result in punishment of an innocent. Islam strongly forbids the zulm of giving false evidence: **"O believers! *Be steadfast for the sake of Allah* and bear true witness and let not the enmity of a people incite you to do injustice; *do justice*; that is nearer to piety. Fear Allah, surely Allah is fully aware of all your actions"** (5:8).

In addition, Islam strictly forbids giving false witness to protect a guilty person *even if* s/he is a loved one: **"O believers! Stand firm for justice and bear true witness for the sake of Allah, even though it be *against yourselves, your parents or your relatives*. It does not matter whether the party is *rich or poor* – Allah is the well-wisher of both. So let not your selfish desires swerve you from justice. If you distort your testimony or decline to give it, then you should remember that Allah is fully aware of your actions"** (4:135). It must be noted that both the above verses end with a stern warning from Allah Himself.

ZULM BY MUSLIM JUDGES

Islam regards justice as the birthright of all humans, regardless of their religion. For judges of every court, the Quran has strict instructions. **"When you judge between people, judge with fairness"** (4:58).

Taima ibn Ubairaq was a Muslim who stole a bag of flour and armor from his neighbor and planted them in the house of a Jew. The theft was reported to Prophet Muhammad[PBUH] and eventually the stolen items were recovered from the Jew's house. Taima ibn Ubairaq had strong tribal support. His fellow Muslim tribesmen pressured Prophet Muhammad[PBUH] to pass a quick judgment against the Jew. However, before the judgment,

Allah revealed to Prophet Muhammad[PBUH] that the Jew was innocent, and indicted Taima ibn Ubairaq. In this context, this verse was revealed: **"Judge between people in accordance with the Right Way which Allah has shown you, so be not an advocate for those who betray trust"** (4:105).[153] As a rule of thumb, regardless of social pressure or the religion or race of the parties involved, a Muslim judge must always execute justice to the fullest.

ZULM ON COMBATANT ENEMY

During the life of Prophet Muhammad[PBUH], the Muslim army had to defend against attacking pagans multiple times. Prophet Muhammad[PBUH] gave detailed instructions to prevent Muslims from committing zulm, both on the battlefield and inside enemy territory. Here are some highlights.[154]

- Do not torture anyone with fire.
- Do not attack any wounded person.
- Do not kill prisoners of war.
- No one should be tied down to be killed.
- Do not loot and destroy the enemy country.
- Muslims are prohibited from taking anything from the people of a conquered country, without paying for it.
- Do not mutilate the corpses of a combatant enemy.
- If the enemy requests, return the dead body of their deceased.
- *Never breach a treaty.*
- Before attacking a state, openly declare war.

ZULM ON NON-COMBATANT ENEMY

Prophet Muhammad[PBUH] said, "Do not kill any old person, any child or any woman"[155] and "Do not kill monks in the monasteries…Muslims have been prohibited from taking anything from the general public of a conquered country, without paying for it. If a Muslim army occupies an area of an enemy country, it does not have the right to use the things belonging to the people without their consent. If the army needs anything, they should purchase it."[156]

FORGIVENESS FOR THOSE WHO DO ZULM

Prophet Muhammad[PBUH] preferred to forgive a *zalim* [person who does zulm] instead of punishing him/her. One excellent example of this occurred during the conquest of Mecca, where Prophet Muhammad[PBUH] forgave almost the entire pagan population, even after they had humiliated, tortured, and killed many Muslims, including close family members of

Prophet Muhammad[PBUH]. These same pagans had once expelled the Muslims, along with Prophet Muhammad[PBUH], from Mecca to an unpopulated area for three years, forcing some of them into starvation. The hardship was so severe that Prophet's wife and uncle died. When the Muslims moved to Medina, these same pagans threatened and attacked the Muslims several times. Many Muslims were killed in those attacks. Still, that did not stop Prophet Muhammad[PBUH] from forgiving the *same* group of pagans.

MISCELLANEOUS TYPES OF ZULM

Compassion is an indispensable part of Islam. Muslims must be sensitive to the feelings of fellow humans and respect their privacy. Muslims are instructed to give gifts to one another and accept gifts from others; they are not allowed to secretly read other people's letters, and must always be polite to everyone. After doing favors for others, Muslims are told not to advertise this or embarrass the recipients by reminding them of the favors. If someone asks some favor or alms, then a Muslim has only two options: either help the needy or *politely* refuse. However, Muslims cannot humiliate the needy person or use sarcasm.

THE WORST ZULM OF ALL

The Quran precisely defines the worst kind of zulm there is. **"Surely committing *polytheism (shirk) is the worst zulm"*** (31:13). Allah alone is our Creator and Sustainer. If a person worships any other imaginary god or human or any other part of creation instead of Allah, or along with Allah, then it is the biggest error of belief, or zulm. Why? Because *zulm* is defined as *putting a thing in a place not its own*, and allocating divinity to a part of creation is the biggest misplacement error.

ISLAM STANDS OUT 9: NO SELF-INFLICTED ZULM

Islam expects you to love yourself. The fact is that unconditional self-love cannot coexist with self-imposed zulm. No wonder Islam forbids zulm on one's own self! Here we see yet another uniqueness of Islam. Many religions encourage self-inflicted suffering to promote spiritual growth. Instead, a Muslim is supposed to become a **"fully satisfied soul"** (89:27). This high status can only be achieved when a believer is satisfied with the self, along with the surroundings. Allah will say to those who qualify for

Paradise: **"[you are] well-pleased with Him and He [Allah] is also pleased with you"** (89:28).

To avoid zulm on the self, Allah does not mandate any worship ritual that is impossible or extremely difficult to perform. For example, Islam does not expect a Muslim priest to observe lifelong sexual abstinence. Instead, Muslims are supposed to get married. Similarly, Muslims are not required to shun the world. They are supposed to fully engage in daily life, provided they do not commit zulm/sins.

KEEPING RELIGIOUS RITUALS EASY AND PRACTICAL

Three companions of the Prophet decided to make the Islamic rituals more challenging in hope to become better Muslims. One person decided that he would not sleep; another one said that he would never break the fast; and the last one stated that he would never marry. When Prophet Muhammad[PBUH] heard their decisions, he said, "I fast and break my fast, I do sleep and I also marry women. So, he who does not follow my tradition in religion is not from me (not one of my followers)."[157] In other words, if a person alters the Islamic rituals by adding zulm, then that person does not remain a Muslim.

SELF-IMPOSED EMOTIONAL ABUSE

What about psychological zulm on one's self? What if, instead of doing one's best to be peaceful, a person allows negative emotions like anger, depression, guilt, or fear to persist? This kind of emotional zulm on self is not allowed. To have a **"fully satisfied soul"** (89:27), a Muslim should continuously do his/her personal best to be happy, peaceful, and contented. Such positive emotions are the consequences if one has unconditional love towards self and others.

The problem is that the ups and downs of life present all kinds of challenges to our inner peace. The good news is that Islam teaches us how to achieve this incredible goal. For example, Prophet Muhammad[PBUH] taught a prayer for inner peace: "O Allah! I seek refuge with You from worry and grief, from incapacity and laziness, from cowardice and miserliness, from being heavily in debt and from being overpowered by (other) men."[158] Islam provides solutions to major emotional problems. Only one instance is described here.

CONTROLLING THE ANGER

Allah says: **"When they [the righteous Muslims] are angry, they forgive"** (42:37). This verse not only points out the problem of anger, it

133

provides the solution: forgiveness. If left unchecked, anger can torment our minds for decades, long after a provocative event has ended. This means we must try our best to forgive. At times, it may involve personal sacrifice and difficult adjustment. But, usually, forgiving and forgetting leads to healthier relationships.

Prophet Muhammad[PBUH] suggested that if you find it difficult to forgive some offender, then pray for that person and ask Allah to forgive the offender. This removes the suppressed anger from the heart.

AMAZING SOLUTION: ISLAM ALLOWS VERY REALISTIC EXCEPTION

What if someone hurts you so deeply you just do not want to associate with that offender or see him/her ever again? Your emotional scars are too deep to overcome. Another reason could be that you are afraid the offender may hurt you again. These situations cause a conflict: (1) Islam insists on forgiveness (2) but in some cases, if a victim makes up with the offender, then the victim would be doing zulm on self. That is also prohibited in Islam. In such situations, how to forgive, without doing zulm on self? Isn't it an impossible riddle to solve?

The beauty of Islam is that it offers a practical solution to this puzzle. Just like the Quran suggests, you still forgive the zalim, *in your heart*, but you do not have to tell the offender. However, if you are emotionally not ready, then you do not have to associate or socially make up with the offender, because that would cause zulm on yourself.

We all have human limitations. At times, we are simply unable to associate with the offender. In the Battle of Uhud, the pagan Wahshi ibn Harb killed the Muslim Hamza, who was also the Prophet's uncle. Later, Wahshi ibn Harb converted to Islam. Prophet Muhammad[PBUH] welcomed him into the fold of Islam, forgave him, and did not punish him for the heinous murder. However, Prophet Muhammad[PBUH] said that he still did not wish to see Wahshi ibn Harb's face. In other words, forgive in your heart, but if you are not comfortable, then you have the right to keep the offender out of your life.

It is interesting that Islam recognizes the human limitation of unbearably painful memories and the necessity to defend ourselves from repeated offense. If you follow the Quran's advice, then handling your anger becomes a win-win situation. In all cases, you save yourself from zulm. (1) you forgive the offender in your heart, Islam regards your forgiveness as a good deed. (2) you still have the freedom to decide if you want to make up with the offender. What a beautiful yet practical solution?

ZULM OF SELF-DESTRUCTIVE HABITS

Self-destructive habits like substance abuse, gambling, and playing the lottery are prohibited in Islam. **"O believers! Intoxicants and gambling … and division by arrows (lottery) are the filthy works of satan"** (5:90).

ZULM OF SELF-IMPOSED FINANCIAL HARDSHIP

Islam strongly advocates charity. A form of charity, *zakat*, is one of the five pillars of Islam. But what if a person donates all their worldly possessions and becomes bankrupt? That would be a financial disaster for the donor and his/her family. This is likely to lead to self-pity and regret, which is a form of emotional suffering. For that reason, both the self-imposed emotional and financial sufferings are prohibited, because Allah praises **"those who, when they spend, are not extravagant and not niggardly, but hold a just (balance) between those (extremes)"** (25:67). How carefully Islam guides the believers to avoid zulm in different areas?

NOT PROTECTING SELF FROM ZULM OF OTHERS

When a Muslim has a choice, s/he is *required* to avoid becoming a victim of zulm. Allah praises those who **"defend themselves when wronged"** (26:227).

How do you defend yourself? Islam provides strict guidelines. The first step is to exhaust all nonviolent options to protect yourself from zulm. One excellent example of this comes from the Treaty of Hudaybia. With profound insight, Prophet Muhammad[PBUH] saved Muslims from an all-out battle that would have caused fatalities on both sides. Instead he forced the Muslims' irreconcilable enemy, Mecca's pagans, to negotiate a peace treaty (described in chapter 9).

Depending on circumstances, another option is to forgive the offender. And the last resort is for Muslims to use violence in self-defense. However, Muslims not allowed to exceed the original zulm caused by the offender.

What if a person is completely helpless to protect self from zulm? Islam regards such a person as a victim, who is neither responsible for zulm on self nor a sinner. However, a victim should continue to have hope in Allah, make his/her best effort to protect self against zulm, be patient, and pray to Allah to provide relief. Allah promises forgiveness to helpless victims. For example, Allah forgave the women who were forced into prostitution (chapter 2).

A GLIMPSE OF ISLAMIC JUSTICE: COMPENSATION FOR ZULM ON OTHERS

Suppose a person illegally acquires someone else's land. For such an offender, seeking forgiveness *only* from Allah is not enough. The first step is to return the land and fully compensate the victim for all damages. Next, one must resolve never to do zulm on anyone in the future, and sincerely repent to Allah.

An alternative to giving compensation is to seek forgiveness from the *victim*. The victim is given a choice to take equal (but not more) revenge or forgive the offender. From the point of view of the victim, forgiving the offender is highly recommended. In that case, Allah may also forgive the offender (based on the offense), and may reward the victim. Otherwise, on the Day of Judgment, the offender would be responsible for the zulm on a fellow human being. No oppression or injustice is too small. **"Whoever has done an atom's weight of evil shall see it"** (99:7–8). This shows the beauty of Islamic justice, where the victim of zulm is compensated unless the victim chooses to forgive.

WHY ISLAM CHANGES ITS OWN RULES

Allah does not mandate any worship ritual that is extremely difficult or impossible to perform. Ritual fasting from dawn to dusk is so important that it is considered one of the five pillars of Islam. Breaking the fast before dusk is a sin. But suppose while fasting a person becomes too sick to continue and has to break the fast to avoid a health crisis, does that make the person a sinner? No. Fasting and other worship rituals are essential, but only if they do not cause undue hardship. **"Allah never wishes injustice to his creation"** (40:31). Here we see that Islam changes its own rules, according to the circumstances, to avoid zulm. Those who are too old or too sick to fast do not have to do so. They have an option to donate to charity or make up a missed fast. No person is responsible for anything beyond his/her capability.

Similarly, Islam provides alternatives for those who are too sick to perform the physical movements of obligatory ritual supplication or *salah*. In relation to the Hajj pilgrimage, Islam provides options for those who do not have the financial or physical ability to travel.

ISLAM STANDS OUT 10: AVOID ZULM IN ALL CASES

The above section shows that if, under certain circumstances, following a rule of Allah may lead to zulm, then Allah changes His own rules and worship rituals to protect humankind from zulm. This shows a general Islamic principle: *if any good intended action is likely to lead to zulm, then under such circumstances, Islam prohibits that particular action.* This principle created a subject called *Maqasid al-Sharia.* For centuries, Muslim scholars have been studying this subject.

LEGAL DECISIONS MUST AVOID ZULM

What if a judge is passing a legal decision based on a Quranic rule but the circumstances indicate that obeying the rule would be zulm? Again, the rule would change because avoiding zulm is an overtly emphasized principle of the Quran.

Here is an example. During the lifetime of Prophet Muhammad[PBUH] two people fought, and one of them bit the hand of the other person. In response, the person pulled his hand away and the biter lost a tooth. The Quran allows equal punishment for the damage—tooth for a tooth—unless the victim chooses to forgive (5:45). In this incident, the person who lost the tooth insisted on punishment and took the case to Prophet Muhammad[PBUH]. Prophet Muhammad[PBUH] refused to punish the person who pulled his hand away. The Prophet said to the plaintiff, "Should he leave his hand in your mouth so that you might snap it …[sic] like a camel?"[159]

This proves an important principle, which is applicable not just in court but also life in general. A Muslim should keep an eye on the *consequences* of all his/her actions, even while obeying the laws of Islamic Jurisprudence.

FREEDOM OF SPEECH AGAINST ZULM

Islam strongly commands: **"Do not slander one another"** (49:12). Is the *victim* of zulm allowed to speak against the offender? The Quran responds to this question with a clear *yes*: **"Allah does not like evil words to be uttered *except* by someone who is truly wronged"** (4:148). This amazing verse allows a person to speak up against any offenders, even if they are religious leaders or belong to the ruling class.

Chapter 3 has a good example of an old woman who interrupted Caliph Umar's sermon. It must be observed here that the woman opposed Caliph Umar with logical arguments and proof from the Quran. Islam does not allow illogical and humiliating verbal attack, which is considered just another form of zulm. Equal credit goes to Caliph Umar, who not only withdrew the proposed law, but publicly admitted his mistake. Only a great person can do that.

Verse 4:148 also proves that the Quran is not authored by a human. If a human had authored the Quran, then, like most leaders, s/he would also have expected blind obedience by all followers, with no questions asked, regardless of whether the command is fair or unfair. Instead, Allah gave *freedom of speech* to individuals to speak up against the zulm of their own leaders, thus avoiding becoming the victims of zulm.

ISLAM RESTRICTS THE MISUSE OF POWER BY RELIGIOUS LEADERS

There are many instances in history, when the priestly class of some religion has claimed to control the divine, and life after death. The priestly class has also claimed that they have the authority to forgive sins and bless whom they choose. They have at times controlled the masses, and even the ruling class. This power has given religious leaders often unmitigated authority to do financial, political, and social zulm. For example, about 500 years ago, in one single temple dedication, to appease the gods, the South American Aztecs performed human sacrifices of an estimated 80,000 people.[160]

Amazingly, in following ways, Islam restricted the authority of the religious leaders and protected future Muslim generations from zulm by the Muslim priest class.

According to Islam, on the Day of Judgment, Allah alone will judge every human, including the Prophets. Only Allah can forgive. The priests do not have any authority or power in these two areas: In worship, no Muslim cleric has the authority to act as intermediary with Allah or to award Paradise.

As in the case of the woman who objected to Umar's law, Islam authorizes the Muslim masses to question the religious leaders and protect themselves from zulm.

Further, Islam does not define any religious hierarchy of the priestly class. In a mosque, any qualified man can lead the congregational prayers.

In summary, Islam limits the authority of the priest class primarily to preaching. They have no power to intervene in divine affairs.

COMPASSION EVEN FOR THE ZALIM

With so much emphasis to avoid zulm in all aspects of life, how should a Muslim treat a zalim? A Muslim should try to guide him/her with compassion to give up zulm. Prophet Muhammad[PBUH] said, "Help your brother, whether he is an *oppressor* or he is an oppressed one."

People asked, "O Allah's Apostle! It is all right to help him if he is oppressed, but how should we help him if he is an oppressor?" The Prophet said, "By preventing him from oppressing others."[161] Yet another example of unconditional love.

THE SUPPORTERS OF A ZALIM ARE ALSO SINNERS

The Quran mandates: **"do not be inclined to those who are *unjust*, lest you be seized by the fire"** (11:113). This verse has far-reaching consequences as a universal rule applicable to every social and political situation. Without the help of supporters and collaborators, no leader/ruler can do zulm on the general population. Suppose a zalim leader plans to do zulm on a group, then the leader should not be able to find Muslim supporters. This is because anyone who chooses to support a zalim leader will also face punishment from Allah. As a result, the leader's plan to do large-scale zulm should fail. What a beautiful insight?

REALITY CHECK

With so much emphasis against zulm, Muslims should be the most humane, just, and conscientious people in the world. They were during the time of Prophet Muhammad[PBUH] and the four guided caliphs.

During the reign of Caliph Ali, a Jew stole his armor. The caliph was also the highest legal judge at that time. To avoid zulm and have an impartial and fair judgment, the case of theft was not presented to Caliph Ali but to another judge of a lower court. The judge asked Caliph Ali to produce witnesses to prove that the armor originally belonged to him. Caliph Ali produced his two sons and his slave as witnesses. The other judge rejected the testimony of both sons, as they were too closely related to Caliph Ali. As a result, Caliph Ali failed to prove the case of theft.

The ruler of the Muslims, who was also the highest judge in the land, failed to prove his own case in a lower court. In Islam, a suspect cannot be punished unless proven guilty beyond a shadow of a doubt. The Jew was so impressed with the honesty and fairness of the Muslims that he converted to Islam.[162] There are hundreds of other examples verifying how Muslims of that era avoided zulm at all costs.

Do Muslims have the same commitment to justice today? The facts are disappointing. In 2015, Transparency International evaluated the level of corruption in 168 countries, out of which 40 were Muslim-majority countries. It is shocking to see that most of the Muslim countries were among the highly corrupt nations. Out of the 12 rated most corrupt, 7 were Muslim majority countries (ordered by most corrupt to less corrupt), namely Somalia, Afghanistan, Sudan, Libya, Iraq, Guinea-Bissau, and Yemen.

How about the most honest countries? Among the least corrupt top 21 countries, there was not a single Muslim majority country. To be uneducated and poor is bad enough, but to be corrupt is a blot and shame. It is worth keeping in mind that every form of corruption is zulm.

Corruption hurts the vast majority of the population. As a result, over the past several decades, millions of Muslims have migrated to Western nations. The irony is that once they settle there, most of the migrated Muslims eventually learn to be as honest as the population of the host country and live with less zulm.

SURPRISE – RAPE *VICTIMS* (NOT THE RAPISTS) ARE PUNISHED!!

So far, we discussed, how strongly Islam emphasizes justice and discourages zulm. Here are a few recent examples that show how some Muslims ignored the above teachings and practiced zulm. The goal is just to prove that the problem exists. Later on, we will discuss a peaceful solution.

In 2001, Zafran Bibi filed a police complaint that her brother-in-law raped her. Here comes a surprise—the Pakistani court sentenced *her* to death by stoning. After she spent more than a year in jail, under international pressure the court finally acquitted her in 2002. No charges were filed against the brother-in-law[163]. In 2001, a Northern Nigerian rape victim, Safiya Husaini, was convicted for having an illicit sexual relationship and a local Islamic court sentenced her to death by stoning. Fortunately, she was later acquitted after a retrial.[164]

What if an unmarried rape victim chooses to avoid punishment by not reporting? That can also backfire, if she becomes pregnant. A divorced Bangladeshi woman was raped and became pregnant. In 2006, she was sentenced to be struck 101 times with a cane because the pregnancy of an unmarried woman was sure proof of sex out of wedlock.[165]

BACKGROUND OF ADULTERY PUNISHMENT

A companion of the Prophet came home and saw that his wife was having sex with another man. The husband went to Prophet Muhammad[PBUH] to complain. This created a problem for the husband because, according to Islam, falsely accusing a chaste woman is a punishable offense. The goal of this rule is to avoid zulm on women.

Prophet Muhammad[PBUH] asked the husband to prove his accusation of *zina* (adultery) by producing four male witnesses who simultaneously saw the sexual act. The husband said that was an impossible condition. Still, the Prophet insisted that without producing four witnesses, the husband would face punishment for slandering.

At that time, several verses of chapter 24 of the Quran were revealed to Prophet Muhammad[PBUH]. According to these verses, if four eyewitnesses prove the charge of adultery, only then will both the adulterous man and woman get caned 100 times. I personally support the opinion that the severe punishment points to the seriousness of the sin of adultery and fornication. However, the nearly impossible condition of securing four genuine witnesses makes the crime of adultery practically unpunishable in this world.

What about the husband who witnessed the scene and was going through the emotional trauma or zulm? The Quran also provided a way to get divorce. If the husband chooses, he can accuse the wife of adultery in court and take an oath that he is speaking the truth. After that, the wife can either accept guilt or deny the charge under oath. If she denies the charge, the court will have to declare her not guilty, and annul the marriage.[166] In either case the lying party will be punished on the Day of Judgment. However, it must be noted that this incident has nothing to do with rape.

The problem started when Muslim scholars defined *"zina* a lot more liberally, where *zina* means *adultery, fornication, prostitution and rape.*"[167] The inclusion of rape with adultery also carried with it the impossible condition of four male eyewitnesses. The consequences of this have been devastating. "For almost 30 years, *hundreds of women* in Pakistan were incriminated and charged with the offense of zina as they inevitably failed to prove rape charges."[168] Pakistani police have proved to be disappointingly immoral in practice, by refusing to register cases under ... rape and recording instead as cases of *Zina* (i.e., adultery).[169]

Legally speaking, there is no similarity between the above incident of zina and rape! *Zina* is an offense when the husband/society/government accuses a woman of having consensual immoral sex. So, the husband or someone else is the accuser/plaintiff and the *woman is the accused*. That is why the Quran specifically limits the discussion to **"those [*husbands*] who accuse their wives [of adultery]"** (24:6). Whereas rape is a crime in which a woman accuses a man of sexual abuse. So, *the woman is the accuser/plaintiff* and a man is the accused. These are two entirely different circumstances. *Zina* is consensual sex, but rape is fully non-consensual. In *zina,* a woman is punished for *choosing* adultery, while a rape victim had no choice.

Allah forgave women who were *forced* into prostitution. How can anyone accuse a woman who was raped or *forced* to have sex? It therefore makes no sense to assign the *zina* witness requirement, and punishment, to the rape victim. This is zulm, without a doubt.

Imagine the psychological effect on Pakistani women when they realized that if they get raped, they would also go to jail and get blamed for promiscuity. In addition, people all over the world blame Islam for cruelty and injustice. Many Muslims (*yes, Muslims*) leave Islam. No one wants to be associated with such an unjust and senseless system.

WHAT DO ISLAMIC HOLY BOOKS SAY ABOUT RAPE?

The Quran does not discuss rape. However, the following hadith acquits the rape victim without the need of four witnesses: "A slave was in charge of the slaves in the khumus and he forced a slave-girl among those slaves against her will and had intercourse with her. Umar ibn al-Khattab had him flogged and banished him and he did not flog the slave-girl because *the slave had forced her.*"[170] So, the hadith does not support the need of four witnesses.

A position paper by *KARAMA* titled "Zina, Rape and Islamic law: an Islamic legal analysis of the rape laws in Pakistan" conclusively proves that the rape law imposed in Pakistan from 1979 to 2006 was incompatible with Islamic law. Why did Islamic scholars previously make and support such a law? It is a question for them. Perhaps they did not fully understand the significance of zulm. No dictionary meaning of the word *rape* can overrule the decree of Allah in the Quran that strictly prohibits zulm.

There are many other examples of zulm as carried out by contemporary Muslim scholars. In Nigeria, Pakistan, and Afghanistan, Muslim scholars banned polio vaccinations, causing immeasurable suffering and death. Before 1988, all over the world an estimated 350,000 people were infected with polio, a virus that can cripple them for the rest of their lives.[171] How can any human allow so much suffering to innocents?

LATELY, WHY HAVE MUSLIMS EMBRACED ZULM?

The problem is obviously not with Islam itself. The problem lies with contemporary Muslim scholars. Some Muslim scholars have refused to acknowledge that zulm is prohibited in Islam. They do not preach: *doing zulm on anyone (including yourself) is a sin.* They should not forget that Prophet Muhammad[PBUH] said, "All of you are guardians and are responsible for your subjects. The ruler is a guardian and responsible for his subjects; the man is a guardian of his family; the woman is a guardian in her husband's house and responsible for her wards; a servant is a guardian of his master's property and responsible for his wards."[172] This means that in every walk of life, Muslims should always be fair and just. These rules establish the foundation of Muslim ethics and moral values. Ignoring them creates an ethical vacuum.

Scholars occasionally talk about charity, taking care of old parents or helping the needy. But this is only a very narrow subset of the concept of zulm. Muslim scholars rarely mention the overwhelming emphasis on zulm in every aspect of human interaction. You can easily verify this claim by browsing the Islamic books section in a library. Just pick up any book on Islam. There is a 95 percent chance that you will not find any reference to zulm at all. If by a great coincidence you do see a chapter that refers to zulm, then again there is about a 95 percent chance that the book you picked up is *The Purest Monotheism: Monotheistic Islam. Polytheistic Muslims*!

On a positive note, credit also goes to some Sufi teachings, which promote love and justice.

IHSAN: ISLAM RAISES THE STANDARD OF JUSTICE

Haqooq ul Ibad, doing adl (justice) and avoiding zulm (oppression), is the minimum duty of every Muslim toward other humans. However, according to Islam, there is more. A Muslim unconditionally loves Allah. Inspired by love, a Muslim may do something extra, something nice for Allah's creation. A loving mother not only feeds and clothes her baby (the minimum requirement to keep the child alive), but she does much more in caring for, loving, and trying to make everything comfortable for the baby. Her motivation is not duty, recognition, or money, but unconditional love for the child. When a person not only fulfills his/her assigned Islamic duty but also voluntarily does more, this is called *ihsan*, the merging point of several Islamic virtues.

EXAMPLE OF IHSAN

The Quran says: **"Allah commands doing justice, doing *ihsan* to others and giving [charity] to relatives"** (16:90). Every good deed can be improved so that it becomes <u>ihsan</u>. Prophet Muhammad[PBUH] said, "Verily Allah has enjoined excellence (ihsan) to everything."[173] The Quran explains: **"Do *ihsan* to your parents, kinfolks, orphans, the helpless, near and far neighbors who keep company with you, the travelers in need and the slaves you own. Allah does not love those who are arrogant and boastful"** (4:36).

When Prophet Muhammad[PBUH] was the ruler of Medina and was surrounded by many companions, a desert Arab approached him and pulled his *rida'* (sheet) so hard that Prophet Muhammad's[PBUH] neck turned red. The desert Arab aggressively demanded, "O Muhammad[PBUH]! Order for me some of Allah's property which you have." At that time, the Prophet Muhammad[PBUH] could have punished the Arab for his aggression, or at least told him how to behave. Instead, Prophet Muhammad[PBUH] lovingly smiled and gave him charity.[174] This is ihsan. Imagine what would happen today if a person behaved in the same way towards a head of state?

Q: Who taught Muhammad[PBUH], *the man,* unconditional love and compassion?

EMPHASIS ON IHSAN

The Quran puts an overwhelming emphasis on ihsan. Allah promises a reward for ihsan on the Day of Judgment: **"Is there any reward for Ihsan other than Ihsan?"** (55:60). In verses 2:195, 3:134, 3:148, 5:13, and 5:93, the Quran repeats five times: **"Allah *loves* those who do *ihsan*"** (5:93). To those who strive on the path of ihsan, Allah promises His help in the form of wisdom and knowledge, right in this life, just as Allah helped Prophet Joseph[PBUH]: **"We [Allah] bestowed on him wisdom and knowledge. Thus do We reward those who do *ihsan*"** (12:22).

Ihsan also has another benefit in this life. Since ihsan is based on unconditional love of Allah, therefore, after you do ihsan to someone, you are guaranteed to feel peace and joy. This is the essential side effect of unconditional love. You can easily verify this by doing ihsan. Ibn Qayyim said, "If you don't find sweetness and joy in the deed [of ihsan] you perform, then doubt its sincerity.[175]

HOW MANY TIMES DOES *JIHAD* APPEAR IN THE QURAN?

Radicals over-emphasize *jihad* (war, among other meanings). While the word *jihad* appears 41 times in the Quran, on *only 12 occasions* is it used to mean *war*. Islamic scholar Ahmed Al-Dawoody presented a detailed breakdown of this usage:

> Seventeen derivatives of jihād occur altogether forty-one times in eleven Meccan texts and thirty Medinan ones, with the following five meanings: striving because of religious belief (21), **war (12)** non-Muslim parents exerting pressure, that is, jihād, to make their children abandon Islam (2), solemn oaths (5) and physical strength (1) [176].

Here we see that the Quran uses the word jihad (war) several times less than the word *zulm* (to discourage oppression). This shows a serious error of incorrectly assigning the priorities.

HOW TO GUIDE TODAY'S MUSLIMS BACK TO JUSTICE

Our goal is not to humiliate or insult Muslim scholars who have ignored zulm. Why? An unnecessary offense against anyone is zulm. Besides, personal verbal attacks are unlikely to be effective. After the four rightly guided caliphs, several Muslim rulers adopted repressive policies. Unlike today, back then, Muslims considered avoiding zulm as a fundamental part of Islam. The public used to ask state officials: "Why do you practice such barbarities [zulm]? Is not all this against the spirit of Islam? Are you not Muslims?"[177] Even if the above questions made sense, directly accusing someone of not being Muslim is offensive. That approach failed to change the course of history.

Proposed Solution

How to *politely* convey the significance of zulm to Muslim scholars? Our goal is not only to tell them to avoid zulm in their own lives but also to teach Muslims to avoid zulm. This book proposes the following two step solution:

Step 1: Let us follow the guidance in the Quran. When Allah commanded Prophet Moses[PBUH] to go and guide Pharaoh, then Prophet Moses[PBUH] prayed: **"O my Lord! *Open my chest* [so I make spiritual progress**

and] make my task easy" (20:25–26). So, the first step is *changing one's own self*. If you wish to teach justice to others, first you must practice justice yourself, in every area of human interaction. That means avoiding doing zulm on others and on yourself.

Step 2: Again, let us follow the guidance in the Quran: **"Strive against them with this *Qur'an*, a *mighty* Jihad [strenuous striving]"** (25:52). The Quran is not a weapon, it is a book of guidance. As a solution, let us use the Quranic teachings and *peacefully* communicate the message of justice. Instead of aggressively accusing the scholars about being wrong, we will just point to their error. The evidence is overwhelmingly in our favor.

"Appendix A" of this book lists the 291 verses of the Quran that condemn injustice and zulm. It also presents questions that will compel Islamic scholars to reassess their thinking. You can give a copy of Appendix A to any Muslim scholar who writes about or preaches Islam. If a number of people do this after every Friday congregational prayer, soon the scholars will realize that Islam does not support zulm. Our peaceful preaching can change the behavior of Muslims all over the world. Do not underestimate the power of Islam.

CHAPTER 8

ESSENTIAL STEPS TO ISLAMIC MONOTHEISM

In previous chapters we discussed that, among the five pillars of Islam, belief holds the highest priority. Without proper belief, practicing the rest of the rituals have no meaning. The following steps will ensure that the essentials of monotheism are included in Islamic belief:

1. **All prayers should be addressed *only* to Allah and none other**. Do not pray to Caliph Ali or Prophet Muhammad[PBUH] or any saints, like Abdul Qadir Jeelani. Do not call on any deceased person to help you or pray for you. Do not visit graves of the holy men to seek their help. Repent your sins, particularly the sin of shirk. Allah will forgive our past sins, *in sha Allah* (if Allah wills).

2. Stay away from *Mawlid* (*Milad*), *Urs* of saints and the traditional rituals related to *Muharram*, which include exaggerated emotions of praise and love of Prophet Muhammad[PBUH], his family, and other saints. In emotional moments, people are often unaware they are reciting the poetry of shirk.

3. **Based on your capability**, try to remove the shirk of desires. Repeatedly seek help from Allah to achieve this goal. This requires *ibadaat* (following Islamic worship rituals), introspection, and abundance of unconditional love.

147

4. The Quran orders Muslims to: **"enjoin what is right and forbid the wrong"** (3:104). When you see Muslims who violate rules 1 and 2, guide them *politely*, without insulting, humiliating or attacking anyone. Ask them the questions presented in chapter 5.

5. Remember that belief in Islamic monotheism is the *first priority*. It is more important than the rest of the worship rituals and rules of Islam.

Please do not use any arguments from this book to emotionally hurt or offend anyone. Physically attacking anyone is out of the question. The purpose of this book is simply to demonstrate the greatness of Islam. However, the challenge is to politely convey this information, without offending other religions and ideologies. That is why, wherever possible, this book cites examples from ancient Greek and Egyptian religions, and intentionally avoids offending any contemporary religion. The Quran prohibits even the minor offense of ridiculing other faiths. **"O believers, *do not insult those*, whom these polytheists call upon besides Allah, lest in retaliation they call bad names to Allah out of their ignorance"** (6:108). If ridiculing is prohibited, then how can a Muslim offend other religious ideologies? Likewise, this book has no interest in criticizing either Sunni or Shia sects of Islam. Instead, this book, simply points out the polytheistic practices in *both* of these sects.

CHAPTER 9

THE CRUCIAL ROLE OF *JIHAD*

The meaning of the word *jihad* has evolved over the last 1400 years. Today, if you ask the definition of jihad, you we will get contradictory answers:

(1) Some Muslim scholars call it "a peaceful internal struggle" or striving by peaceful means.

(2) According to the Encyclopedia Britannica, "Jihad is a religious duty imposed on Muslims to spread Islam by waging war."[178]

(3) Some Muslim scholars claim that jihad is limited to *defensive* war only (*Jihād ad-dafʿa*).

It should be noted that 'internal struggle' as described in case 1 can co-exist with cases 2 and 3. This chapter will not discuss jihad as an internal struggle. Instead, we will do a comparative study of cases 2 and 3: aggressive, armed jihad vs. jihad only as a defensive war. The disagreement is more than a simple etymological issue. Both aggressive-jihad (case 2) and defensive-jihad (case 3) have strong ideological support that sharply divides Muslims.

The case for defensive-jihad is based on the Quran, ahadith and writings of some supporting scholars. On the other hand, the case for aggressive-jihad draws inspiration from the ideologies of Syed Abu Ala Maududi (1903–1979) and Sayyid Qutb (1906–1966). Both of these men are among the highest-ranking scholars who have given philosophical support to contemporary radical Islam. Maududi was the founder of *Jamat-e-Islami* and Qutb was a leading member of Muslim Brotherhood. Maududi said about Jamat-e-Islami: "It is not a missionary organization or a body of preachers or evangelists, but an organization of *God's troopers.*"[179] Similarly, according to Luke Loboda: "Sayyid Qutb remains a significant and influential thinker in the Muslim world to this day. Professor Muhammad Qutb, Sayyid's brother, was a teacher and mentor to the young Osama Bin Laden."[180]

This book will *not* be discussing the above two political parties because a political party may change its agenda over time. Instead, the criticism is limited to the radical ideology of Maududi and Qutb.

How to find out which of the above two meanings of jihad is correct? In order to logically present the arguments in digestible segments, this chapter will present the top 5 goals of aggressive-jihad along with justifications based on the ideologies of Maududi and Qutb. Each aggressive-jihad goal will be immediately followed by a logical refutation based on defensive-jihad ideology. The point-counterpoint format will help the reader to objectively evaluate both sides.

Similar to jihad, the term *Islamic government* holds different meanings for different groups. When there is no confusion about its meaning, I use the term *Islamic government*. When relevant, I will use the term *radical rule* to describe government based on the ideologies of Maududi or Qutb.

What if a government is based on Islamic principles (like love and justice), instead of a radical ideology? Then it will be called *Islam-inspired government*.

AGGRESSIVE JIHAD GOAL 1

Maududi said: "the goal of the Islamic Jihad is to eliminate the rule of an un-Islamic system and *establish in its place* an Islamic system of state rule. Islam does not intend to confine this rule to a single state or to a handful of countries. The aim of Islam is to bring about a *universal revolution.*"[181] This goal can be proven in the Quran itself. In his exegesis of the Quran, he explained that when the Arabic word *iqamat* is used with respect to something that is not material but spiritual in nature, then it means to "practically enforce" the concept. Therefore, the words, *aqeemat-e-deen* as used in the verse **"establish the Deen [religion] of Al-Islam and make no division (sects) in it"** (42:13) means that Muslims should enforce

Islamic religious law on the rest of humankind. Maududi said that *the real object is to establish the din* [religion] *and keep it established.*[182] In other words, once it is enforced, do jihad to sustain it. Maududi said that the Quran *"demands from its followers that they should struggle with their lives for the intellectual, cultural, legal and political supremacy of the true Faith."*[183]

CRITIQUE AS OFFERED BY DEFENSIVE-JIHAD IDEOLOGY:

Maududi refused to defend his exegesis of verse 42:13 when challenged by another Islamic scholar, Wahiduddin Khan (1925– 2021). Khan wrote an article exposing the logical errors in the writings of Maududi, along with his misinterpretation of Arabic text, and provided his own explanation of verse 42:13. In May 1962, Khan mailed the article to Maududi and asked for his comments. They exchanged correspondence until April 1963, yet Maududi failed to justify his stance.[184] Later Khan published his articles, along with this correspondence in an Urdu book *Tabeer Ki Ghalti*. In this book, Khan explained that *aqeemat-e-deen* does not mean to "practically enforce sharia law on others." Khan quoted Imam Raghib that it means "to perform a job to perfection." Khan further said that *no recognized exegesis* of the Quran substantiates Maududi's interpretation of verse 42:13. To prove the point, he quoted 6 Urdu exegeses of the verse 42:13 by other famous scholars:

> ***Establish the Religion*** by Adul-Quadir
> ***Establish in Religion*** by Rafiuddin
> ***Remain steadfast in Religion*** by Abdul Haq Haqqani
> ***Remain steadfast in Religion*** by Ashraf Ali Thanwi
> ***Remain steadfast in Religion*** by Nazeer Ahmad
> ***Establish in Religion*** by Mehmood Hasan

If any of the above exegeses had implied the meaning of enforcing religion, it would have also provided an explanation like Maududi's interpretation.

Khan also quoted a hadith to prove that the addressee of aqeemat-e-deen is the individual, not humankind in general. In support, Khan also quoted ten exegeses of some of the foremost scholars of Islam, who clearly explained that aqeemat-e-deen is meant for the individual only: Aloosi Baghdadi, **Imam Razi**, Ashraf Ali Thanwi, Abul Alia, Mujahid, Abu Hayan, Khazn, **Qurtubi**, Qami Nishapoori, **Ibn Kathir**, and Hafizuddin.[185] The names of some prominent scholars are shown in bold.

Readers are encouraged to check English exegeses of the verse 42:13 by various authors and to keep a tally of how many exegeses *explicitly* support Maududi's claim and how many do not.

WHAT DOES QUTB THINK ABOUT AQEEMAT-E-DEEN?

Qutb was probably more radical than Maududi in his thinking. His ideology has influenced millions, particularly Arabic-speaking Muslims. Qutb was an Egyptian, and his mother tongue was Arabic. Qutb also wrote an exegesis of the Quran. But when it comes to explaining aqeemat-e-deen, even Qutb does not support Maududi. He simply states: **"steadfastly uphold the faith"**[186] (42:13).

Qutb did not add an explanation that the verse means to conquer the world to enforce Islamic rule. This is the case of major disagreement between Maududi and Qutb.

It is of interest to note that Maududi's mother tongue was not Arabic, and that his primary followers do not know the Arabic language.

Q: How can Maududi claim that aqeemat-e-deen means that Muslims should wage jihad to enforce Islamic religious law on humanity, when the Arabic-speaking Qutb did not make the same claim? Is Maududi's explanation meant only for those who cannot understand the Quran in Arabic and will accept his interpretation without questioning?

MAUDUDI'S EXEGESIS CONTRADICTS THE QURAN

To claim that Muslims are required to impose Islamic rule by violent jihad worldwide is a sweeping statement. History has shown us that no one has been able to rule the whole world. Men like Alexander, Genghis Khan, Napoleon, and Hitler managed to conquer and rule large areas (by the way, none of these conquerors were Muslim). But they all failed to maintain a permanent empire, despite the unimaginable bloodshed and suffering they caused. To claim that Muslims are required to conquer all seven continents is an extremely serious goal. In the present age of nuclear armaments, attempting to do so would surely result in more bloodshed and suffering than that of the above four conquerors combined. Therefore, Maududi's interpretation contradicts the important theme of the Quran to avoid zulm, as emphasized in 291 verses (see Appendix – A).

CONCLUSION

The above discussion argues that Maududi's exegesis contradicts the concept of zulm. Also, many reputable scholars, like Ibn Kathir, did not support Maududi's interpretation. This suggests that Maududi's interpretation was based on personal opinion. But no one can change the foundation of Islam by personal opinion. Why? Because the Quran protects the religion of Islam from *evolving with time* and thereby becoming a polytheistic or oppressive religion. Allah says: **"I have perfected your religion for you, completed my favor upon you and approved Al-Islam as a Deen [religion]"** (5:3). Because of this verse, no deviant sect, after Prophet Muhammad[PBUH] can argue that Islam can be perfected by adding new basic ideas. In his last sermon, Prophet Muhammad[PBUH] also said that Islam has been perfected.

In that same sermon, Prophet Muhammad[PBUH] summarized all of his Islamic teachings. And he did not say anything about conquering the world. He did not even use the word *jihad*. Serious students should read the Urdu book *Tabeer ki Ghalti*, which exposes several flaws in Maududi's writings and his ideology of enforcing Shari'ah law over humankind.

Q: If the goal of Islam were to establish radical rule, then all previous Prophets of Islam would also have attempted to establish it. The Quran does not contain any prayer by a Prophet that seeks Allah's help to establish a political government over the whole world. Before a battle, some Prophets prayed for victory. But none prayed to conquer the world. Is the goal to establish a global political government not important enough? Let's think about this issue.

JIHAD IS ONLY A DEFENSIVE BATTLE

According to the Quran, the goal of armed jihad, or *quital*, is a defensive war to protect ourselves and our allies from the zulm of an attacker, not world domination. The Quran says: **"Permission to fight back is hereby granted to the believers *against whom war is waged and because they are oppressed*"** (22:39). The following incidents from the life of Prophet Muhammad[PBUH] conclusively prove this point.

In the seventh century, the two greatest superpowers were the Persian Sassanid Empire and the Byzantine Empire. Byzantium was the eastern wing of the Roman Empire and Caesar Heraclius was a Christian, whereas the Persian Chosroes was Zoroastrian. To both empires, Islam was a double threat, both as powerful rule and as new religion.

After 629 CE, Prophet Muhammad[PBUH] sent peaceful delegations to the tribes near Syria to invite them to Islam. These tribes were aligned with the Byzantine Empire. Against the commonly accepted international law of that time, the tribes killed 15 members of the Muslim delegation. Also, the Roman governor of Busra killed the ambassador of Prophet Muhammad[PBUH].

At that time, killing a delegation or ambassador was regarded as an open declaration of war. In retaliation, Prophet Muhammad[PBUH] sent an army of 3,000 soldiers. The Roman Emperor did not take any chances. He mustered an army of 100,000. The battle was fierce; still, the Romans utterly failed to defeat the small Muslim army.[187]

When the Muslim army began to withdraw, the Romans decided not to chase them into the desert. This gave immense prestige to the Muslims, and several border tribes chose to embrace Islam.[188] Under these circumstances, another showdown was expected so that the Romans could regain their lost prestige.

In 630 CE, Prophet Muhammad[PBUH] heard the news of a massive buildup by the Roman army. Once again, the desert-dwelling, small Muslim population was pitted against the overwhelmingly resourceful Romans with hundreds of years of governing and large-scale warfare experience. It should be noted that all along the Romans were very aggressive, while the Muslims only defended themselves.

Under these circumstances, Prophet Muhammad[PBUH] encouraged Muslims to volunteer in the army and donate generously. Several verses of the Quran, like: **"O believers! What is the matter with you that when you are asked to march forth in the way of Allah, you cling to the Earth?"** (9:38) were revealed, encouraging the Muslims to voluntarily join the defensive war, or jihad. We must note here that these verses of the Quran and related hadith were applicable *only* under threatening circumstances.

The Muslims donated generously, and also put together a volunteer army of 30,000. Imagine the difficulties of a 15 days trip across the desert to Tabuk in unbearable summer heat.

When the Muslim army reached Tabuk, the Romans changed their mind about attacking an army of 30,000 Muslims and did not show up to face them.[189] This was another significant victory for the Muslims. Prophet Muhammad[PBUH] then received delegations from the neighboring tribes of Ailah, Jarba', and Adhruh,[190] who wished for Arab protection while traveling by sea and land, particularly from the Romans. They were willing to pay taxes to Prophet Muhammad[PBUH], but the tribes did not wish to convert to Islam. Nonetheless, Prophet Muhammad[PBUH] signed protection treaties with them.

Historian Bernard Lewis explains that even non-Muslims preferred Arab rule to that of Byzantium, because *the new yoke was far lighter than the old, both in taxation and in other matters. Some even among the Christian population of Syria and Egypt preferred the rule of Islam.*[191] Why were the Muslims so fair to the people they ruled? The explanation is obvious: back then the Muslims practiced justice and refrained from zulm on anyone.

THE SERMON IN TABUK DID NOT TALK ABOUT CONQUERING THE WORLD

After the no-show by the Roman Army, which was considered the most powerful army of that time, Prophet Muhammad[PBUH] gave a famous sermon in Tabuk (Appendix B). Here is an interesting point: The content of this sermon is *not* what you might expect from a victorious military general and head of state, particularly after the Muslims had earlier paid such a heavy emotional and physical toll at the hands of the Romans.

According to the aggressive-jihad goal, if Muslims were supposed to conquer the world to establish radical rule, then the subject of the sermon would have included topics like recognition of Muslim sacrifices, need of enforcing Islamic law on the rest of the world, and instructions on how to continue the armed jihad on Roman lands. The sermon would have leveraged success at Tabuk to increase Muslim resolve to conquer the world.

Surprisingly, these topics were not *even hinted* at in the sermon. Instead, it offered spiritual guidance to Muslims. Hate, arrogance, and oaths of revenge were out of the question.

To understand this point, a contrast can help. At the moment of conquest, without exception, all warrior leaders swim in adrenaline. On such occasions, it is human nature to arrogantly boast with pride and anger. For example, Genghis Khan (1162–1227) said: "The greatest pleasure is to vanquish your enemies and chase them before you, to rob them of their wealth and see those dear to them bathed in tears, to ride their horses and clasp to your bosom their wives and daughters."[192] If you compare this quote to Prophet Muhammad's[PBUH] victory speech in Tabuk, it becomes obvious that the Prophet of Allah spoke at a different level.

Challenge Q: When the Muslims army reached Tabuk, the Roman lands were unprotected. In his Tabuk sermon, why didn't Prophet Muhammad^{PBUH} quote the verse of aqeemat-e-deen (as interpreted by Maududi) and order Muslims to conquer the world? Was the goal of taking over the world not important enough?

AFTER THE SUCCESS IN TABUK, THE REVELATION OF JIHAD VERSES STOPPED

When Prophet Muhammad^{PBUH} was putting together an army to defend against the Roman threat in Tabuk, it was the season to harvest the dates from palm trees, where a delay can cause damage to the crops. The summer heat made the trip to Tabuk very difficult. And the Muslims knew that the Romans were overwhelmingly powerful. The whole idea seemed like a futile losing battle.

During this difficult time, several verses of the Quran were revealed to encourage the Muslims to help the cause, including: **"March forth whether you are equipped lightly or heavily and make *Jihad*"** (9:41).

Note that as soon as the Roman threat in Tabuk was over, the jihad ended, and no *new* verse was revealed to encourage the Muslims to continue the attack on unprotected Roman lands. It is misleading to quote verses like 9:41 as if they are applicable for all times.

Q: Before the Tabuk expedition, Allah had encouraged the Muslims to participate in jihad against the Romans as in *Surah Tawbah* (9:41). If Muslims are supposed to conquer the world, then why, after the Muslim army reached Tabuk, was no new verse of the Quran revealed to encourage the Muslims to attack adjacent defenseless Roman territories? How can anyone still justify Maududi's explanation of aqeemat-e-deen?

PROPHET MUHAMMAD^{PBUH} DID NOT ATTACK THE ROMAN TERRITORY

Prophet Muhammad^{PBUH} stayed for 20 days in Tabuk before retreating the Muslim army back to Medina. It is important to note that the Tabuk Expedition (630 CE) was the last battle in which Prophet Muhammad^{PBUH} (d 632 CE) personally participated. By that time, most of the Quran had been revealed. If violent jihad were a permanent requirement for Muslims, Prophet Muhammad^{PBUH} would have attacked the Roman lands, wouldn't he?

Avoiding violence in Tabuk was certainly not an exception. As a rule, Prophet Muhammad[PBUH] always preferred peace over confrontation. For example, in the Battle of the Trenches, Mecca's pagans attacked the Muslims in the city of Medina. Prophet Muhammad[PBUH] chose to defend the city by digging protective trenches instead of engaging in direct combat. Thus, he managed to limit bloodshed. The only times Prophet Muhammad[PBUH] chose violence were when a nonviolent option would have resulted in greater zulm.

Q: Before the Battle of Badr, the Quran encouraged the Muslims to carry out jihad against the attacking pagan army (8:5–6). Allah helped the Muslims with thousands of angels. As a result, the Muslims won the battle, even though they were outnumbered and ill-equipped. As soon as the Battle of Badr was over, the verses of the Quran encouraging war stopped. If Maududi's theory is correct, immediately after the Battle of Badr ended, why did Allah not encourage the Muslims to take over Mecca from pagan control?

Q: After the battle of Uhud, when the Muslims reached Hamra al-Asad, why did they not continue to attack Mecca, which was under pagan rule? Similarly, after the pagans retreated in the Battle of the Trenches, why did the Muslim army not attack Mecca?

Q: Maududi's opinion of global dominance contradicts the words and actions of Prophet Muhammad[PBUH]. Who is right?

AGGRESSIVE JIHAD GOAL 2

The second purpose of jihad is to follow in the footsteps of Prophet Muhammad[PBUH], who waged armed jihad against non-Muslims across Arabia. In the words of Maududi, "Who can deny the fact that he [Prophet Muhammad[PBUH]] subdued entire Arabia by means of both preaching and the sword."[193] The guided caliphs also conquered large territories beyond Arabia, including Persia, Egypt, and Syria. The books of hadith, like *Sahih Bukhari* and *Sahih Muslim,* contain entire chapters on jihad. For example, "Whoever is wounded in Allah's cause.... will come on the Day of Resurrection with his wound having the color of blood but the scent of musk."[194] There is an abundance of evidence of the role of armed jihad as an essential element of Islam.

CRITIQUE AS OFFERED BY DEFENSIVE-JIHAD IDEOLOGY:

The Quran tells Prophet Muhammad[PBUH] that **"thou art not charged to oversee them [the non-Muslims]"**[195] (88:22) and the Quran precisely describes his duty: **"then the duty of Our Messenger is *only* to convey [the Message] clearly"** (64:12). These verses again support the statement that Prophet Muhammad's[PBUH] purpose was not to use jihad to subdue the whole world. Prophet Muhammad[PBUH] participated in many battles. But every one of those battles was in self-defense. Non-Muslims had attacked Muslims, broken a treaty crucial to Muslim survival, or were preparing to attack.

The worse pagan attacks resulted in the battles of Badr, Uhud, and the Trenches. Chiragh Ali points out that the battleground of Badr was very close to the city of Medina, where Prophet Muhammad[PBUH] lived with the Muslims. This proves that the pagan army must have started several days earlier and almost reached Medina, where the Muslims came out to defend their city. Therefore, it is obvious that the pagans were the aggressors.[196] Similarly, the battleground of Uhud was very close to the city of Medina. Likewise, the Roman attacks and threats resulted in the Tabuk expedition.

The Tabuk incident did not permanently subdue the Byzantine Empire. It continued to intimidate Muslims across the border. In 632 CE, Roman pressure increased to the point that even when Prophet Muhammad[PBUH] was on his deathbed, he dispatched another Muslim army as a show of force. According to historian Al-Mubarakpuri, "His [Prophet Muhammad's[PBUH]] aim was to scare Byzantines and to implant confidence into the hearts of the Arabs who were settled at the borders of the Byzantines."[197] It should be noted that, once again, the goal of the Muslim army was not to conquer the Earth. Roman aggression continued during the reign of the four guided caliphs, who had to fight back in self-defense.

The Persian Empire was just as aggressive. Emperor Khosrow Parvīz II belonged to the 400-year-old Sassanid Dynasty. He was so powerful that at one time he almost subdued the Roman Empire.

In 628 CE, Parvīz ordered his governor, Bazan, in Yemen to send two soldiers to arrest and bring Prophet Muhammad[PBUH] to the emperor's court. This was a serious threat, because disobeying the Persian emperor meant a full-fledged punitive attack by the Persians.

When the two soldiers reached Medina and conveyed the emperor's message, Prophet Muhammad[PBUH] told them to wait until the next day. That night, the angel Gabriel informed Prophet Muhammad[PBUH] that Emperor Parvīz had been assassinated by his own son. The next morning, Prophet Muhammad[PBUH] informed the Persian envoy, "My Lord killed your lord."[198] The soldiers were stunned. If the news had not reached Yemen, how could Prophet Muhammad[PBUH] know about the assassination?

The soldiers hurried back to Bazan and conveyed to him the response of Prophet Muhammad[PBUH]. Soon after that, Bazan received a letter from the new monarch, Shahryar, confirming the assassination of Parvīz. Bazan realized that only a messenger of Allah could have known about this so swiftly. He, along with many other Persians in Yemen, accepted Islam.[199] It must be noted that these are all historical events, not mythology.

During the reign of the four guided caliphs, confrontations with the Persian Empire continued. Byzantines joined hands with the Sassanid Empire against the Muslims. Heraclius married off his grand-daughter Manyanh to Yazdegerd as a symbol of the alliance.[200] No matter how many times the Muslims defeated the Persians, they kept coming back with renewed attacks. Caliph Umar once said, "I wish that between the Suwad and the Persian hills there were walls which would prevent them from getting to us and prevent us from getting to them…*I prefer the safety of the Muslims to the spoils of war.*"[201] Under these circumstances, Caliph Umar had no choice but to take over the Sassanid Empire once and for all.

What was the secret of the military success of the early Muslims? British scholar Marmaduke Picktall (1875–1936) said: "The 'wars' of Islam in the Prophet's lifetime and in the lifetime of his immediate successors were all begun in self-defense and were waged with a humanity and consideration for the enemy which had never been known on Earth before. It was not the warlike prowess of the early Muslims which enabled them to conquer half the then known world and convert half that world so firmly that conversion stands unshaken to this day. *It was their righteousness and their humanity, their manifest superiority in these respects of other men.*"[202]

SURPRISE: THE FIRST MAJOR PEACEFUL TRANSFER OF POWER IN HISTORY

Some scholars give credit to America for the first peaceful transfer of power. "*Peaceful transfer of power from one party to another that occurred in United States—the first such transfer of power in history.*"[203] But this statement is simply not true. More than a thousand years earlier, Prophet Muhammad[PBUH] took over power in the city-state of Medina without a single drop of blood shed. Please note the odds against him.

1. Prophet Muhammad[PBUH] did not inherit power through a dynasty.

2. He belonged to a different tribe than the people of Medina, an important factor for Arabs with thousands of years of tribally-based succession of rulers.

3. Residents of Medina were not all Muslims. At that time, Medina was a multi-religious society consisting of the polytheists of Medina, Jews, and Muslims.[204]

4. Prophet Muhammad[PBUH] was not even a citizen of the city of Medina. He came from a different city-state, run by a different government. So it was just like a foreigner taking over as the head of state.

5. At that time, Medina was wracked by generations-old inter-tribal wars between Banu Aus and Banu Khazraj. Prophet Muhammad[PBUH] promised to bring peace between the two warring tribes. Because of his good reputation, both tribes almost unanimously accepted Prophet Muhammad[PBUH] as their leader.

   The entire city, celebrated his arrival by singing a famous song, that is still popular today. Though there was some political opposition, even in such a war-torn environment, there was absolutely no violence.

   Though they did not have voting similar to modern democracies, the population's enthusiastic participation in welcoming Prophet Muhammad[PBUH] and lack of violent opposition proves Prophet's popularity. Unlike most politicians, he *immediately* made peace between the two tribes and fulfilled his promise.

   When Thomas Jefferson was elected president of the United States, only property owners/taxpaying[205] white men were allowed to vote. Women and slaves were not allowed to vote.

6. Prophet Muhammad[PBUH] did not execute political opponents of Medina and allowed them freedom of speech, provided they were nonviolent. After taking power in Medina, his rule was threatened by a political opponent, Abdullah bin Ubai, who was a hypocrite Muslim and had many followers. One of Ubai's most aggressive actions was taken during the Battle of Uhud. Initially, Ubai travelled

with Prophet Muhammad[PBUH] and other Muslims to go to the battle ground to face the army of Mecca's pagans. However, right before the battle, Ubai and his 300 followers walked back to Medina, leaving only 700 Muslims to face a 3,000-strong, well-equipped pagan army. Besides reducing the headcount, his action hurt Muslim morale.[206] Ubai persistently tried to overthrow Prophet Muhammad[PBUH] and in so doing hurt the Muslims. Still, Prophet Muhammad[PBUH] did not persecute Ubai, but allowed him full freedom of speech. Abdullah bin Ubai remained a politically active opponent till his death.

7. Prophet Muhammad[PBUH] fought only defensive battles. He *did not use violence to acquire power in Medina*. He did not repress his opponents who were non-violent.

Q: Throughout history, has anyone *peacefully* taken power over a foreign nation with equivalent odds? How about in the future? Realistically speaking, can we imagine anyone in the future peacefully becoming the head of state under similar odds?

Q: Who taught Muhammad[PBUH], *the man*, that it is possible to become the head of state without violence?

THE SECRETS OF THE "PEACEFUL TRANSFER OF POWER"

Earned Public Approval

Before claiming power, Prophet Muhammad[PBUH] established his reputation as an honest and wise person who would always pursue justice, and who avoided zulm at all costs. He proved his skills as a successful leader of Muslims in Mecca. By word of mouth, his reputation reached the city of Medina and other areas.

Immediately after reaching Medina, Prophet Muhammad[PBUH] made peace treaties with neighboring Jewish tribes, and with other settlements in the vicinity of Medina. He even consulted his subjects on important issues. The Quran ranks *consultation* as a praise-worthy act: **"who have pledged their obedience to the Lord, …*who conduct their affairs with consultation among themselves*"** (42:38).

Planned to Avoid Future Problems

The desert town of Medina had few resources, including a very limited water supply. Prophet Muhammad[PBUH] ensured that the Muslims migrating from Mecca were given the resources they needed, and respectable status in society. From any perspective, this was an extraordinary achievement. He lived in peace with the Jewish tribes until they broke their agreements. Even non-Muslims preferred the rule of Prophet Muhammad[PBUH]. For example, non-Muslim tribes made agreements with him in Tabuk.

Used Wisdom During Calamities

The migration of Prophet Muhammad[PBUH] and the Muslims to Medina, however, caused a new problem for the people of Medina, the animosity of the overwhelmingly powerful and resourceful pagans of Mecca. They attacked Medina on several occasions. Abdullah bin Ubai and his followers raised serious concerns about this new animosity, however, Prophet Muhammad[PBUH] used his wisdom and foresight to peacefully avoid any domestic conflict in Medina. He did not wage jihad to solve every problem. After Prophet Muhammad[PBUH] took over power, there was a significant decrease in overall violence. After the Battle of Hunain, the original residents of Medina unanimously agreed that they were far better off after the migration of the Muslims from Mecca.[207]

Q: Why did Maududi not follow the hadith of the peaceful transfer of power as exercised by Prophet Muhammad[PBUH] and the first three caliphs?

Q: Why did Maududi recommend jihad to acquire power when it is possible to peacefully elect the head of state, as in modern Western democracies and as witnessed in the appointment of the three guided caliphs?

AGGRESSIVE JIHAD GOAL 2 (CONTINUED)

Every Muslim is supposed to follow the instructions of Prophet Muhammad[PBUH] and emulate his actions. Total obedience to Prophet Muhammad[PBUH] is an essential part of Islam; it is not an option. For example, the ahadith tell us how Prophet Muhammad[PBUH] prayed *salah*, and today Muslims copy his actions. Similarly, Prophet Muhammad[PBUH] ruled as head of state. Therefore, all Muslims are supposed to have a caliph. For that purpose, according to Maududi's quote above, armed jihad is required.

CRITIQUE AS OFFERED BY DEFENSIVE-JIHAD IDEOLOGY:

When Prophet Muhammad[PBUH] migrated to the city of Medina, he was surprised to find that the date palm farmers there were manually cross-pollinating the trees. Prophet Muhammad[PBUH] was not familiar with the process, so he expressed his surprise. The farmers thought that Prophet Muhammad[PBUH] had prohibited manual pollination and refrained from the activity. As a result, date production was reduced. When Prophet Muhammad[PBUH] learned about this, he said, "That was only my thought. If it will do any good, then do it. *I am only a human being like you* and what I think may be right or wrong. But *when I tell you: 'Allah says,' I will never tell lies about Allah...* If it is one of your worldly matters then it is your affair, but *if it is one of the matters of your religion, then refer to me.*"[208]

The above hadith points out that:

1. The religious instruction from the Quran and the ahadith, which have come through Prophet Muhammad[PBUH], are true. Muslims are required to obey his religious commands.
2. When it comes to worldly affairs, however, unless Islam specifically prohibits an action, Muslims have the freedom to accept whatever the new knowledge offers. This is one of the beauties of Islam, which allows Muslims to adapt to changing times. However, it should never lead to zulm on self or others.

How do we determine which comments made by Prophet Muhammad[PBUH] addressed worldly affairs and which constituted religious decrees?

For example, Prophet Muhammad[PBUH] never traveled by car, train, or plane. Does that mean that today's Muslims cannot travel by car, train, or plane? Islamic scholars have suggested that if Prophet Muhammad[PBUH] specifically *ordered* any religious action, then it became part of Islam and must be obeyed. However, if he only *practiced* a non-religious action, without ordering it, then all it means is that the action is permitted. Such action may or may not become a religious decree. It is true that Prophet Muhammad[PBUH] traveled by camel and horse, but he never specifically *said* that camel or horse are the only ways to travel. Therefore, according to Islam, all modern means of travel are also permitted.

Muslims should regard such riddles or confusion as tests from Allah. The Quran says: **"Do the people think that they will be left alone on saying**

'We believe,' and that they will not be *tested*? We [Allah] did *test* those who have gone before them" (verse 29:2–3). However, based on the guidance of Islam, we are responsible for making right choices.

The fact that Prophet Muhammad[PBUH] was caliph means that a Muslim can also become a caliph. Prophet Muhammad[PBUH] never explicitly *ordered* that Muslims should have a caliph, or explained how a caliph should be selected.

Such instructions are necessary to establish an Islamic government. Why did Prophet Muhammad[PBUH] ignore such important questions? The fate of the entire Muslim population depends on their government. It has only one explanation: *establishing an Islamic government is not a requirement for Muslims.*

A comparison to Islamic instructions can illustrate the point. Prophet Muhammad[PBUH] gave complete instructions on how an *individual* should worship. The book of hadith, *Sahih Bukhari*, contains about 20 chapters with several hundred ahadith, which give details on how to perform the salah, ablution, call to prayer, and the night prayer. Prophet Muhammad[PBUH] described what to pray before going to sleep and after waking up. In other words, Prophet Muhammad[PBUH] fully explained how an individual should pray to Allah.

The primary source of divine knowledge, the Quran, does not say how Muslims should select the caliph. The Quran has some general guidance (like avoiding zulm) but the exact procedure is not defined. Similarly, why is there not a single hadith that answers the most important question about establishing an Islamic government: *how all Muslims of the world should select a caliph?* This question cannot be answered from the examples of the guided caliphs either. Wahiduddin Khan points out: "including Umar bin Abdul Aziz there were five Muslim heads of the state who can be called the guided Caliphs. *All of them were assigned the power in different ways.*"[209]

Does Islam provide all the basic information about *establishing* and *operating* an Islamic government? Let us leave out all *ijtihad, ijmah,* and *qiyas* by the scholars. We are only looking for what Allah has revealed on this subject, not opinions of the scholars. It turns out that neither the Quran nor the hadith answer the following basic questions:

Q-1: Even after 1400 years, Muslims have failed to settle the issue of how to select a caliph. It is not just the question of which individual will be caliph, but what is the standard procedure for selection? Western democracies have exactly one process to select a president or prime minister. If there is more than one way to select the Caliph, then the *exact*

THE CRUCIAL ROLE OF JIHAD

procedure is not defined. The answer cannot be vague, because it can lead to civil war. Other related questions are: (1) How many years can a caliph stay in power? (2) How do people replace an incompetent caliph?

Q-2: In the 21st century, governing a country has become a complicated endeavor. In this age, it is impossible for one caliph to single handedly govern the entire nation. Modern countries divide the governance into branches. Each branch has separate, independent powers and responsibilities that do not conflict with powers/responsibilities of other branches. Also, every branch has some degree of check over other branches. According to *trias politica* model, the government is divided into *executive*, *legislative*, and *judicial* branches. In some countries these branches are further divided. For example, Germany has six main bodies. What is the Islamic way of dividing the duties of one caliph into different areas, so he can govern the nation in best possible way? How many branches of government will be there? How each branch will check other branches?

Q-3: What form of government and economic system does Allah recommend for Muslims (socialist, capitalist, communist or other)? Western countries have different types of democracies (electoral, parliamentary or presidential). Which democracy does Islam recommend?

Q-4: What will be the structure of the Islamic judiciary? Will there be lower and higher courts? How many levels of courts should there be? How will judges be selected?

Q-5: How will the legislators of Islamic law be elected/selected? How long each legislator will serve? Who will judge that the laws approved by the legislators are not zulm?

Maududi artificially introduced the idea that verse 42:13 mandates that Muslims are required to impose radical rule all over the world. However, this leads to another problem: once the radical rule is imposed, *how to govern*?

Q: Allah wanted humans to worship Him, so the Quran and ahadith provided the step-by-step procedure for worship. If Allah wanted Muslims to conquer the world and establish radical rule, then why do the Quran and ahadith not provide answers to the above key questions?

Islam allows independent reasoning (*ijtihad*) by scholars who can provide answers. Since the ijtihad about the government of a country will directly influence the lives of its citizens, the ijtihad should also have the overwhelming approval of citizens, as Prophet Muhammad[PBUH] and the three caliphs received. Otherwise, it will lead to violence and chaos.

Some organizations have proposed Islamic constitutions[210], but unlike under the rule of Prophet Muhammad[PBUH] no other constitution has: (1) received the approval of the overwhelming majority of citizens; (2) anticipated future problems (like adapting to modern technology and economic models); or (3) used wisdom to avoid calamities and solve problems nonviolently. Prophet Muhammad[PBUH] allowed full freedom of speech, fulfilled his promises to his citizens, and refrained from killing his nonviolent political opponents. Any government based on Islamic values must obey the same guidelines.

AGGRESSIVE JIHAD GOAL 3

According to Qutb, the world is divided into two distinct parts. The first is: "If we look at the sources and foundations of modern ways of living, it becomes clear that the whole world is steeped in *Jahiliyyah*, [Ignorance of the Divine guidance]…This Jahiliyyah is based on *rebellion against God's sovereignty* on Earth. It transfers to man one of the greatest attributes of God, namely sovereignty and makes some men lords over others."[211]

The second is: "The *Islamic society* is, by its very nature, the only civilized society and the Jahiliyyah societies, in all their various forms, are backward societies."[212] Islamic society is called *dar-ul-Islam* (abode-of-peace), which is "the homeland where faith rules and the *Shari'ah of God holds sway*."[213]

As far as the Jahili societies are concerned, they are, *dar-ul-harb* (abode-of-war) or a "place where the Islamic Shari'ah is not enforced and where *Islam is not dominant becomes the home of Hostility*."[214] In other words: the "rest of the world is the home of hostility (*Dar-ul-Harb*). A Muslim can have only two possible relations with Dar-ul-Harb: peace with a contractual agreement, or war."[215]

The goal of jihad is therefore to eradicate dar-ul-harb and replace it with dar-ul-Islam all over the world.

CRITIQUE AS OFFERED BY DEFENSIVE-JIHAD IDEOLOGY

This goal is identical to Goal 1. The only difference is that Qutb gives a different reason to conquer the world, since he disagreed with Maududi's explanation of aqeemat-e-deen.

166

When it comes to the idea of dividing the world into two adversaries, the best critical response comes from Wahiduddin Khan. He argues that the terms dar-ul-harb and dar-ul-Islam were not used either in the Quran or in any hadith. Instead, they were introduced by the Islamic Jurisprudence (*fiqh*) more than a century after the death of Prophet Muhammad[PBUH]. The most significant books of fiqh were written in the 2nd century after the death of the Prophet[216]. Here the writers of fiqh were making an *ijtihad*, the process of making a legal decision by "personal reasoning" based on the Quran and ahadith. However, ijtihad is permitted specifically *only for new* issues for which *no guidance is available either in the Quran or hadith.'*[217]

For example, a hadith says that Muslims should pray five times a day. Therefore, scholars cannot make ijtihad and overrule the hadith by claiming that Muslims should pray six times a day. Based on this limitation of ijtihad, Khan points out that during the lifetime of Prophet Muhammad[PBUH], the "state of war" between Mecca's pagans and Muslims in Medina existed for about six years. During this period, Mecca was an independent non-Muslim state, and fulfilled every single requirement the writers of fiqh assigned to dar-ul-harb. During the same period, Prophet Muhammad[PBUH] was the head of state in Medina and followed Shari'ah law, and fulfilled every requirement of the dar-ul-Islam, as defined by the writers of fiqh.

During these eventful years, Mecca's pagans attacked Medina several times, and many verses of the Quran were revealed, yet no verse defined these two sides in terms of dar-ul-harb and dar-ul-Islam. The Quran describes Paradise as *dar-ul-Salam* (Home-of-Peace) in verse 10:25. But this description is not used in reference to any land on Earth. Verse 14:28 refers to Allah's punishment as abode-of-loss, but this term does not refer to any land on Earth, as Muslims' enemy territory or dar-ul-harb. Therefore, it is not applicable to the current discussion.

Similarly, Prophet Muhammad[PBUH] never classified Mecca as dar-ul-harb and Medina as dar-ul-Islam. If the Quran and ahadith did not divide the world between the abode-of-war and the abode-of-peace, even *during an ongoing war*, why do the writers of fiqh make this division? Next, let us evaluate the contrast in a hypothetical case. If the *situation had not existed during the lifetime* of Prophet Muhammad[PBUH], only then is it possible to make such ijtihad. This means the ijtihad of abode-of-war and abode-of-peace should be discarded. Such a rejection of ijtihad is permissible. Khan quotes Prophet Muhammad[PBUH]: "If someone adds a new idea to *Islam* [the religion], which is not already present, then reject it."[218]

167

Khan makes another strong argument in the same context. The Quran talks in terms of **"O humankind"** [114:1 and many other verses]. Allah does not see the world as divided in terms of dar-ul-harb and dar-ul-Islam. According to the Quran, irrespective of where a person lives, every *individual* will be judged only by his/her own belief and actions.[219]

In the following verse, the Quran puts Muslims, Christians, and Jews in the same group, where everyone is treated under the same principles: **"The final result [of going to Paradise] will neither be in accordance with your desires [Muslims] nor in accordance with the desires of the People of the Book [Jews and Christians]"** (4:123). According to this verse, whoever does wrong will be punished. The Quran does not describe non-Muslims as permanent enemies. The Quran orders Muslims to be kind to orphans, travelers, prisoners, and neighbors, regardless of their religion. In contrast, the fiqh sharply divides the world into the abode-of-war and abode-of-peace.

These two concepts contradict one another. The fiqh divides humanity into two adversaries: Muslims vs. non-Muslims. Or more precisely, Muslims vs. the potential enemy. Khan laments that this concept was adopted by the majority of Muslim scholars throughout history. Khan concludes that such an interpretation gives the wrong idea that Muslims are the chosen people of a superior race, while all non-Muslims are inferior and the targets of jihad. He explains that when the Quran says, **"the best group"** *(Kahirul Umma)* (3:110), it means only those Muslims who properly act and believe according to the teachings of Islam.[220]

Does Khan have the right to criticize the highly reputable authors of Islamic Jurisprudence? *Yes, he does!* Doubt and confusion are part of our test, and Muslims are supposed to ponder to find the right answers based on facts and logic.

The Quran describes mistakes (judgmental errors) made by several Prophets including Nuh and Dawood. Later, those Prophets asked for forgiveness and Allah forgave them. If Prophets can make mistakes then the authors of Islamic Jurisprudence can also make mistakes. Are ordinary Muslims also allowed to reject the advice of scholars? It is interesting to note that the Quran gives Muslims the freedom to reject wrong ideas instead of blindly following them: **"You shall not follow anyone *blindly* in those matters of which you have no knowledge, surely the use of your ears and the eyes, and the heart - all of these, *shall be questioned* on the Day of Judgment"** (17:36). In other words, we are responsible to use our senses of ears, eyes and heart (or intellect) to critically evaluate what we learn. To support his arguments against the abode-of-war and abode-of-peace dichotomy, Khan has successfully provided proof by referring to the Quran and ahadith.

After all, following any school of Islamic Jurisprudence is optional (chapter 5). If you find following a particular school of Islamic Jurisprudence is helpful in your worship rituals, then by all means follow that school. However, it is not binding on Muslims to support the mistaken concepts of abode-of-war and abode-of-peace.

Disagree? **"Produce proof of your claim, if you are truthful"** (2:111).

BACKGROUND OF THE TREATY OF HUDAYBIA

Kaba is a stone building located in the city of Mecca, Saudi Arabia. Several centuries before Prophet Muhammad[PBUH], it was Prophet Abraham[PBUH] who rebuilt the Kaba and preached the religion of Islam to Arabs there. He told them to worship Allah alone, without doing *shirk*. However, with the passage of time, some Arab tribes started worshipping various gods and goddesses along with Allah. They regarded Prophet Abraham[PBUH] as their patriarch and they visited Kaba on pilgrimage. Muslims regard Abraham as a Prophet of Allah and, similar to non-Muslim Arabs, Muslims also regard Kaba as their holiest site.

For centuries the pagans in Mecca regarded the area surrounding Kaba as a holy sanctuary. Inside the sanctuary, every tribe was allowed to make pilgrimage—regardless of whether a tribe was a friend or an adversary. All tribes were allowed, irrespective of which god or goddess they worshiped. After the Muslims[221] and Prophet Muhammad[PBUH] migrated to Medina, however, the pagans in Mecca singled out Muslims and prohibited them from entering Mecca, even on pilgrimage.

Two Options of "Defensive jihad"

By 628 CE, the pagans in Mecca had attacked the Muslims in Medina several times. In defense, the Muslims fought three major battles: in Badr, in Uhud, and in the Battle of the Trench. After these battles, Prophet Muhammad[PBUH] had only two options remaining:

A. To wait for the next major pagan attack. In response, Muslims would be forced to fight another defensive battle. Arab tradition was to sustain the cycle of revenge and to keep fighting for decades. In addition, the pagans wanted their religion to dominate Islam. This meant that the attacks would continue one after another until one side was nearly annihilated. This option would have resulted in tremendous carnage on both sides.

B. Since the Muslim migration to Medina, the number of Muslims there had been steadily increasing. By 628 CE, they were probably in a better position to launch an attack on the pagans in Mecca and take over Mecca once and for all. This too would have resulted in bloodshed on both sides.

Either option would have been justified, because the Muslims would be defending themselves against the pagans, who had acted aggressively against them for the previous six years. But the Prophet rejected both options. Instead, he chose a *nonviolent* option; he decided to defy the ban on Muslim entry into Mecca. He planned for Muslims to travel to Mecca to make Umrah (pilgrimage), an entirely peaceful activity.

Discovering a Non-violent Solution

To make the pilgrimage, the Prophet led a Muslim caravan from Medina to Mecca. When the pagans learned the intention of the approaching Muslims to do Umrah, they dispatched a heavily armed unit of 200 horsemen to intercept the caravan and prevent the Muslims from entering Mecca. Rather than confronting the pagan army, the Prophet changed the route of the caravan.[222] Thus he avoided another opportunity to wage a defensive jihad.

The Muslim caravan managed to avoid any confrontation and successfully camped on the edge of the Kaba sanctuary zone at a place called Hudaybia. This created an unexpected problem for the pagans. According to the English philosopher Martin Lings, "if they [Mecca's pagans], the guardians of the sanctuary, were to hinder the approach of over a thousand Arab pilgrims to the holy house [Kaba], this would be a most flagrant violation of the laws on which all their own greatness was founded."[223] The pagans tried to prove that the Muslims did not qualify for sanctuary status because they came to attack, but their own observers confirmed that the Muslims were a peaceful caravan of pilgrims. This shows the beauty of the Prophet's strategy. Even when it was justified to fight, he tactfully avoided even defensive jihad, and nonviolently *forced* a recalcitrant and powerful enemy to make peace.

NEGOTIATION HAS HIGHER PRIORITY THAN VIOLENCE

Next the Prophet proposed a peace treaty, not just to make pilgrimage, but also *to end the 6 years of animosity* between Mecca's pagans and Muslims in Medina. He proposed that the pagans and Muslims would not attack one another. The pagans had to agree because the Prophet's strategy ruled out violence as an option for the pagans.

Still, the pagans added some unfair conditions to the peace treaty. For example, the treaty included terms for refugee extradition that were unfair to the Muslims. Also, Muslims were not allowed to make pilgrimage that same year, but only in the following years. This in particular was not an easy condition for the Muslims who had traveled through the desert for pilgrimage who were then prohibited from praying in the pious house of Allah (Kaba) at the last minute.

THE ANALYSIS OF THE TREATY OF HUDAYBIA

It is important to note that the Prophet never compromised the two fundamentals of Islam:

1. Monotheism.
2. Doing justice and avoiding zulm.

The treaty provides the following guidance for us today:

1. If a peaceful alternative/negotiation is possible, waging jihad is zulm.[224]
2. Just like Prophet Muhammad[PBUH], depending on the circumstances, the Muslims are allowed to make tradeoffs to avoid zulm.

Prophet Muhammad[PBUH] was probably the first person in history who managed to find a solution to conflict that influenced the lives of thousands of people *without violence*. He did not just propose a theoretical concept. He presented a practical example in the form of the treaty of Hudaybia. All this is history, not mythology.

HOW DID ALLAH RATE THE TREATY OF HUDAYBIA?

This treaty was such a significant event that the Quran not only mentions it, **"O Prophet, Surely We [Allah] have granted you a *manifest victory***

(as the treaty of Hudaybia)" (48:1), but Allah named a chapter of the Quran (*al-Fath*) after the treaty.

During the lifetime of the Prophet, Muslims had to fight several defensive battles, and many times they were victorious. The Quran does not, however, call any battlefield triumph a *manifest victory*. Only the peace treaty is granted that high status. It's something to think about.

News of the extremely unusual peace treaty traveled fast. For generations, the desert Arabs had been most familiar with revenge, bravery and the art of battle. But a skillfully negotiated peace treaty gave them an unusual message: *Islam is a religion of compromise, tolerance, and peace*. Islam spreads and thrives best in a peaceful environment. People started becoming Muslim at an unprecedented rate. According to Mubarakpuri, when the Prophet "went out to Al-Hudaibiyah [he had] with only 1,400 men, but when he set out to liberate Makkah, two years later, he had 10,000 men with him."[225]

Q: Today, do Muslims still follow in the footsteps of Prophet Muhammad[PBUH] and practice similar compromise, tolerance, and peace?

Q: Maududi and Qutb preached aggressive jihad. However, when pagans were no longer attacking Muslims (as in Tabuk and after victory in Badr), Prophet Muhammad[PBUH] refrained from waging aggressive jihad. In 628 CE, he even rejected defensive jihad; he preferred the Treaty of Hudaybia and thereby avoided bloodshed. How can anyone still justify that Islam approves attacking non-aggressive pagan lands?

RESTRICTIONS ON JIHAD—ZULM IS NEVER ALLOWED!

According to Maududi and Qutb, continuous jihad is necessary to conquer the world and sustain radical rule. Instead, Allah says: **"permission to fight back is hereby granted to the believers against whom war is waged and *because they are oppressed* … [Muslims] have been unjustly expelled from their homes only because they said, 'Our Lord is Allah.'"** (22:39–40). These *muhkamat* verses prove that jihad is reserved for defensive battle. Also, the purpose of jihad is to prevent zulm on Muslims and allies, not for world domination.

Another condition, even during retaliatory battle, requires that Muslims *not exceed the original zulm*. But that is not all; Allah prefers peace and patience over violence: **"If you have to retaliate, *let your retaliation be commensurate with the wrong which was done to you;* but if you endure with patience, *the best reward indeed is for those who endure with patience*"** (16:126). The Quran also puts forth another condition, that jihad must stop as soon as opponents offer peaceful terms: **"If the enemy is inclined towards peace, do make peace with them"** (8:61).

Author Louay Fatoohi argued, citing the Quran and ahadith, that a peaceful non-Muslim is not an enemy,[226] and Allah mandates: **"If anyone from the non-Muslims asks you for asylum, grant it to him so that he may hear the Word of Allah and then escort him to** *his place of safety*: **this should be done because these people do not know the truth"** (9:6).

Based on the above verses and other evidences, Fatoohi successfully proved that "armed jihad is a defensive reaction rather than an offensive action."[227]

Challenge Q: If Muslims obey the above muhkamat verses from the Quran, they cannot attack a peaceful non-Muslim nation. How then can Qutb justify jihad to attack peaceful non-Muslim nations, based on man-made ijtihad supporting abode-of-war and abode-of-peace?

HELPFUL NEW TERMS

Difference between an Islam-inspired government and Radical Rule

While describing political duties, Maududi said, "If the Muslim Party commands enough resources, it will eliminate un-Islamic governments and establish the power of *Islamic government* in their place."[228] I believe that the use of the term *Islamic government* in the above quote is misleading, because Maududi's version of government (or radical rule) has little to do with the rules set by Prophet Muhammad[PBUH] and the four guided caliphs. The most important difference is that neither the Quran nor Prophet Muhammad[PBUH] ever preached that Muslims should conquer the world to establish Shari'ah law, whereas Maududi believed that it is the duty of Muslims to keep fighting until the whole world is subdued and *radical rule* is established. In this book, *radical rule* is defined as a government based on the ideologies of Maududi and Qutb.

In contrast, an *Islam-inspired government* will be based on fundamental Islamic principles. Its leaders will believe that avoiding zulm is an essential element of Islam. That is what Prophet Muhammad[PBUH] and the four caliphs believed and practiced. The leaders will **"conduct their affairs with consultation among themselves"** (42:38) to make sure that their laws are not zulm on anyone, particularly religious minorities, women, orphans, the elderly, and other vulnerable segments of society. Just as Prophet Muhammad[PBUH] made a peace treaty with the Jews who were in the minority in Medina. The leaders of the Islam-inspired government will always allow any criticism of their man-made government. If necessary, they will change their laws and avoid zulm. After all, the Islam-inspired government is based on Islamic values and guidance given by Allah.

On the other hand, radical leaders are *only* interested in waging jihad. They are completely immune to zulm and the suffering of both sides caused by the ensuing perpetual battle.

Definition of the word 'Shari'ah' as used in this book

In the last 1400 years, the meaning of the words *Shari'ah* and *fiqh* have evolved. This book contains quotes from authors who may have used these words differently. To avoid confusion, I define the word *Shari'ah*^aditb as *the rules, ideologies, and moralities <u>revealed by Allah</u> and preserved <u>only</u> in the Quran and ahadith.* Shari'ah^aditb does not include any man-made laws or ideas.

Here the superscript *aditb* stands for: *as defined in this book.*

Shari'ah^aditb are the laws of Allah, therefore Muslims have to obey them. The fundamentals of divine laws never change. For example, Muslims should pray to only one God and Muslims must avoid zulm.

Definition of Fiqh^aditb

To respond to situations and issues not covered by Shari'ah^aditb, qualified Islamic scholars have used guidance from the Quran and ahadith to make new rules and laws. This book calls *only* the *man-made* laws and rulings fiqh^aditb. To achieve this goal of making laws for new situations, the scholars used ijtihad, ijmah or qiyas and other helpful permitted techniques.

1. Since fiqh^aditb is man-made, it can be wrong or change with time and situation.
2. Shari'ah^aditb provides general principles, while fiqh^aditb addresses specific situations.
3. Fiqh^aditb can never overrule Shari'ah^aditb. The only exception would be in a specific situation when following Shari'ah^aditb would lead to zulm.

Islamic Jurisprudence is the combination of laws from Shari'ah^aditb and fiqh^aditb. This meaning matches the definition of fiqh found in Brill's Encyclopedia: *"the science of religious law in Islam….* In addition to the laws regulating ritual and religious observances (ibādāt), containing orders, and prohibitions, it includes the whole field of family law, the law of inheritance, of property and of contracts and obligations, in a word provisions for all the legal questions that arise in social life (muāmalāt); it also includes criminal law and procedure and finally constitutional law and laws regulating the administration of the state and the conduct of war."[229]

A madhab is a school of thought within fiqh[aditb] (Islamic Jurisprudence). The major Sunni madhhabs are Hanafi, Maliki, Shafii and Hanbali.

Definition of Shari'ah Law

Shari'ah law is a combination of Shari'ah[aditb] and fiqh[aditb], including recent ijtihad and *fatwa* (religious rulings by a scholar to address new circumstances).

AGGRESSIVE JIHAD GOAL 4:

MUSLIMS CAN OBEY ONLY ALLAH'S LAWS, NOT MAN-MADE LAWS

Maududi said: "Din [obedience and submission] … actually means the same thing as state and government; Shari'ah is the law of that state and government… Whenever you accept someone as your ruler and submit to his orders, you have entered that person's Din. If you accept that Allah is your ruler, you have entered Allah's Din; *if your ruler is some particular nation you have entered that nation's Din.*"[230]

To decide to obey the law of a land is a major decision, as it also determines which god you are worshipping. Maududi poses a question, *"As a matter of belief can we accept one ruler, even if in practice we obey another?"* To this he responds, *"This is shirk!"*[231] If you obey the law of Allah or Shari'ah, only then can you be a Muslim. If you obey man-made laws, you are doing shirk.

According to Maududi: "the *Shari'ah is a complete scheme of life* and an all embracing social order where nothing is superfluous and nothing is lacking."[232] Maududi said that Prophet Muhammad[PBUH] established a "full-fledged system of government with a detailed law, *covering all aspects of life*, from beliefs and rites of worship to personal conduct, collective morality, culture, and civilization, economic, and social life, politics and judiciary, peace and war."[233] That is why the famous Urdu song says, *"deen hamara deene mukammal* (our religion is a complete religion)."

Sayyid Qutb arrived at the same conclusion, using different logic. He argued that any country that ignores the laws given by Allah and replaces them with man-made laws is in a state of *Jahilia* (those who ignore the Divine guidance). Qutb says, *"Jahilia is worship of some people by others*; that is to say some people become dominant and make laws for others ... Islam on the other hand is people worshipping God alone and deriving concepts and beliefs, laws and regulation, and values from the authority of God ... *the foremost duty of man is to dispose Jahilia from the leadership of man.*"[234] To ignore the laws of Allah and replace them with man-made laws is challenging the sovereignty of Allah. In the words of Qutb: "Jahilia is based on rebellion against God's sovereignty of Earth."[235]

Qutb describes the widespread influence of Jahilia as: "Our whole environment, people's beliefs and ideas, habits and arts, rules and laws is Jahilia, even to the extent that what we consider to be Islamic culture, Islamic sources, Islamic philosophy and Islamic thought are also constructs of jahiliyyah!"[236] He believed it is the duty of all Muslims to impose Shari'ah law all over the world and convert the world into dar-ul-Islam. Qutb said, in case of any resistance, "*a Muslim will remain prepared to fight against it.*"[237]

CRITIQUE AS OFFERED BY DEFENSIVE-JIHAD IDEOLOGY:

ISLAM *FULLY* PERMITS USE OF MAN-MADE LAWS AND RULES

Allah has total control over every single event: **"*all powers* belong to Allah"** (2:165). Allah even has complete and continuous control over the movement and spin of every single electron in the entire universe. He is not dependent on anyone's help: **"Allah is Self-Sufficient"** (112:2), because everything is already under Allah's control.

For example, we do not have to worry that tomorrow the sun will not rise in the east. If Allah wanted to, He could have made every human on Earth a perfect Muslim (verse 10:99). It is beyond human capability to challenge the sovereignty of Allah. However, as a test, Allah gave humans the freedom to choose between right and wrong. Allah also created human society, where we *need* the services of one another to survive. **"It is We [Allah] Who distribute the means of their livelihood in the life of this world, *raising some [humans] in rank above others, so that one may take others into his service*"** (43:32). This means following man-made rules is also by Allah's design. There is nothing wrong in following the rules of your employer, provided you are not violating Islam. However, obeying the unlawful instructions of a drug-smuggling employer would be zulm and sin. The following address this point.

1. **Q:** If following man-made laws is shirk, then why did Prophet Joseph^{PBUH} ask for a job from a non-Muslim king? **"Place me (in authority) over the treasures of the land, surely I am a good keeper"** (12:55).

2. **Q:** After Prophet Joseph^{PBUH} started working for the Egyptian king, why did he not overthrow him to establish dar-ul-Islam?

3. **Q:** Why did Allah let Prophet Joseph^{PBUH} follow the rules of the non-Muslim king as in this verse: **"Thus, We [Allah] showed Joseph^{PBUH} how to plan this; he would not have been able to take his brother under the *King's law* unless God had wanted it to be so"** (12:76).

4. Before the Battle of Badr, Prophet Muhammad^{PBUH} led the Muslims to a particular location and told them to wait for the approaching pagan army. A Prophet's companion, Al-Hubab asked Prophet Muhammad^{PBUH} if the choice of location was a command from Allah or just a war strategy. Prophet Muhammad^{PBUH} said it was a strategy. Al-Hubab suggested another location, where drinking water wells would be available only to Muslims and not to the approaching enemy army. Prophet Muhammad^{PBUH} changed his decision and followed this advice. Here Prophet Muhammad^{PBUH} followed a man-made rule.[238]

5. Prophet Muhammad^{PBUH} allowed Medina farmers to cross-pollinate the date palm trees and let them follow a man-made rule.

6. While signing the Treaty of Hudaybia, Prophet Muhammad^{PBUH} agreed not to perform *Umrah*, a worship ritual, that year. Here we must note that the pagans interfered with Umrah, a worship ritual, and Prophet Muhammad^{PBUH} agreed to it. Why? Because Prophet Muhammad^{PBUH} wanted to avoid a bigger zulm. Even if the pagans' terms of agreement were unfair, Prophet Muhammad^{PBUH} accepted those man-made rules.

7. When signing the Treaty of Hudaybia, the pagan negotiator objected that the word *Prophet* should not be written before the name of Muhammad^{PBUH}. Still, Prophet Muhammad^{PBUH} agreed to the man-made rule.

8. Why did Maududi and Qutb both follow man-made laws in their own countries? For example, they followed the man-made traffic rules by traveling on the right side of the road and stopped at intersections at a red light. None of these are part of Shari'ah law.

9. When Qutb visited to the United States in 1948, and Maududi visited the U.S. in 1979, did they not obey man-made laws by filling

out man-made visa application forms and following American time zones?

10. In the above quote, Qutb strongly condemned when "people become dominant and *make laws for others.*" Qutb also advocated establishing dar-ul-Islam all over the world. But dar-ul-Islam is ijtihad, which is a man-made concept or rule. How can anyone claim that ijtihad made by a human is the word of Allah? As discussed above, the concept of dar-ul-Islam is mistaken. Why was Qutb trying to become *dominant* and enforce a man-made concept of dar-ul-Islam over other people?

It is ridiculously impossible to reject all man-made rules.

Q: Suppose you are planning a plane trip. A man-made airport rule states that passengers should come to the airport two hours before the departure of the flight. How can you reject this man-made rule? Would you arrive at a barber shop two hours late?

ISLAMIC JURISPRUDENCE DOES NOT HAVE ALL THE NECESSARY RULES TO GOVERN A COUNTRY!

One of the main goals of Islam is to teach correct belief and proper behavior. Therefore, we will find *all* necessary guidance in Shari'ah[aditb] and fiqh[aditb] explaining how to maintain the proper monotheistic belief, how to perform worship rituals (*'Ibadah*), and, when interacting with others, emphasize unconditional love and avoiding zulm.

Over the last century, some radical Muslim scholars have tried to promote jihad to establish their version of radical rule. Khan thinks their ideology was a reaction to the collapse of the Ottoman Empire and they wished to overthrow their inept governments. A couple of generations later, the idea evolved into a full-fledged ideology. For that purpose, these scholars created literature that Shari'ah is 100 percent complete and all that the Muslims have to do is to wage jihad to impose it. Otherwise, Islam will remain incomplete. According to Khan, these scholars have misinterpreted verses of the Quran and ahadith. Their logic is baseless.[239] It is important to recall that Shari'ah[aditb] and fiqh[aditb] do not have answers to the basic questions Q-1 to Q-5.

The twenty-first century has emerged with new challenges. What are the laws against computer viruses or industrial pollution, for example? The four schools of Islamic Jurisprudence do not have the answers to such questions. How can Maududi and Qutb then claim that Shari'ah is a complete set of laws?

WHAT IS ALLAH'S LAW AND WHAT IS NOT?

How do you judge a court case if the applicable law is not available in the Quran and ahadith? This problem was identified during the time of Prophet Muhammad[PBUH]. When he sent Muadh ibn Jabal as an Islamic judge to the people of Yemen, he explained that Muadh should base his judgment on the Quran. If a certain case is not discussed in the Quran, he should base his judgment on ahadith. If it is still not found, then he should exercise ijtihad. The very fact that that ijtihad was allowed proves that all necessary laws are not available in Shari'ah[aditb]. It also opens the door for the Islamic-inspired laws to adapt to new situations.

Muslims should not make the mistake of assuming that laws made by jurists (fiqh[aditb]) are laws of Allah. The founders of the four schools were neither God nor His messengers. The Quran points out mistakes made even by Prophets. If Prophets can make mistakes, so can jurists. All humans are susceptible to human error. Here are a few shortcomings of the *madhabs*:

1. At times, the laws of madhabs contradict one another. For example, two madhabs require women to cover their faces, while the other two madhabs do not. [240] How can you make a law with contradictory instructions?
2. Sometimes laws of madhabs can be mistaken, as proven in the cases of dar-ul-Islam and dar-ul-harb. This does not mean that all madhabs are wrong. But they may contain parts that are not correct.

CLOSING A LOOPHOLE

Islam permits ijtihad by scholars. On the one hand, ijtihad allows flexibility to adapt to ever-changing circumstances in the modern world. On the other hand, it can also cause serious problems, because wrong ijtihad can misguide large numbers of Muslims and do zulm!

Since the Quran is a book of Allah, it should not ignore a *potential future* threat of this magnitude. It turns out that the Quran warns against all forms of corruption introduced by ignorance: **"You shall *not follow anyone blindly* in those matters of which *you have no knowledge*, surely the use of your *ears, and the eyes, and the heart* - all of these, shall be questioned on the Day of Judgment"** (17:36). The Quran puts the *responsibility* on individual Muslims to *think*, instead of blindly following leaders or scholars. This means every Muslim has the *authority* to reject unfair guidance or rules proposed by scholars. This verse also offers the solution that every Muslim should use the full powers of intellect, by observing and studying (use of eyes), listening to others (use of ears), and pondering with your mind and heart (logic and reasoning). On the Day of Judgment, humans will be asked if they fully used the capabilities given to them by Allah before choosing between right and wrong. Since the Quran cannot be altered until the end of the world, then for all times to come, if a person studies the Quran with understanding, eventually he or she will be able to find the truth, *in sha Allah.*

What if someone is intellectually challenged or too young to make correct choices? Allah assures: **"Allah never wishes injustice [*zulm*] to his creation"** (40:31). No one will be judged unfairly.

IS THIS ISLAMIC RULE OR A MAN-MADE RULE?

In 1956, Maududi's party Jamat-e-Islami approved a constitution that was enforced in Pakistan for a short time.[241] The constitution proposed the positions of president, an elected *shura* council, and prime minister. In contrast, the rule of Prophet Muhammad[PBUH] was followed by four guided caliphs, not a *president* or *prime minister.* The English words *president* and *prime minister* appear nowhere in Shari'ah[aditb], fiqh[aditb], or the four madhabs. This was a man-made constitution based on ijtihad.

Nothing about this was wrong in itself, because Islam allows ijtihad. The problem arose when Maududi wrote a book regarding this constitution and called it *Islamic law and constitution.* This leads to a serious problem. How can ijtihad by Maududi and his supporters become an essential element of Islam? Ijtihad is a man-made method to solve new legal issues when they arise. As proved earlier, ijtihad can be mistaken or contradictory. The ijtihad of any scholar can never change Islam. Human ijtihad should never be projected as a decree of Allah.

Similarly, Qutb said: *Nationalism here is belief, homeland here is dar-ul-Islam, the ruler here is God and the constitution here is the Qur'an.*[242] Again, dar-ul-Islam comes from ijtihad, not from the Quran and ahadith. It is wrong to claim that the notion of dar-ul-Islam is an essential element of Islam. Presenting man-made ijtihad as decrees from Allah is a characteristic of radical rule.

Similarly, many contemporary scholars claim that Muslims are required to establish an *Islamic State* (a country ruled by Islamic government). Again, this term has no relation to Shari'ah[aditb]. Pakistani scholar and thinker

Qamaruddin Khan said, "The claim that Islam is a harmonious blend of religion and politics is a modern slogan, of which no trace can be found in the past history of Islam. The very term, 'Islamic State' was never used in the theory or practice of Muslim political science, before the twentieth century."[243] Therefore, *Islamic State* is just another man-made term.

PROPHET MUHAMMAD[PBUH] HAD THE CONSENSUS OF THE PEOPLE OF MEDINA

Before taking over as head of state, Prophet Muhammad[PBUH] had the approval of the *overwhelming* majority of Medina's citizens. He even made an agreement with the Jews and did not ignore the religious minorities. Allah defines the righteous as those **"who conduct their affairs with consultation among themselves"** (42:38). When it comes to the constitution, not just a majority but the overwhelming percentage of citizens should support it. For example, in the United States, the two most dominant rival political parties are Democratic and Republican. During elections they compete against each other. Yet, both these parties fully support the U.S. constitution. Maududi's *man-made* constitution affected every citizen in his country and, therefore, every citizen had the right to criticize, verify, protest, reject or accept it. In reality, Maududi's constitution was never approved by an overwhelming percentage of citizens.

WHICH ISLAMIC GOVERNMENT IS CORRECT?

Allah did not instruct Muslims to establish an Islamic government. Therefore, Allah did not specify how to run an Islamic government. According to The Oxford Encyclopedia of the Islamic World, *"the original Islamic sources [the Quran and hadith] rarely convey much on how to form states, run governments, and manage organizations."*[244] Radical leaders had to invent different man-made ways of governing. By nature, humans have disagreements. No wonder Qutb's Muslim Brotherhood never adopted Maududi's model of president and prime minister.

But that is not all. ISIS has established a totally different version of governing, where Al-Baghdadi (1971-2019) was the caliph. Similarly, the Taliban's Mullah Omar is *Amirul-Momenin*, not caliph or prime minister or president. As can be clearly seen, there are many differences among the above four types of governance.

GRANTING GOD'S STATUS TO A HUMAN

To claim or imply that Maududi's man-made constitution was the word of Allah or 'Islamic' is grossly misleading; some people assumed the constitution was given by Allah. Similarly, man-made radical rule should never be called Islamic government or described as a nation led by Allah. There are serious consequences of such erroneous claims:

- Muslims may think that following the constitution and supporting radical rule is their religious duty. Many will even be willing to die for the cause.
- When people believe that radical rule is Allah's rule, criticizing the government becomes apostasy. The citizens and the press cannot complain about corruption, zulm, mismanagement or poor economy.

THE QURAN STRICTLY FORBIDS ASSIGNING FALSEHOOD TO ALLAH

Since the Quran is a book of God, so it must point out an outrageous *future* error in which man-made rule is falsely claimed as the word of Allah. Such a claim can misguide millions of people. Of course, the Quran points this out. **"Who is more unjust than one who invents a falsehood against Allah?"** (39:32). Also, the Quran warns people against blind following and suggests full analysis before following their leaders (verse 17:36 above).

During the time of the four guided caliphs, the people did not confuse ijtihad with the commands of Allah. An old woman publicly rejected an ijtihad of Caliph Umar. The irony is that contemporary Muslims support an ijtihad even if it allows gross injustice, because that man-made ijtihad is presented to them as the word of Allah. They then believe it is their Islamic duty to obey without question.

For example, unjust rape law in Pakistan (chapter 7) was based only on man-made ijtihad, yet a large number of Pakistani Muslims have supported this unjust law as if it is the word of Allah.

Challenge Q: Why did the Pakistani Muslim community not object that Maududi's ijtihad-based man-made constitution was not the word of Allah and should not be called *Islamic*? Why did the Muslim community not object that dar-ul-Islam is a man-made concept, and Qutb should not present dar-ul-Islam as *Islamic* government? Can Muslims no longer distinguish between the word of God and the word of man?

AN ISLAM-INSPIRED GOVERNMENT SHOULD BELIEVE

This is what we should see under an Islam-inspired government:

1. Allah, Prophet Muhammad^PBUH, and the four caliphs can never suggest any law or rule that leads to zulm. Any hadith that claims that the Prophet or the four guided Caliph promoted zulm is suspicious.
2. Ijtihad is man-made rule. It should never be attributed to Allah.
3. The people should have full authority to criticize man-made ijtihad. They *should* verify if the ijtihad leads to zulm and reject it if it does. In such cases, scholars should revise their ijtihad.
4. While making the constitution for the nation, public consent must be obtained. This includes the consent of non-Muslim minorities, as well as other suppressed sections of society. Muslims do not have right to do zulm on non-Muslims. As discussed earlier, many non-Muslims preferred the rule of Prophet Muhammad^PBUH because he believed in justice. Today, if a fair and just rule is initiated, then, once again, the people of all religions will support.

LAWS OF ALLAH IN THE QURAN

The Quran does provide some basic rules. For example: **"You shall give full measure, when you measure and weigh with even scale"** (17:35), and **"Do not spy on one another, nor backbite one another"** (49:12). In almost all cases, an individual can easily obey the guidance of the Quran, even if local law does not support Quranic rules. However, Allah will judge the violators on the Day of Judgment.

The Quran also states some laws and assigns *worldly* punishments to the violators. Since the Quran is applicable until the end of the world, its laws are always mandatory. These stern laws of the Quran are called *hudood*.

For example, **"Male or female, whoever is guilty of theft, cut off the hand of either of them as a punishment for their crime"** (5:38). Since the Quran itself mandates this punishment, must this punishment for stealing *always* be enforced, without exception? According to Prophet Muhammad^PBUH, the strict *hudood* punishments should not be imposed when there is the *slightest* doubt or a *reasonable excuse* for committing the crime. Prophet Muhammad^PBUH said, "Avoid the *hudood* as much as possible. Whenever there is a mild chance release him [suspect]. For *releasing by an error on the part of the judge is better than punishing anyone without error.*"[245]

Once, during the reign of Caliph Umar, the kingdom was afflicted with a severe drought. A rich farmer sent some slaves to Caliph Umar with a sealed letter. The caliph broke the seal to read the letter. The message said that the slaves who had brought the letter to Caliph Umar had stolen and eaten fruits from a garden owned by the farmer. The letter asked Caliph Umar to punish the slaves by cutting off their hands. The caliph asked the slaves for an explanation. The slaves said that their master did not feed them enough and they were on the verge of starvation. Caliph Umar acquitted the slaves and they were not punished. Next he wrote a letter to the farmer. He said if the farmer had not participated in the famous Battle of Badr alongside Prophet Muhammad[PBUH], Caliph Umar would have the farmer's hand cut off for ignoring the duty of looking after the slaves. Caliph Umar was famous for his strict adherence to the rules of the Quran and ahadith. It is inconceivable that he would have overlooked the *hudood* imposed by Allah.

Instead, analysis reveals that Caliph Umar followed another law of Allah that was also applicable to this case and which held *higher priority*: the law of doing justice and avoiding zulm. For example, Allah strictly commands: **"when you judge between people, judge with *fairness* [the opposite of *zulm*]"** (4:58). Caliph Umar was facing two mutually exclusive options:

Option 1: He could implement the *hudood* for theft by amputating the hands of the slaves who ate the fruit to avoid starvation and thereby do gross injustice or zulm on the slaves.

Option 2: He could do justice but ignore the hudood law for theft.

Caliph Umar chose justice (option 2) because of its much higher priority in the Quran. His choice was in line with a similar decision made by Prophet Muhammad[PBUH], who ignored the *hudood* of a tooth for a tooth (see chapter 7). If the application of any hudood or law leads to injustice or zulm, the *rule of Islam changes to protect the victim*. In the above case, a tyrant victimized slaves to the brink of starvation. As a result, a law of the Quran adapted to protect the victims, and the tyrant himself deserved punishment.

Here is another example. The Quran strictly prohibits vulgarity, fornication, and adultery. However, Allah forgave women who were forced into prostitution (chapter 2).

Conclusion: The laws in the Quran are immutable, however, there are exceptions to the application of hudood punishments:

1. If applying hudood leads to zulm or injustice, then hudood cannot be applied.

2. If the government is inefficient and does not provide gainful employment to *every* eligible citizen or take care of the vulnerable people in society, like the disabled and orphans, then hudood for theft cannot be imposed, because the government is responsible for failing to provide 100 percent employment. This means that before imposing hudood, a Muslim country should be technologically advanced because only then can the government collect enough taxes to take care of a today's highly populated society and provide employment on a large scale. Until a Muslim country achieves these goals, the country can only run on normal laws, which are far more lenient than hudood. In addition, let us not forget that Caliph Umar threatened to punish the farmer rather than the slaves. This should make us all ponder: If radical rule fails to uplift citizens to the highest possible standard of living, provide full employment and take care of orphans, the handicapped, women, and religious minorities in a much better way than in other countries (within a reasonable time), then the incompetent radical rulers and their supporters deserve the hudood punishment for mismanaging their nation. Shouldn't this be the case?

3. If a judicial process is so corrupt that an innocent is likely to be convicted, hudood punishment should *never* be imposed. The sad reality is that Muslim countries are among some of the most corrupt in the world. Until a Muslim country joins the *most* honest and transparent countries in the world, its judicial process cannot be trusted enough to apply hudood laws. Something to think about.

AGGRESSIVE JIHAD GOAL 5:

Over the last two centuries, look what has been happening to Muslim countries around the world. Who can ignore the merciless exploitation and mass murder of Muslims? Others have occupied Muslim countries, so Muslims have had to wage jihad to survive. Muslim morality is also under attack from the heinous evils of prostitution, gambling, alcohol, drugs, promiscuity, elder abuse and neglect, and child abuse. On the ideological front, the Western ideas of secularism and separation of church and state are becoming popular in some Muslim countries. Maududi never approved Western ideas of anthropocentrism, secularism, socialism, and capitalism.[246] Along the same lines, Qutb criticized the highly industrialized and technically advanced U.S. as "abysmally primitive in the world of the senses, feelings and behavior."[247]

If Muslims want to survive as Muslims, then jihad is the only option left to save themselves and Islam. So the fifth goal of jihad is survival.

CRITIQUE AS OFFERED BY DEFENSIVE-JIHAD IDEOLOGY:

SIGNIFICANT ROLE OF THE MODERN AGE

The modern age has had an overwhelming impact on our thinking, our lives and our governments. We think in terms of socialism, secularism, democracy, communism, capitalism, liberalism and human rights.

In the early period of Islam, when the Muslim kingdom was expanding, Muslims were ardent learners from other cultures and civilizations. According to American chemist and historian George Sarton, "The Arabs began to encourage learning of all kinds. Schools, colleges, libraries, observatories and hospitals were built … and were adequately staffed and endowed.… In the same time, scholars were invited to Damascus and Baghdad without distinction of nationality or creed. Greek manuscripts were acquired in large numbers and were studied, translated and provided with scholarly and illuminating commentaries. The old learning was thus infused with a new vigor and the intellectual freedom of men of the desert stimulated the search for knowledge and science."[248] Soon Muslims became leaders in all areas of innovation and scholarship. In the words of Murad Hofmann, "They [the Muslims] made epoch-making results in all areas of arts and sciences—including mathematics, optics, botany, surgery, ophthalmology, hygiene, lexicography, history, sociology."[249] There was a time when Western Europe lagged behind Muslims! Bernard Lewis, in *The Muslim Discovery of Europe,* describes this era and justifies the title of his book, "in which the European is not the explorer discovering the barbaric people in strange and remote places but himself an exotic barbarian discovered and observed by an enquirer from the lands of Islam."[250]

From the fifteenth century, however, the tables began to turn. With the dawning of the modern age, Muslims lagged behind the West. According to Bernard Lewis, "The Renaissance, the Reformation, the technological revolution passed virtually unnoticed in the lands of Islam."[251] Missing out on transformation to the modern age was a costly mistake on the part of

Muslims. This rude awakening came to them at the turn of the 19th century.

In 1798, Napoleon's army landed in Egypt, the British defeated Muslim King Tipu in India in 1799, and the French conquered Algeria in 1830. Slowly, one by one, Muslim countries lost the upper hand, their independence, and their obsolete modes of governing and managing their kingdoms. Naturally Muslims felt anger and hatred toward their aggressors. Unfortunately, the majority of Muslim scholars and leaders failed to notice that the greatest cause of Western victories was not Middle Ages-style brute force and bravery, but the power of management, industrialization, and science. The West had discovered better ways of managing commerce, business, and government. They learned the delicate art of peaceful transfer of power, which gave them stability and resilience. Their heads of state were scrutinized based on performance. Citizens were empowered to choose their government. Technology gave the West superior military might.

Early Muslims had responded to foreign occupation with armed jihad and fought with great courage and sacrifice. Author Michael Bonner describes several armed-jihad-based efforts by Muslim leaders like Shamil (1796–1871) in the Caucasus against the Russians, Ahmad Urabi (1841–1911) in Egypt against the British, and Sanusiyya in Libya against Italy. But these "efforts [of armed-Jihad] were doomed."[252]

As discussed, there is nothing wrong with waging jihad in self-defense. However, Islam gives higher priority to finding peaceful solutions. Did Muslims try to negotiate before waging jihad? In addition, jihad is not the ultimate solution to every problem. One such challenge is the influence of the modern age. Here one must bear in mind that most aspects of the modern age are very positive. Instead of resisting them, Muslims need to adapt to them. These issues are just as relevant today as they were a couple of centuries ago.

THE COST OF MISSING OUT ON THE MODERN AGE

The West did not reach its present state of domination by coincidence. Its leaders certainly are not perfect, and have caused many atrocities and made serious mistakes. However, unlike Muslim countries, they did not reject modernity. The West is constantly inventing, learning, experimenting, discerning, and adapting. The West not only invented electricity, modern communication and transport, like the telephone, automobile, railway, and aircraft, it also discovered cures for the plague, malaria, tuberculosis, and other infectious diseases. The West is responsible for the invention of Braille, training guide dogs for the blind, and creating innumerable other amenities for the overall betterment of our lives.

Industrialization led to the unprecedented production of goods, and created millions of jobs in raw material procurement, manufacturing, distribution, transportation, communication, power generation, retail, advertising, and repair. This abundance of goods and jobs brought prosperity to the people, both in cities and remote villages. Jobs, in turn, provided governments with taxes to build infrastructure and fund social programs, including education, health care and housing. The West can afford to provide food for the needy and care for the orphans. Factories became heavily dependent on research to improve their end products. This boosted research labs and universities. With modern agricultural machinery, crop output increased and food became more plentiful. It now takes only a fraction of the population to produce enough food to feed an entire nation, something that was inconceivable in the middle ages. Mutual dependency of the blue-collar factory workers and the managers created dignity of labor.

In due course, the complexities of running a country became too much for one king to handle. In the West, people discovered the solution of dividing government primarily into executive, judicial, and legislative branches. In this way absolute power was split. Each branch of government had some degree of check on the other two branches. The judiciary and legislative were developed along the lines of protecting the weak. Capitalism allowed free competition, forcing businesses to constantly improve their products and management skills. Freedom of speech and a free press forced government and businesses to do introspection and self-correction.

As democracy flourished and human rights were recognized, governments adopted secularism, racial barriers started to dismantle, a large percentage of poverty was removed and, in many areas, women won their equal rights. During elections, people chose the most popular party. This created a positive competition among political parties. People utilized the freedoms of speech and freedom to create non-profit voluntary organizations to serve the weaker segments of society, including disabled persons and children with special needs. As a result, average citizens were able to play a productive role in building their communities. People generally respected the law and disciplined themselves. Overall corruption was reduced. People had a chance to realize their potential, and consequently experienced greater job satisfaction.

Challenge Q: How do the proponents of radical rule plan to provide the above benefits to all their citizens?

Any nation willing to accept modernity and compete has had the full opportunity to benefit. This included the late comers, like Japan, Singapore, Taiwan, Hong Kong, and South Korea. Here it is interesting to note that all the above changes are exactly according to Islam because progress reduces the zulm in the society. It is simply wrong to claim that Islam is incompatible with the modern age.

It is in fact easy to be Muslim and live in the modern West. At present, literally millions of Muslims are living in the West and devoutly practicing Islam. Mosques and Islamic schools are being built. International Muslim organizations like Islamic Relief have headquarters in the West. In some cases, it is a lot easier to be a Muslim in Western countries than in many overtly corrupt Muslim countries ruled by theocratic regimes. For decades, Muslims have been taking refuge in the West. It is true that many Western nations allow legal gambling, alcohol consumption and even prostitution. But these are optional activities and a Muslim does not have to participate.

The majority Christian West has given freedom to Islam because the West is mainly secular. How can Muslim-majority countries refuse to provide freedom to non-Muslim religions in the same manner, when the Quran says: **"Woe to those who give less [than due] but when they take a measure from [other] people, take in full"** (83:1–3)? Isn't that clearly zulm?

The modern age has also resulted in new problems, like high divorce rates, loneliness, domestic and other criminal violence, and substance abuse. But modern knowledge and research are being used to solve these new challenges through innovation and ingenuity. For example, the ongoing effort to control industrial pollution. No doubt, the overall benefits far exceed the negative side effects of modernism.

CONTRADICTION: RADICALS REJECT MODERNISM BUT DEPEND ON MODERN CONVENIENCES

Like most people, Muslims also depend on modern necessities and comforts. The sad reality is that Muslims have ended up in a contradictory state of simultaneously rejecting and depending on modernism. According to Nobel Laureate novelist VS Naipaul, this is "the confusion of a people of high medieval culture awakening to oil and money, a sense of power and violation and a knowledge of a great new encircling civilization. That civilization could not be mastered. It was to be rejected; at the same time, it was to be depended on."[253]

A good example of such rejection-cum-dependency was exhibited by Maududi himself. Toward the end of his life, he traveled to the U.S. to seek medical treatment. He did not depend on the traditional Graeco-Arabic medicine (*Unani-tibb*) practiced by Muslims in South Asia, nor did he trust the allopathic hospitals in various Muslim countries. He preferred to seek treatment in the U.S. It is hard to believe that the same man called it shirk to "accept one ruler, even if in practice we obey another." Also, it is contradictory behavior when Maududi asked his followers to create Islamic government by sacrificing their lives, but he himself traveled to the abode-of-war to save his own.

Q: When Maududi realized that he had to travel to the U.S. to seek a cure, as a founder of the *Jamat-e-Islami*, why did he not suggest any plan that would provide similar medical facilities to all citizens under his version of the Islamic government? Did only he deserve modern conveniences? What about the rest of the citizens?

Challenge Q: If the West is evil, why do radical Muslim leaders depend on the Western inventions of electricity, television, cell phones, computers, planes, water purifying plants, modern medicine, and cars? If radicals destroy the West to establish radical rule, how will the citizens get modern conveniences? Will radicals wait till Muslims reinvent them?

Muslim nations do not just depend on the West for consumer goods, they also depend on the West to learn natural and applied sciences, to gain technical knowledge, and to learn how to industrialize, efficiently manage government, peacefully transfer power, maintain freedom of the press, develop a comprehensive legal system, manage businesses so they contribute without exploiting consumers, and more. All this is beneficial knowledge that reduces zulm. It is an Islamic duty incumbent on every Muslim to learn and use knowledge to benefit the world. If Muslims adapt to the modern age, they will be less dependent on the West. In that case, Muslim nations will be in a better position to negotiate with the West. They need not migrate to the West to survive.

According to statistics from the mid-1990s, it has been estimated that the exports of Finland, a European country of 5 million, exceeded the exports of the entire Arab world of 260 million, excluding oil revenue.[254] It means Finland alone out-exported the entire Arab world, even with a population ratio of 1:52 in favor of the Arab world. Taking note of this fact should be an eye opener for all Muslims around the world.

IS VIOLENCE THE ONLY WAY TO MAKE POLITICAL CHANGE?

How have other countries responded to Western supremacy? In the 19th century, Japan faced the same scenario as Muslims did. Japan was primarily an agricultural society ruled by an emperor, and was surprised by ships coming from Europe and America. Instead of launching an immediate attack (similar to modern-day armed jihad), the Japanese used an alternative approach with amazing results. With a planned strategy, Japan avoided foreign occupation, so there was no need for a violent war of independence. Also, Japan fully caught up with the progress made by the West. This Japanese transformation occurred during the *Meiji* Restorations (1868–1912). How did Japan achieve this amazing feat in just 44 years?

Before 1868, Western Europe and the U.S. had forced Japan to sign an unfair treaty. One of the clauses stated that instead of the Japanese, Western courts would judge any crime involving foreigners in Japan. Thus, foreign courts had the power to do injustice to Japanese nationals.

Also, the Japanese military was no match for Western firepower, and Japan had very little technological development. Land was owned by local feudal lords (*daimyo*) who exercised tremendous control over the powerless common man.

Another power bank was the Japanese elite warrior class called *Samurai*. The essential first step for the Meiji emperor was to consolidate his own power. Meiji began their reforms by offering the daimyo and Samurai a yearly stipend. In return, the daimyo were requested to give up their lands. Samurais were told not to wear their swords in public, and all social classes of Japan were declared equal. Many Samurais were absorbed into business and professions.[255] Thus the emperor managed to take the land from the feudal lords and power from the Samurai, without any major war. Just imagine how many people would have suffered had there been a large-scale civil war to achieve the very same goals.

This Japanese strategy was based on sincerity, wisdom, patience and effort. The Meiji emperor realized that Japan needed modern education from the

West. To speed up this process, the emperor adopted a two-fold learning strategy. He sent Japanese experts abroad to learn banking, education, and political systems, along with treaty structures. The emperor also invited Western scholars (*yatoi*) to teach English, science, and journalism in Japan. Foreign engineers built railroads.[256] By 1872, a national system was introduced to educate every citizen.

History shows that kings are overprotective of their thrones. Usually, the most important goal of a king is to pass the throne to his oldest son and thereby continue the dynasty. The welfare of their country remains a secondary priority. In contrast, the Meiji emperor put the interests of Japan first, endangering his own throne. He not only initiated but implemented the process of creating a Western-style democracy. In 1881, a government bureau was formed to study the various modern political systems and to draft a constitution. Japanese experts studied the constitutions of many countries, including the United States, England, Spain, and France. They selected the constitution of Germany and Prussia, and based on that, they drafted the Japanese constitution, which was promulgated in 1889.[257] It was the first constitution in any Asian country. It gave the people limited freedoms of speech, religion, and assembly. It created an independent judiciary and a democratically elected parliament called the *Diet*.

The Meiji emperor also overhauled the Japanese legal system and adopted criminal and civil codes similar to those of France and Germany. It is interesting that Japan did not blindly follow just one Western country. Instead, they shopped around for solutions most suitable to Japan. The Meiji emperor also practiced religious tolerance. His rule allowed Christian missionaries to operate in Japan. Equal credit goes to the people of Japan, who wholeheartedly supported the modernization programs. Combined efforts of temples, government offices, and private schools quickly put Japan near the highest literacy rate in the world. Industries started sprouting, with textile became the largest Japanese industry. The postal system, banking system, public schools, and hospitals were modernized. Not only did trade, art, and literature flourish, but they also created many jobs in various sectors.

Western powers could not ignore this exponential Japanese growth. In 1894, they revised their unjust treaties with Japan. With their self-respect protected, naturally Japan managed to preserve its traditions, cultures, and religion. Today, only 2% of Japanese are Christians.[258]

It is just as important to note what the Japanese did *not* do. They did not launch terrorist attacks on the Western powers that were superior to Japan in warfare technology. That would have resulted in retaliatory attacks, and the deaths of innocent Japanese. Further, once violence is triggered, it may take decades before the cycle of violence and counter-violence subsides.

There is an unmistakable similarity between the restraint of the Japanese in the late 19th century and the Treaty of Hudaybia, with which Prophet Muhammad[PBUH] avoided a direct attack and saved lives on both sides. He proved by practical example that Islam is a religion of peace and compromise. As a result, without violence, most of Arabia converted to Islam. Eventually the pagans became powerless, and no major battle was needed to conquer Mecca. This is an example of the positive effect of using wisdom instead of senseless bravery and random violence to solve a problem.

Here is an interesting contrast. In late 2010, citizens of many Arab countries decided to protest against their inept and corrupt rulers. Instead of a Meiji-like planned and patient restoration, the citizens began what was to be known as the Arab Spring, triggering a series of demonstrations, protests, riots, coups, and civil wars. Overall it made the situation far worse, creating many negative side effects. Also, they projected Islam as a religion of senseless violence.

The late modernization of Japan is not an exception. Similarly, Singapore, Taiwan, South Korea, and Hong Kong have made galloping progress in the last 50 years. These countries are called The Four Asian Tigers. To live with dignity, Muslim countries need to make similar well-planned and patient efforts at modernization. But this will not happen by wishful thinking and random violence.

IN THIS DAY AND AGE, IS VIOLENT JIHAD THE BEST OPTION?

Surprisingly, the past century has offered an unusual choice, allowing common people to make *major* political changes, and that too without resorting to violence. Similarly, the modern age has also allowed rival countries to forgive centuries-old animosity and make peace. These options avoid bloodshed and make the world, in general, a better place.

Wisdom of Foreseeing the Mutual Benefit

Throughout history, political decisions have leaned toward the indiscriminate use of military power to maximize exploitation of the weak. More recently, there are numerous examples of prudent political leaders and citizens who have opted for mutual benefit instead of exploitation and revenge.

In World War II, by the time Japan surrendered to U.S., both sides had paid a heavy toll. U.S. had the upper hand. Still, U.S. did not colonize Japan and try to collect taxes and run the Japanese government or punish Japan till the end of the world. Similarly, Japan was the victim of two nuclear bombs, and had lost an incredible 2.3 million lives.[259] Its industry and infrastructure were nearly destroyed. But the Japanese government and its citizens did not launch an endless war to get even with America and take revenge for every single drop of blood. The U.S. and Japan chose to become allies instead of adversaries.

With the Treaty of San Francisco in 1952, the Allies ended all occupation of Japan. There was no need for a Japanese struggle for independence, suicide bombings, or emotionally loaded sermons to seek revenge. This wisdom tremendously benefited both sides in the form of economic growth, millions of jobs, and rapid technological development. There was no need to waste resources to annihilate each other.

The credit for this historical cooperation goes to the leaders *and* citizens of *both* sides. They envisioned that cooperation is better than warfare, even if countries practice different religions, speak different languages, and come from different races, customs, and cultures. In this case, both sides put up with some unfairness and still chose not to take revenge. Without ample forgiveness and wisdom, it would have been impossible to enjoy the benefits of cooperation and peace.

Similarly, Prophet Muhammad[PBUH] made several compromises just so Mecca's pagans would agree to sign the peace treaty of Hudaybia. He did not try to take revenge for the pagan atrocities against Muslims in early phase of Islam in Mecca and later on in form of attacks in Medina. The same principle, just several centuries ahead of his time.

Another outstanding example of cooperation over conflict comes from Western Europe. At the end of World War II, Germany was occupied by four countries: Russia, the United States, France, and England. Hitler had caused tremendous damage to these countries and Germany had lost millions of lives. These four countries had every reason to take revenge and punish Germany. Besides, the Cold War between NATO and Russia was an ongoing cause for hostility. Yet with wisdom and foresight on all sides, Germany regained its full sovereignty as a single nation in 1990. There were no major terrorist attacks or costly war for independence (compare that to violent independence struggles in some countries). No further resources were lost in fighting against each other.

European Union (EU) is another example of peaceful coexistence. Hostility among European nations goes back centuries. And World War II caused havoc across Europe. Only six years after WWII, the European Coal and Steel community (ECSC) was created to facilitate cooperation among six nations. As of September 2016, initial efforts had grown into what is now the EU, with 28 member states. It is interesting to note that the European Union includes former enemies like Germany and France. Instead of wasting lives and resources to continue to fight or to take revenge, these countries have become close allies for mutual benefit. For the first time in history, so many countries created a system that permits free movement of people, capital, services, and goods across borders. The credit for this landmark achievement goes to the leaders *and* citizens of all participating countries.

Relationships Between Contemporary Muslim Countries

As of 2010, there were 49 Muslim majority countries.[260] Did they also make peace agreements with their neighbors, similar to the EU? In a recent example, Iran and Iraq fiercely fought each other from 1980 to 1988, primarily over a border dispute. During this extremely costly war, 1.5 million people lost their lives.[261] Ironically, after the war, the borders of Iran and Iraq remained unchanged. The end result was all loss and no gain to either side.

This is not an isolated case. Many Muslim countries are currently involved in coup attempts, violent separatist movements, and civil wars. Why do Muslims engage in such carnage, while other countries have managed to find peaceful solutions to their disputes? I believe that one answer is because contemporary Muslim scholars do not teach Muslims to avoid zulm and do justice. Instead, many try to establish radical rule by waging jihad.

Muslim radicals do not have to attain power in order to wield political influence. For example, in Pakistan, regardless of which party is in power, terrorist attacks and threats interfere with government decisions. As a result, Pakistan has enforced absurd laws, like jailing rape victims instead of their rapists.

Q: Countries in which jihad has been used to establish radical rule have nearly been destroyed, like Afghanistan under the Taliban (1996–2001). In contrast, after only a few decades of effort, Taiwan,[262] Singapore, South

Korea, and Hong Kong have outperformed every single Muslim country, per the Human Development Index 2015. Why are non-Muslim governments better than (so-called) divinely guided radical rule? Something to think about!

All news is not bad news. One exceptional case of cooperation among Muslim countries deserves credit. In 1971, 7 isolated Arab states, including Dubai, successfully joined to create the United Arab Emirates. Naturally, they made progress.

Political Agitation Without Violence

As late as the 1960s, the U.S. openly practiced racial segregation and discrimination against African Americans. To protest this injustice, Dr. Martin Luther King Jr. along with other leaders did not carry out or encourage racially motivated riots, violent demonstrations, an armed separatist movement or terrorist attacks. Instead, they appealed to the conscience of the white majority using a Gandhi-like style, in a nonviolent civil disobedience movement. They set the course in the right direction to deliver African Americans from injustice.

In the 1960s, the U.S. was very affluent and considered nearly the sole superpower. It had played a major role in defeating Germany and Japan in WWII. Still, the civil rights movement managed to change the laws of this superpower and the thinking of a large number of Americans. Much of this was achieved in over just two decades. Sentiments changed from hate and superiority to sympathy and equality. Had MLK and other leaders started a violent separatist movement, it is difficult to imagine the damage it would have done to the United States, particularly to the African Americans. The beauty of their movement was to reach the goal, minimize damage, and win compassion for the victims of injustice, which they rightfully deserved.

An earlier example is India's independence movement led by M. K. Gandhi. In 1914, Gandhi returned from working in South Africa to a pre-partitioned India under British rule. Gandhi realized that in India, the Britishers are far less in number and cannot rule without collaborating with the Indians. He also noticed that Indians were divided, weak, and had low morale. Instead of prematurely starting a violent freedom movement, he used patience and worked to promote the unity and self-improvement of Indians. In 1918, he united poor farmers and laborers against an excessive land tax. This cause was genuine, easy to understand, and affected many lives, and protest was nonviolent. Gandhi quickly gained nationwide sympathy and support.

He continued to campaign to ease poverty, promote women's rights, end caste untouchability, and promote ethnic unity. He also promoted volunteerism to serve society, and simple living. These practices offered self-esteem to Indians without material advantage. Finally, when the time was right, in 1942, he started a nonviolent movement for Indian independence. His timing and strategy rendered the superior military might of England nearly powerless. Only after 33 years of nonviolent protest, Gandhi and his followers freed India without a blood-soaked destructive war for independence between Indian and British armies. A great achievement indeed!

NEW DIFFERENCES BETWEEN ISLAM-INSPIRED GOVERNMENT AND RADICAL RULE

Extreme proponents of radical rule (like the Taliban) have absolutely no concept of how to run a modern government. They have failed to create governments like Japan and the Four Asian Tigers. Their goal is to wage jihad and topple government. Whether they fail or succeed at this, large-scale jihad adversely affects all citizens. Depending on the degree of jihad, radical rule in various countries does not provide employment, except perhaps for jihadi warriors. The reality is that, just to survive, people have to earn a living, by legitimate or illegitimate means. For example, during the Taliban Era (1996–2001), prostitution flourished; "the ban on female beggars to enter shops, inns and other trading premises has even further affected their income, *forcing a number of them to enter into prostitution* for their survival and survival of their children.'[263] In the 21st century, if a radical leader attains power but fails to modernize his country and utilize the full available potential to improve the standard of living of its citizens, then such a leader and his supporters are nothing but zalim. Sooner or later, the citizens are bound to demand their rights, and the government will never be stable or peaceful.

In contrast, in an *Islam-inspired government*, it is the duty of a Muslim caliph to use all available resources and provide the highest possible quality of life to all citizens. The Prophet Muhammad[PBUH] and the four caliphs lived very simple lives, so their personal expenses did not burden the national treasury. To them, the basic needs of all citizens held the highest priority. Caliph Umar said, "If a dog dies hungry on the banks of the River Euphrates [on the edge of Umar's kingdom], Umar will be responsible for dereliction of duty."[264]

Since the time of Caliph Umar, many scientific and political discoveries have made human life easier, safer, healthier, and longer. There is no reason why Muslims should not benefit from these advancements as well.

Q: The fact that Japan and the Four Asian Tigers developed without large-scale violence proves that Allah created ways for countries to *peacefully* make political and economic progress. Why have Islamic leaders ignored this unique gift of Allah and emphasized only jihad? Why do they ignore the lessons from the treaty of Hudaybia?

Q: Both Maududi and Qutb wrote a great deal about jihad. Did they author any useful book on how Muslim countries can exceed the West in industrialization or improving the citizens' quality of life? If outspoken leaders like Maududi and Qutb ignored these essential issues, then who will guide Muslims how to catch up with the West?

RADICALS HAVE NO CONCEPT OF MODERN WARFARE

As quoted earlier, Maududi said that Jamat-e-Islami is "an organization of *God's troopers.*" And Qutb said that "a Muslim will remain prepared to fight [to impose dar-ul-Islam all over the world]." Both preached that Muslims should launch *immediate* attacks. Problem is that these radical leaders have had no idea about modern warfare. One would think that before attacking the world, they might carry out some preparation. They might conduct research and manufacture the *most advanced* modern weaponry, including nuclear/hydrogen bombs, multiple independently targetable reentry vehicles (MIRV), anti-ballistic missiles (ABM), aircraft carriers, submarines, satellites, drones, planes, military robots, missiles, laser weapons, and so on. So that they are better equipped than the West and the rest of the world. Instead radicals' main means of attack has been suicide bombings, and their primary defense is creating human shields against attacks by their opponents. They do little damage to the enemy. However, when industrialized countries retaliate, they cause tremendous damage to Muslims.

Challenge Q: Radical ideology has presented no proof that the Quran orders Muslims to conquer the world. When radicals acquire power, they do not know how to effectively govern a country. They cannot answer Q-1 to Q-5. They do not possess the necessary weaponry to conquer the world. So, what is really their goal? To wage jihad by suicide bombing and make Muslims around the world pay the price?

CHAPTER 10

PERSECUTION OF MUSLIMS BY MUSLIMS

Suppose a Muslim teenaged son refuses to pray *salah* and ignores all verbal preaching. Will the father become a better Muslim if he exercises physical punishment and compels the son to pray salah? Where should the father draw the line and leave the son alone? Rampant enforcement of Islamic rules on a Muslim by individuals and non-state actors has resulted in physical and emotional persecution of Muslims. In this case, both the oppressed and the oppressor are Muslims. Here are some examples.

Persecution within a family: On December 11, 2007, in Mississauga, Canada, Muhammad Parvez told the police that he strangled his 16-year-old daughter, Aqsa Parvez, because she refused to wear the traditional Islamic scarf (*hijab*). In 2010, Muhammad Parvez and his son, Waqas Parvez, were each sentenced to life imprisonment.

Death threats for minor offenses: Pakistani actress Veena Malik posed semi-nude in a British magazine. She received death threats. Similarly, Tunisian teenager Amina Tyler posed topless in a magazine and received death threats.

Persecution within the same sect: Ideological disagreements can result in violent persecution. In Bangladesh, at least 64 people, including University Professor Mohammad Yunus and two Jhalakathi judges, were killed by a radical party. The same party carried out more than a thousand bomb attacks across the country between 2000 and 2005[265].

Persecution of Muslim minority sects: Hardliners believe that *only* their sect is the guided one and it is their religious duty to persecute other so-called misguided Muslim sects. Sometimes a Muslim government joins in the persecution effort to impose the majority version of fiqh[aditb] on a minority sect. For example, in *Islamic Law and Constitution*, Maududi declared that members of the Ahmadiyya sect of Islam are non-Muslims. Since the title of the book contains the words *Islamic* and *Constitution,* some people have interpreted that Allah declared that Ahmadiyyas are non-Muslim. This has led to a very serious problem. Some Muslim scholars preach that apostates should be killed.

With persistent preaching through generations, such aggressive ideology influences crowd behavior and can lead to terrorist attacks and riots. In Pakistan, inter-sectarian conflict has cost hundreds of lives of Shia and Ahmadiyya Muslim minorities. In Iraq, violence between majority Shia and minority Sunni sects is a never-ending source of destruction and suffering.

Psychological and emotional abuse: Some community and household elders severely restrict the freedoms of women and children. For example, some children are only allowed to study the Quran and nothing else. Women are not allowed to leave their homes, even to attend schools or go to work. No one considers how, if left unsupported by family, these women can earn an honest living? What about their feelings of helplessness and frustration? Such restrictions take a phenomenal emotional toll. It is hard to imagine the economic and social impact of the lost potential.

Targeted killings: Mohamed Brahmi was a Tunisian politician. In 2013, he was shot dead in front of his family.

Indirect Muslim persecution: News, pictures, and videos of the above incidents and hundreds of similar incidents from the Muslim world go viral on the internet. Muslims are perceived as exceedingly intolerant and violent people. Average Muslims suffer because non-Muslims, in general, hold dangerously negative views of them. Thus Muslim oppression indirectly hurts Muslims all over the world.

Senseless and insensitive religious rulings: (1) The Moroccan Cleric Zamzami issued an Islamic religious ruling (*fatwa*) that a husband can have sex with the corpse of his wife within six hours after her death.[266] (2) Izzat Atiya of Egypt's Al-Azhar University suggested a novel way to avoid promiscuity in the office. A woman should breast feed her male colleagues five times, so they treat her like their mother.[267] Such *fatwas* are zulm and can never be Islamic. Utterly bizarre *fatwas* give the impression that

Muslims are weirdos. They become the target of sarcasm and ridicule. Imagine a young Muslim girl who gets bullied by her classmates about such fatwas. Such Muslim scholars are responsible for causing the emotional persecution of Muslims in general.

WHY SO VIOLENT, SO INTOLERANT, SO WIDESPREAD?

In all of the above cases, Muslim oppressors completely ignored the emphasis of the Quran on unconditional love and avoiding zulm. Why? The most obvious reason is not hard to see. Over the last two centuries, Muslim scholars have been emphasizing obedience to Islamic rules and the establishment of Islamic government through jihad. To such scholars, Islam is entirely made up of military-like 'dos and don'ts'. According to these hardliners, one who follows more rules and who more severely punishes the violators is a better Muslim. They believe that strict punishment discourages others from violating rules.

This lopsided approach holds the following conceptual errors.

MONOTHEISTIC BELIEF IS MORE IMPORTANT THAN THE REST OF THE RULES

If a person does not have proper belief in Islamic monotheism, then following the rest of the Islamic rules is completely irrelevant (chapter 5). This important point is emphasized and re-emphasized in the Quran. In verses 6:83-88, Allah refers to the following 18 Prophets by name: Ibrahim (Abraham), Ishaq (Isaac), Ya'qoob (Jacob), Nuh (Noah), Dawood (David), Sulaiman (Solomon), Ayub (Job), Yusuf (Joseph), Musa (Moses), Haroon (Aaron), Zakariya, Yahya (John), Isa (Jesus), Ilyas (Elias), Ismail (Ishmael), Al-Yas'a (Elisha), Yunus (Jonah), and Lut (Lot) [PBUT]. Allah concludes this message: **"If they [the above-mentioned Prophets] had committed *shirk all their deeds would have become void*"** (6:83–88). This is a very serious warning, because anyone whose good deeds are wasted will be sent to the hellfire.

Prophets are not ordinary people. Allah guides them: **"We [Allah] chose them [the Prophets] for Our service and guided them to the Right Way"** (6:87). While they are Prophets, they spend their lives in worship and other good deeds. It is impossible that any Prophet would ever do shirk. But, the above verses of the Quran convey an important message for

201

humankind: *a sincere belief in monotheism has a higher priority than all the other good deeds combined.* A Muslim's highest priority should be to have true Islamic monotheistic belief. All other rules and regulations have lower priority. This is a very significant conclusion.

SHIRK BY DESIRES CANNOT BE JUDGED BY ANY HUMAN

Shirk is not only committed by words and deeds, but also by desires (chapter 5). Shirk of words and deeds are obvious and can be easily detected by another person. For example, if a Muslim prostrates to the Egyptian god Ra; this would be a clear sign of shirk. But the shirk of desire is private, and can be so subtle that even the person himself or herself may not be aware of it. Only Allah knows who commits the shirk of desires. It is impossible for any human to judge the shirk of desires in someone else. On the Day of Judgment, a verbal claim to be a Muslim would be of no advantage: **"*most of them* who believe [claim to be a Muslim] in Allah also commit shirk"** (12:106). The only way to remove the shirk of desire is by serious self-analysis and prayer, according to one's capability. An individual can only do this by personal choice. It is impossible to force an unwilling person to carry out self-analysis.

In conclusion:

1. If one commits shirk, then obedience to every other Islamic rule is meaningless.
2. If a person does not follow many human-judgeable Islamic rules but avoids shirk, then Allah may still forgive that person: Chapter 6 has an example of a sinner who had had himself cremated. Still, Allah forgave the sinner, only because he was free of shirk. If a person does not commit shirk, then the mercy and forgiveness of Allah is infinite and completely beyond human comprehension. However, having no shirk does not mean a person has freedom to commit other sins (chapter 5). Also, a person who tries to get rid of shirk of desires is naturally attracted to perform worship rituals, that too without external coercion.

Challenge Q: According to the Quran, what is more important for a Muslim: (1) To wage jihad and impose radical rule all over the world; OR (2) Become completely free from all *shirk* including the *shirk* of desires. If (2) is more important then, why did Maududi and Qutb emphasize establishing radical rule and ignore preaching against the shirk of desires?

BEST DISCIPLINE: GUIDANCE BY THE CONSCIENCE

Sumerian King Ur-Nammu (reigned 2047–2030 BCE) of Mesopotamia is credited with the oldest existing legal laws, called the Code of Ur-Nammu. He assigned matching legal punishments to various crimes. In this case, the punishment serves as a deterrent against committing crimes. This same idea still drives today's penal codes. However, in civilized society, most citizens are guided by their own conscience and choose to avoid crimes. Legal punishment is rarely required.

MUSLIMS GUIDED BY CONSCIENCE

Islamic monotheism is a captivating spiritual experience. A dedicated Muslim feels deep in his/her heart that God exists and He is One. The next stage is when the believer does not knowingly sin because Muslim is guided by one or both of these motivations: (1) s/he is inspired by unconditional love to do only as Allah commands; and/or (2) s/he is afraid of Allah's punishment.

The fear of Allah that prevents a Muslim from sinning, or doing zulm is called *taqwa,* or *God consciousness.* It is highly unlikely that such a person will sin or do zulm by choice, even if the law of the land is not a threat.

Caliph Umar used to patrol the streets at night to make sure that all his duties as a ruler were fulfilled. On one occasion, he overheard a conversation between a young woman and her mother, who were milk-sellers. The mother told the daughter to mix water into the milk to increase its volume for extra profit. When the daughter refused, the mother reminded her that it was safe at night because no one would find out, so there was no threat of legal punishment. The daughter responded, *"How can we escape the notice of Allah and our own conscience?"*[268] Here the taqwa, or God consciousness, prevented her sin.

INFLUENCE OF BELIEF ON AN INDIVIDUAL

Before Islam, some Arabs were avid alcohol users and drinking was part of their culture. Islam did not immediately ban alcohol. In the beginning, Prophet Muhammad[PBUH] only introduced the concept of monotheism. With time, the message of monotheism began to sink into the hearts of the people. About 16 years after becoming a Prophet, finally, Prophet Muhammad[PBUH] received the divine command to ban alcohol. By that time, people were so firm in their belief in Allah that they immediately quit drinking. At the very time when the verse of prohibition was revealed, some residents of Medina were engaged in actual drinking. As soon as they heard about the verse, instead of finishing the drink in their cups, they poured it out. People broke the containers used to store alcohol. Instead of swallowing, some spat the drink from their mouths.[269] Rarely was any violation thereafter reported.

Compare this to the failed attempt at prohibition in the United States in the early 20th century. The primary reason for the Muslims' high morals was taqwa. It works far better than any modern alcohol rehabilitation program. In such a society, punishment is rarely needed as a deterrent.

Similarly, Islam also has a severe punishment for stealing. But during the reign of Prophet Muhammad[PBUH] and the first four guided caliphs, even when the Islamic kingdom extended widely, hardly any cases of theft were reported.

Taqwa is a far better method of disciplining people than forcefully imposing Islamic 'dos and don'ts.'

AVOIDING SINS, INCLUDING POSSIBLE *FUTURE* SINS

In 637 CE, Muslim armies surrounded the city of Jerusalem. At that time, Jerusalem was ruled by the eastern wing of the Christian Roman Empire and their patriarch, Sophonious, realized that any resistance against the Muslims would be futile. He agreed to surrender the city, provided that the leader of the Muslims, Caliph Umar himself, came in person. To satisfy this condition, Caliph Umar traveled from the city of Medina to Jerusalem and met Sophonious in the Church of the Holy Sepulchre. After accepting the surrender of Jerusalem, Caliph Umar wanted to thank Allah by offering salah. Patriarch Sophonious offered to let Caliph Umar pray inside the church. Caliph Umar declined the invitation. He explained that if he prayed inside the church, then future Muslim rulers might demolish the entire church and replace it with a mosque. Instead, Caliph Umar prayed in the courtyard of the church.[270] From Jerusalem, Caliph Umar went to Bethlehem and issued a command to protect the Church of the Nativity and ensure the safety of Christians and their clergy.[271] There too Caliph Umar prayed outside the church.

After these incidents, Muslims ruled Jerusalem for hundreds of years. During this period, at times, there were serious animosities between Muslims and Christians, including the Christian Crusade attacks on Muslims, and the Muslims recapture of the city. Indeed, sometime later, Muslim rulers built mosques at the sites where Umar had prayed, in the courtyards of the Church of the Holy Sepulchre and the Church of the Nativity. To this day, both original churches still stand.

The Church of the Holy Sepulchre is no ordinary church. Christians believe that it stands on the location where Jesus was crucified, buried and resurrected. It must be noted that at the time of Caliph Umar, Christians initiated hostilities by repeatedly attacking Muslims. Still Caliph Umar did not take revenge by demolishing churches.

It should come as no surprise that Caliph Umar protected the churches. The Quran prohibits even ridiculing other religions: **"insult not those whom they (the disbelievers) worship besides Allah"** (6:108). So attacking their places of worship is out of the question. Many ahadith mandate that Muslim rulers should protect non-Muslims and their places of worship (chapter 7). But Caliph Umar went further. He not only refused to pray inside the Church of the Holy Sepulchre, but also explained his reason why. His explanation protected the churches from destruction by future Muslim rulers, because there was a strong temptation to build a mosque at the location where Caliph Umar prayed. No doubt the foresight and compassion of Caliph Umar saved the Church of the Holy Sepulchre, the Church of the Nativity, and many other places of worship.

What made Caliph Umar so far-sighted? The reason is that a Muslim is required to avoid not just obvious sins, but also those actions that may lead to sinful consequences, including encouraging others to sin. However, we are not responsible for what we are not aware of and what we cannot control. Such insights come with taqwa. Naturally, such a person with taqwa will be overly cautious to avoid all kinds of sin and zulm.

Conclusion: When a Muslim commits a sin but not a crime (where no one suffers, for example he misses salah), then one can encourage discipline through monotheism, self-analysis, and taqwa rather than physical punishment. A salah motivated by unconditional love to please Allah is better than a salah performed under the threat of human punishment.

AVOIDING POLITICAL ZULM

The art of peaceful transfer of power to a rival party (other than in the early Islamic period) is a recent phenomenon, and only some modern governments have mastered this delicate art. The only other alternatives are violent revolt, dynastic succession or the unfair acquisition of power.

While Islam leaves it to Muslims to choose the best method of governing based on location and time period, Islam still provides clear guidelines on the fundamentals of good governance: *under all circumstances, avoid zulm*. The early Muslims diligently followed these guidelines.

Here is one example: Soon after the death of Prophet Muhammad[PBUH], the residents of Medina, known as the "Helpers of the Mecca migrants" (*Ansar*) arranged a meeting and proposed that the next caliph should be an Ansar. In this meeting and in the city of Medina, the Ansars were in an overwhelming majority. Traditionally, succession of Arab rulers was based on tribal dynasty. Therefore, this was a crucial decision.

Later, the Ansars realized that if the caliph was not chosen from the tribe of Quraish, it could lead to civil war. Immediately, the Ansars gave up their claim.[272] Why? Because it would have led to zulm. The reward for this sacrifice was the second *major* peaceful transfer of power in history. Later, Abu Bakr was confirmed as Caliph by the residents of Medina and other Muslims. Such remarkable unity is only possible when people believe in Islam with proper understanding and self-analysis. Today, if Muslims relearn these skills, they can again establish stable, peaceful governments, and may even surpass the West.

BELIEF IN ISLAM PREVENTS SOCIAL ZULM

A Muslim with taqwa conducts self-evaluation and is always looking for ways to improve. Such a Muslim *invites* criticism from others, and if an objection is valid, Muslim immediately changes his/her actions. Since the believer holds a firm belief in Allah, self-pride does not prevent such a person from admitting personal shortcomings, even publicly.

As early as the 7th century, Islam gave freedom of speech to ordinary people. On non-religious personal issues, Muslims can reject the advice of any scholar. Prophet Muhammad[PBUH] once asked a Muslim woman, Barira, to return to her estranged husband, Mughith. She asked Prophet Muhammad[PBUH] if it was his personal advice or a command of Allah. Prophet Muhammad[PBUH] said it was only his personal recommendation. In response, Barira refused to go back to her husband because she did not love him.[273] Her decision was fully permissible under Islam, just like the hadith about date palm pollination in the earlier story. However, when Prophet Muhammad[PBUH] conveys a command from Allah, obedience becomes mandatory for all Muslims. Otherwise, Muslims have total freedom of speech, to question, criticize, accept, or reject the ijtihad or fatwa of any Islamic scholar.

On one occasion, Caliph Umar's sermon was interrupted by a young man who wanted to know why Caliph Umar was wearing two pieces of cloth, as the treasury distributed only one piece to every male. The young man raised the question "*I want to know what right had the caliph to get a share twice the share of an ordinary Muslim?*"[274] Before Caliph Umar could speak, his son Abdullah stood up and explained that the caliph was tall, and one piece of cloth was inadequate to cover him, so Abdullah gave his share of cloth to Umar. This incident shows that the caliphs lived just like other citizens and did not waste wealth on luxuries. Also, back then, the citizens had the right to publicly question the finances of their caliph.

At that time, the overwhelming majority of Muslims, including the caliph, believed in pure monotheism. Consequently, motivated by conscience, people effortlessly disciplined themselves. The conscience of the caliph was telling him that he was responsible for his actions. The caliph knew that if he took more than his share of cloth, it would be zulm, and everyone has the right to point out zulm, even if the caliph himself is the suspect. It is better to be questioned about zulm in this life than on the Day of Judgment.

Conclusion: I suggest that everyone should have the freedom to criticize Shari'ah law. What if a person points to zulm in fiqh[aditb] and is justified in doing so? Reasonable freedom of speech should never be considered offensive. As in the above case, if one woman can reject the advice of Prophet Muhammad[PBUH], then today people can reject or object to the opinions or fatwas of Muslim scholars. Let people also criticize Shari'ah[aditb]. What if they point to a particular situation where applying Shari'ah[aditb] leads to zulm? No Islamic scholar has the authority to allow, approve, ignore, or condone zulm.

PROPER RESPONSE TO VIOLATION OF AN ISLAMIC RULE WITHIN A FAMILY

Suppose that a father has correct belief in Islamic monotheism and he also knows that Islam strictly prohibits zulm. What should his reaction be if his daughter refuses to wear the hijab? The father's immediate concern should be whether his daughter has the correct monotheistic belief or not. If she does not, the father should forget the hijab and advise her about monotheistic belief. After all, without monotheism, obeying other rules of Islam have no meaning. If she has the correct monotheistic belief, the father still has no right to force her to wear the hijab by verbal or physical abuse, because enforcement can cause emotional rebellion against Islam, including against monotheistic belief, which would be a much greater loss. If the daughter continues to refuse the hijab, then the father should pray for her with hope and patience. *When appropriate*, the father should continue to advise her. He should not sever ties with her, for then he would be unable to guide her in the future. Besides, Islam prohibits severing family ties. The Quran contains a story about Prophet Noah's son who refused to convert to Islam; still the Prophet did not kill him.

If Islamic rules are obeyed out of fear of another human, then Allah may reject the obedience, like the three people who became a martyr, a scholar, and a big donor to get the approval of others, but Allah rejected their good deeds (chapter 2).

If little children refuse to obey rules, then on rare occasions, light punishment may work, just like when they refuse to go to school. But we must remember that the bond of unconditional love must always remain. Above all, *Allah neither does zulm nor authorizes zulm*.

DOES ISLAM MANDATE WORLDLY PUNISHMENT FOR APOSTASY?

In this context, an apostate is a person who leaves Islam to join another religion or who becomes an atheist. On the Day of Judgment, Allah will punish those who do shirk. The question is: are Muslims required to punish apostates *in this world*?

To find the answer, let us first check the Quran. According to Abed Awad, a Professor in Rutgers Law School, "Nowhere in the Quran does God command earthly authorities to execute anyone who has converted from Islam."[275] If that were the case, most of the exegesis of the Quran would have said so. Instead, many verses of the Quran are amazingly tolerant of other beliefs.

Allah gave *full freedom to every human*: **"whosoever wills, let him believe and whosoever wills, *let him disbelieve*"** (18:29).

In other words: **"There is no compulsion in religion"** (2:256).

Allah does not force Islam on humanity: **"If your Lord had pleased, surely all those who are in the earth would have believed, all of them; *will you then force men until they become believers?*"** (10:99).

208

If someone rejects the invitation to Islam, then Muslims should peacefully accept that person's choice, just as Prophet Muhammad^{PBUH} said to the pagans: **"To you be your religion and to me my religion (Islam)"** (109:6).

In this world, Islam grants full freedom to every individual to remain true to his/her own *inner belief*. If a person is forced to convert to Islam or remains Muslim under threat of worldly punishment, still his/her false faith may be rejected on the Day of Judgment. That is why the Quran: (1) prohibits the use of force to promote conversion to Islam; (2) rejects the hypocrisy (to become Muslim just for worldly gain or to harm Muslims); and (3) did not assign worldly punishment for apostasy.

The Quran limits capital punishment to *exactly two situations* and no more: **"If anyone killed a person not in retaliation of *murder*, or to *spread mischief in the land* [*zulm* on a large scale that affects society] — it would be as if he killed all humankind and if anyone saved a life, it would be as if he saved the life of all humankind"** (5:32). This verse also mandates that murder for any other reason is strictly prohibited.

Then why have writers of fiqh assigned the death penalty to punish apostates? Awad explained that the "Prophet's growing tribe frequently battled outsiders, from competing Arabian religious tribes to Jewish groups. That means a Muslim who decided to abandon his religion was not simply making a personal choice to follow another God. He was turning his back on his tribe at a time of almost perpetual war."[276] To writers of fiqh he said, "it was an act of treason against the community. It was a political crime and not a restriction on one's freedom of conscience."[277]

Then Awad quoted the hadith 9.424A of Bukhari in which the Prophet did not punish the apostate who was not a political threat. Similarly, in the treaty of Hudaybia, the Prophet agreed that Muslims can leave him and join the pagans of Mecca without threat of execution by Muslims. Awad concluded, "Allah the most merciful and wise said it best: *There is no compulsion in religion*. And that should be the last word."[278]

HOW TO END INTER-SECT AND INTRA-SECT VIOLENCE

I am not an Ahmadiyya or Shia, and I am strongly against all kinds of shirk. Still, I do not have any authority to physically or emotionally hurt anyone who disagrees with me. As a Muslim, my duty is only to guide others. When

Allah speaks so strongly against zulm, how can any Muslim do zulm on others?

How to Guide an Apostate and When to Leave him/her Alone

It makes no sense to blame the Shia and Ahmadiyya sects for polytheism and declare them apostates when a significant percentage of Sunni Muslims also worship deceased saints or fail to warn others against Mawlid. Instead of blaming any specific sect, the best approach is to guide the apostate.

The most important condition is to stay away from any verbal or physical abuse or threat. Only in a non-threatening environment can a person be introspective and change his/her self. Islam has a very powerful and logical concept of monotheism. Try to trigger critical thinking by asking questions. If the apostate continues to reject your guidance, then leave him/her alone. **"To you be your religion and to me my religion"** (109:6). Some people take their time to understand the message of Islam. Pray for them. Beyond that point, the duty of the guide ends. Avoid violence at all costs. Remember, *Allah neither does zulm nor authorizes zulm.*

The sad reality is that several Muslim countries enforce the death penalty for apostasy. Such an attitude encourages persecution of Muslims by both state and non-state actors.

HOW TO RESPOND TO WEIRD RELIGIOUS RULINGS

The insensitive fatwas are serious problem. Oddball scholars may cite their own interpretations of the Quran. Citing a fabricated hadith is the least of the problem. A majority of Muslims can also get confused. Fortunately, the solution is simple. Just because one scholar *claims* something strange, does not mean Allah or Prophet Muhammad[PBUH] also said the same thing. All Muslims have to do is show the scholar Appendix A and ask him questions 1 and 2. Next, ask him how he can propose a hadith that suggests that Prophet Muhammad[PBUH] contradicted the concept of justice in the Quran and did zulm. Tell him that hadith must qualify the criteria of Ibn Jauzi.

CHAPTER 11

SUPPRESSION OF MUSLIM WOMEN

Throughout history, men have most often been considered stronger, better educated, and more important workers than women. Men have also had an undisputed upper hand in commercial centers, the labor force, the military, and other major job markets. In comparison, generally, women have been considered weaker, less educated, delicate and vulnerable. They are the ones who get pregnant, and by nature, are committed to looking after the children. In many parts of the world, women still depend on men for financial support, and sometimes even for survival. This allows men ample opportunity to manipulate and exploit women.

Since time immemorial, many men have taken unfair advantage of them, leaving behind a trail of pregnant women. Surprisingly, way back in the seventh century, Islam trampled social customs and empowered women by giving them many rights. The Quran says: **"women shall have rights similar to the rights against them, according to what is equitable"** (2:228).

According to Scottish Orientalist William Watt, Prophet Muhammad[PBUH] began "instituting rights of property ownership, inheritance, marriage, education and divorce, gave women certain basic safeguards."[279] This stabilized society, but many men did not like losing their edge and wanted to continue exploiting women. Early on, they started looking for loopholes in Islam, but changing the Quran is beyond human capability. Instead, they fabricated ahadith. This reopened the door of women exploitation. This chapter covers some controversial issues regarding women's rights in Islam.

WHY DOES ISLAM ALLOW UP TO FOUR MARRIAGES?

Polygyny existed long before Islam. Holy scriptures of other religions and mythologies describe Prophets and gods practicing polygyny. For example, the Christian version of King Solomon,[280] and King Dashrath, father of the Hindu god Ram.

In pre-Islamic Arabia, some people combined polygyny with another zulm of exploiting orphan girls. Here is what the Quran says about the exploitation of orphans, especially girls:

"Render unto the orphans their possessions and *do not substitute bad things* [of your own] for the good things [that belong to them] and *do not consume their possessions* together with your own. This verily is a crime (4:2)

"And if you have reason to fear that *you might not act equitably* towards orphans, then marry from among *other women* such as are lawful to you—[even] two, three or four: but *if you have reasons to fear* that you might not be able to treat them with equal fairness then *[only] one* or [from among] those whom you rightfully possess this will make it *more likely* that you will not deviate from the right course" (4:3).

Aisha[PBUH], wife of Prophet Muhammad[PBUH], explained that the above verses were revealed to protect the *rights of the orphans*. In Arabia at that time there were no organized orphanages. The relatives or tribal elders were responsible for sheltering orphans and guarding their inherited wealth. When the orphans became adults, then the guardians were supposed to hand over the inheritance to the orphans.

This arrangement made orphans vulnerable in several ways. For example, if a guardian was attracted to an orphan girl's beauty or wealth, then the guardian himself could marry her. He may also prevent the orphan girl's marriage to someone else, because after that she may claim her inheritance. According to Aisha[PBUH] in the above verses and verse 4:127: "they (the guardians) were forbidden to marry the orphans unless they paid them a full appropriate mahr [dowry], otherwise they were ordered to marry other women *instead of them*."[281] These verses were intended to prevent zulm in several areas, including:

1. The zulm of unethically acquiring the inheritance of an orphan by an ill-intended wedding to the guardian, or substituting the orphan's inheritance with inferior items, and other such tricks. Any such action would violate the decree: **"do not consume their possessions"** (4:2). Those who follow the Quran's guidelines have no reason to prevent an orphan girl's marriage to someone else, because that would be zulm.

2. The verses prevent the zulm of child molestation and suggest the alternative that the guardian could marry other available woman and leave the orphan girls alone.

3. Before Islam, Arab men had no upper limit to the number of wives they could have. The Quran restricted the maximum number of wives to four.

4. The verses *strongly* encourage monogamy. It also tells the reason to avoid polygyny—to protect multiple wives from zulm! This includes both physical and emotional zulm. The Quran concludes that *the best option* is only one marriage, because monogamy **"...make it *more likely* that you will not deviate from the right course"** (4:3).

Just like in most of the Quran, the theme of the above two verses is to protect orphans, particularly orphan girls, from zulm *in all circumstances*. Nowhere does the Quran encourage polygyny. No story in the Quran describes any previous Prophet or any man who had more than one wife. Allah clearly prefers for men to have only one wife; this means Muslims do not have to live in a society where polygyny is legal.

We now live in an overpopulated industrialized world with fast-paced lifestyles. House and family sizes are reducing. For individual survival and the prosperity of the nation, both men and women must become self-supporting. In such an environment, large households in which polygyny is practiced are slowly becoming obsolete.

In the present age, if a Muslim society plans to sustain the practice of polygyny, the ruling class and Muslim clergy must keep women repressed, vulnerable, and defenseless. To achieve this goal, they employ religious pretexts. As a result, instead of rebelling, women have to succumb to polygyny. Such clergy legally and socially enforce several rules on women, including sexual segregation, wearing the veil, and limiting women's freedom of movement and speech. They prohibit or severely limit women's education and job opportunities. They have no concept that Islam considers these actions to be zulm. We must not forget that the same repressed, uneducated, emotionally, and often physically abused women also become mothers. This perpetuates zulm through generations, negatively affecting the entire society. In this age, no nation can progress under such constraints.

The best option is to follow the guidance of the Quran, that a Muslim male should marry **"[only] one ... this will make it *more likely* that you will not deviate from the right course"** (4:3). As always, Islam stands against zulm, because *Allah never does zulm on anyone* and **"He [Allah] does not like those who do *zulm"*** (42:40).

AUTHORITY OF MEN COMES WITH RESPONSIBILITY

One of the basic principles of business management is that when a manager is given some authority, s/he should also be held responsible for fulfilling the related duties.

Amazingly, this recent principle is also in accordance with Islam. When a person does not have the freedom of choice (or authority), then he or she is not responsible for the committed sins. For example, we had no authority to control the sin of Adam and Eve, so we are not responsible for their actions. On the other hand, when humans have authority and choice, they are responsible.

If Allah blesses us with abilities and opportunities, then it is our responsibility to use our maximum potential so that we benefit our own self as well as others. Prophet Muhammad[PBUH] said that every man would be questioned about, *"his life and how he spent it, his knowledge and how he acted upon it, his wealth and how he acquired it and spent it, his body and how he used it."*[282] The Quran says, with emphasis, that: **"on that Day [of Judgment], you shall be questioned about the *blessings* [given by Allah]"** (102:8).

Allah has blessed men and women in different ways. These blessings are also obligations. Husband and wife have responsibility toward each other. In his famous last sermon, Prophet Muhammad[PBUH] said: "O People, it is true that you have certain rights with regard to your women, but they also have rights over you. If they abide by your right then to them belongs the right to be fed and clothed in kindness. *Do treat your women well and be kind to them for they are your partners and committed helpers."*[283]

214

In comparison to women, Allah gave men an upper hand in many areas. Think of these advantages as blessings of Allah. At the same time, this is a serious test. Men are obligated to fulfill the related duties that come with the advantages. More abilities in some areas simply mean more responsibility for men. It is not a reason to feel superior. Under any pretext, men should not misuse Allah's blessings to exploit women or do zulm. At the same time, women should not put up with any zulm they can avoid. They should use tact and wisdom to amiably avoid zulm. In extreme cases, Islam also allows women to seek divorce. Of course, women should not do zulm on men either. The Quran says: **"And they (women) have rights (over their husbands as regards living expenses, etc.) similar (to those of their husbands) over them (as regards obedience and respect, etc.) to what is *reasonable*, but men have a degree (of responsibility) over them."**[284] (2:228). It should be noted that this verse also assigns responsibility to men by making sure that women's rights are retained in an **what is *reasonable*** (2:228).

HUSBAND IS ACCOUNTABLE FOR EVEN HURTING THE FEELINGS OF HIS WIFE

In pre-Islamic days, besides regular divorce, Arabs also employed a humiliating form of divorce called *zihar*. The husband would say to his wife, "You are to me like the back of my mother." This meant that the wife was forbidden to her husband just like his mother, implying that the wife was not even worthy of his intimacy. Though Islam has permitted divorce as a last resort to avoid zulm, but humiliating women is inconceivable.

The husband of Khawlah did zihar on her. She was devastated, and went crying to Prophet Muhammad[PBUH] to complain. At that time, the following verses were revealed. It is interesting to note how Allah offered consolation to the woman. **"Allah has indeed heard the words of the woman, who pleaded with you against her husband and made her complaint to Allah and Allah has heard what you said to each other. Allah hears all and sees all"** (58:1). The last sentence assures her that Allah knows her full situation.

The next verse addresses the psychological pain of zihar. It prohibits the age-old unjust pagan tradition of zihar as means to divorce. The verse also promises forgiveness. **"Those of you who divorce their wives by *zihar* should know that they are not their mothers. Their mothers are only those who gave birth to them. Surely the words they utter are *absurd*** *and false.* **Allah could punish them for this but He forgave them, surely Allah is All-Pardoning, All-Forgiving"** (58:2).

The next verses describe the strict penalties for the husband if he wishes reconciliation. **"...free a slave or...fast two consecutive months or...feed 60 poor..."** (58:3–4). Multiple options allow reconciliation and provide opportunity even to the poor.

In summary, *men are responsible for causing the wives emotional pain.* Husbands should be very careful because, in the same verse, the Quran reminds the husband: **"violators shall have a painful punishment"** (58:4).

DOES ISLAM PERMIT WIFE-BEATING?

The following verse discusses beating the wife. **"...the righteous women are truly devout ones, who guard the intimacy which God has [ordained to be] guarded. And as for those women whose ill-will you have reasons to fear, admonish them and leave them alone in bed; then *beat them* and if thereupon they pay you heed, do not seek to harm them"**[285] (4:34). Austro-Hungarian-born Muslim scholar Asad explained that the *beating...should be more or less symbolic—with a toothbrush or ... with a folded handkerchief.*[286]

However, this interpretation is controversial. Some scholars cite a hadith that beating has restrictions, like a husband should avoid hitting on the face and without leaving a mark on the body and breaking bones. Which opinion is correct?

The answer is in the Quran itself. The interpretation that a husband can beat his wife without breaking the bones contradicts with the over-emphasized concept of zulm in Islam. Therefore, no hadith or exegesis of the Quran can authorize zulm, under any circumstances. We can only conclude that in the above verse, the Quran talks about merely symbolic beating, say by touching a hand with a folded handkerchief. The above verse also mentions **"... guard the intimacy..."** (4:34). If a wife does not guard intimacy, which may lead the family to break up, then the husband can emphasize the point by gently using a handkerchief. This is a purely symbolic gesture, and should never even give the impression of using force or threat. Even verbal threat of physical harm is zulm.

The symbolic beating is supported by a strong hadith. Abdullah Ibn Umar, a companion of Prophet Muhammad[PBUH], said that beating can only be with a *miswak* (a small stick used as a toothbrush) as a warning. Any man

216

who exceeds this limit should be aware that Prophet Muhammad[PBUH] avoided hitting a disobedient slave girl even with a miswak because he was afraid of the punishment from Allah (chapter 4). If Prophet Muhammad[PBUH] was afraid, every Muslim husband should also fear Allah's punishment.

Islam presents these kinds of challenges, which force us to think and ponder. When a person sincerely uses intellect, then, with the help of Allah, that person is bound to make the right choice. Such riddles are part of Allah's test.

What about the hadith that claims the husband can beat the wife without leaving a mark or breaking bones? Such hadith contradicts the Quran and the two ahadith quoted above. It also promotes zulm. According to Ibn Jauzi's guidelines, any hadith that goes against accepted principles should be discarded (chapter 5). It must be noted that Prophet Muhammad[PBUH] himself never beat any of his wives. He would *never* order zulm on anyone and violate the principle of zulm emphasized in the Quran.

ISLAM-INSPIRED LOVE AND MARRIAGE

Man's higher status in the family means he is responsible for using all his abilities to keep monotheism, peace, and unconditional love in the household. That is why in his last sermon, Prophet Muhammad[PBUH] assigned the duty of feeding and clothing the family to men, not to women. Of course, women have every right to earn money, but they do not have to.

Suppose there is an argument between husband and wife, and the issue is not settled before bedtime. Since Allah has blessed men with many advantages, it is their obligation to take the initiative to keep love and peace in the family. The author recommends that the husband should try to make peace, even if the wife is totally wrong. *Yes, even then*! The husband does not have to agree to do what the wife wants; still he should try to make up with her. Who said that in family arguments, first you have to unanimously judge who was guilty and only then can you make peace? This condition uselessly delays the peace process.

Most of the time in families, peace can be made without having to settle an argument. That is how children resolve their disputes. They do not over-analyze until one party is unanimously proven guilty. The man could take the initiative by expressing unconditional love for his wife, in a way that she knows. Say, by lovingly caressing her. Try it! If that happens, the wife should reciprocate with unconditional love. Prophet Muhammad[PBUH] said, "Each one of you is a shepherd and is responsible for those under his care."[287] You would be surprised at the power of unconditional love. Most arguments would end right there.

Even during arguments, unconditional love should always be there in one's heart. Even if a woman is physically weaker, financially dependent and has less education, still she has the right to express herself and disagree with her husband. However, there are some concerns neither husband nor wife should ignore; like incidents of promiscuity, the welfare of children and health. Both the husband and wife are responsible for guiding the family toward Islamic monotheism. If the wife, husband or children do not listen, then the best option is to gently but persistently keep explaining, without severing ties.

LOOPHOLE OF EXPLOITATION: TEMPORARY MARRIAGES

Some Shia and Sunni scholars allow temporary marriages. Shia call this *muta`h*. Brill's Encyclopedia defines *muta`h* as a "contract (aqd) in which a man and an unmarried woman decide how long they want to be married to each other and how much money, or bride-price, is to be given to the temporary wife. Unlike in the case of permanent marriage (*nikah*) a temporary wife is not legally entitled to financial support (*nafaqa*) above and beyond the bride-price, even in the event of pregnancy, unless it is agreed upon beforehand."[288]

After the contract period is over, the marriage terminates without the need for divorce. "Shia jurists distinguish temporary marriage from permanent marriage by stating that the objective of muta`h is sexual enjoyment, while that of nikāah is procreation."[289] There are, however, some conditions on the woman, including that the woman must be unmarried and chaste (*afifa*) and "*there is no obligation on the man to provide food and home for the woman.*"[290] In case of pregnancy, children go to the father.[291] Muta`h "need not be witnessed or registered... Presently, however … Iran requires its registration, ostensibly to ascertain the legality of a woman's claim in case she may become pregnant."[292]

Similar to the Shia muta`h, some Sunni scholars approve *misyar* marriage. It varies slightly in conditions. For example, there must be two legal witnesses. Still "Misyar marriage, in its legal definition, falls short of traditional obligations of Islamic marriage, including co-habitation of husband and wife and welfare provisions from husband to wife."[293] In both cases, the bottom line is that a Muslim man is allowed to have sex outside marriage, in exchange for money, that too without any marriage responsibilities. Since some Muslim scholars permit temporary marriage, many Muslims do not even regard it as a sin. Besides, the wives cannot complain because they think it is allowed in Islam. However, many scholars strongly oppose temporary marriage.

Impact of muta`h and misyar on society

One does not have to be a genius to agree with Brill's Encyclopedia that, "muta'h in many cases can only be described as *legalized prostitution*."[294] Similarly, according to scholar Al-Nasr, "Misyar marriage would be aligned with *legal prostitution*."[295]

Muta`h and misyar have become lucrative businesses, in constant demand. This means there must be an adequate number of unmarried girls available who are looking for bride-money, members of Muslim clergy to conduct these ceremonies, middlemen to connect girls with male customers, hotels that provide rooms for this purpose, and agents who keep recruiting new girls and women.

This is also emotional zulm on the men's housewives and their children. Faithful housewives can catch venereal diseases from their straying husbands. This is also extreme zulm on the children born as a result of muta`h and misyar, who grow up without their biological father. No one would respect them or their mothers. According to a report published in October 2010, in Egypt alone 900 children were abandoned by their Saudi fathers as a result of misyar marriages.[296]

Of Course, Muta`h and Misyar are Not Allowed in Islam

In support of muta`h, Shia scholars have been quoting the following verse: **"All women other than these [mentioned earlier] are lawful provided you seek them in marriage with gifts from your property (dowry), *desiring chastity and not lust*. Give them their dowry as an obligation for the benefit you have received from your marriage relationship"** (4:24). These scholars claim that marriage implies muta`h.[297]

Disagreeing scholars argue that this verse talks about regular marriage, in which the groom has many responsibilities besides paying the dowry to the bride, including full financial support and a share in his inheritance for his wife and children. In the exegesis of this verse, Ibn Kathir quoted two ahadith in which Prophet Muhammad[PBUH] prohibited the pre-Islamic practice of muta`h. It must be noted that the above verse itself puts a restriction on marriage that men should be **"desiring chastity and not lust"** (4:24).

Let's face it, if a married man forgets his faithful wife and pays money to do muta`h with a young, unmarried girl, then walks away without accepting any responsibility, this has to be lust. What else could it be? Since the above verse prohibits lust, therefore it is clear that the verse is discussing permanent marriage, not muta`h.

Muta`h and misyar are zulm, therefore, no supporting scholarly interpretation can be accepted. Besides, such interpretations contradict other parts of the Quran as well. In Islam, marriage is a sacred bond, because Allah **"created for you mates from among yourselves that you may find comfort with them and He planted love and kindness in your hearts"** (30:21). If a man follows the instruction in this verse and sincerely loves his wife and finds comfort with her, then why would he seek a temporary mate in muta`h or misyar? The Quran recommends **"marriage with chaste free believing women and also chaste women … is made lawful for you, provided that you give them their dowries and *desire chastity, neither committing fornication nor taking them as mistresses*"** (5:5). And prostitution is strictly forbidden, **"Do not force your slave-girls into prostitution for your own worldly gains"** (24:33).

What if someone quotes a hadith to justify muta`h and misyar? That would violate Ibn Jauzi's recommended guidelines, because that hadith would contradict the accepted principle of avoiding zulm. Such hadith cannot be accepted.

Q: What do you think of a radical government that legalizes muta`h or misyar, but cannot provide women means to independently earn an honest living? As a result, these women are often forced to trade their bodies and chastity for bride-money. Is the government fulfilling the responsibility to care for its citizens? Does radical rule have other responsibilities besides legalizing muta`h and misyar?

WHO IS RESPONSIBLE FOR THE PLIGHT OF ZUBEIDA BANO?

An Indian photojournalist, M. A. Soofi, interviewed 72-year-old Zubeida Bano, who came from a middle-class, cultured Muslim family of Delhi,

India. Unlike in poor families, Zubeida Bano could have had a chance to get education and employment. However, like millions of other Muslim women, except on rare occasions her father never allowed her to go outside the house. She did not get any job-oriented education. She was never married. After her father died, she became homeless. The saddest part is that she described herself as *'worse* than beggars.'[298] Home-confined women like Zubeida Bano are told that Islam expects them to remain uneducated, and any sort of rebellion is blasphemy. For sure, if Marie Curie or Joan of Arc had been born in the same environment, they would have ended up in the exact same situation as Bano. A young woman in such circumstances would have been a perfect candidate for muta`h, misyar, or a brothel.

Many Muslim scholars restrict women's education and employment in hope to avoid promiscuity. As a result, they have created several generations of vulnerable and repressed women. This has negatively affected the entire Muslim population.

It is unrealistic to claim that if radical rule is established, the government will provide financial help to all unsupported women. We must recall that radical rule rejects modernism. Without extensive industrialization, they can never collect enough taxes to support such large-scale social programs.

So who is responsible for the suffering of Zubeida Bano and millions of other helpless and isolated Muslim women? The answer is—the radical Muslim scholars and their followers who restrict women's education and employment.

On the other hand, if women's education and employment were encouraged, these women could become self-supporting. They would contribute to building nations and they would pay taxes. If they get married they would raise responsible and educated children. Zulm would be drastically reduced.

What about concerns over promiscuity? For that, the scholars should encourage *discipline through self-analysis* or taqwa. If a Muslim woman still chooses to become promiscuous, it would be her personal choice. The scholars would share no blame.

CHAPTER   12

WHERE HAVE TODAY'S MUSLIMS GONE WRONG?

Muslims, in general, have suffered a great deal over the last two centuries. Here are some of the reasons why, along with a possible solution.

1. Many Muslims leaders and their followers have rejected modernism. As a result, much of the Muslim world has fallen behind, and Muslims have failed to improve their governments over time. They have become desperately dependent on others for modern conveniences and knowledge. Consequently, Muslims are often easy targets for exploitation.

2. The ideology of Qutb and Maududi has encouraged Muslims to wage a never-ending *jihad* against all governments. Muslim countries have become the primary targets of terrorist attacks. To fight back, Muslim governments have become overtly repressive and authoritarian.

3. The idea that Muslims must wage *jihad* to impose Shari'ah law around the world has yielded an unfortunate side effect. Many Muslims now ignore the Quranic emphasis on unconditional love and justice. Instead, they have openly embraced zulm. This has resulted in a moral vacuum in much of the Muslim world. It has encouraged cruelty, corruption, insensitivity, violence, and intolerance.

4. The education and employment of most Muslim women are severely restricted. As a result, about half the Muslim population has failed to realize its full potential.
5. Most Muslims no longer realize that monotheism is the first priority of Islam, and nobody can be *compelled* to believe in Islamic monotheism. Instead, many scholars have tried to enforce other low priority 'dos and don'ts' on common Muslims. This has led to inter-sectoral and intra-sectoral conflicts.
6. Some Muslims blindly obey the orders of Muslim scholars as if they are commands of Allah. They no longer distinguish between the word of man and the word of Allah. This gives scholars unmitigated power to commit zulm.

THE SOLUTION

The problems we face are not due to Islam. On the positive side, Muslims are generally very committed and sincere. All of the problems here described can be solved, *in sha Allah*, if Muslims once again (1) make monotheism their first priority and (2) speak out against zulm. Passing a copy of Appendix-A to the Muslim scholars would make a fine first step toward achieving this goal.

CHAPTER 13

REQUEST TO SCHOLARS: GUIDE MUSLIMS BACK TO ISLAM AND PEACE

M uslim scholars should emphasize:

1. Monotheism as the first priority
2. The essential roles of unconditional love and avoiding zulm
3. Muslims are not required to conquer the planet to establish Islamic government.

Other Islamic 'dos and don'ts' are lower priority. It is counterproductive to overemphasize lower priority rules (like those regarding beards and veils) because people forget the importance of monotheism. When facing the challenges of everyday life, many Muslims have lost sight of Islamic priorities; this shuts the door on compromise and trade-offs. Muslims have overlooked the lesson of the Treaty of Hudaybia.

What is the point of preaching lower priority rules if Muslims continue to commit shirk?

IMPORTANT NOTE: The purpose of this book is *not* to humiliate Muslims scholars, but to help them. That is why this book points out the shortcoming of some Muslim scholars, while also providing peaceful solutions. The Quran provides essential guidance during desperate circumstances: **"Never give up hope of Allah's Mercy"** (12:87).

APPENDIX A

If you agree with the following message, please email or print this message and share it with Muslim scholars.

From the book *The Purest Monotheism: Monotheistic Islam. Polytheistic Muslims**.
(* All Muslims are not polytheists. Inspired by verse 12:106 and Hadith of 73 sects).

AN IMPORTANT MESSAGE FOR MUSLIM SCHOLARS

The Quran says: **"Allah does not love those who do *zulm*"** (3:57). Allah emphasized the concept of justice because the word ع د ل (justice) appears 18 times in the Quran. Similarly, Allah strongly discourages zulm or ظ ل م (injustice, oppression, putting a thing in a place not its own). The Quran references the word *zulm* an impressive 291 times, to discourage it.

The word *zulm* appears in the following verses. *Only* the verses that use these words in the above meanings are included below. If the word *zulm* appears more than once in a verse, then the verse number is repeated.

Question 1: The Quran says that **"Allah wills no injustice [word *zulm* used here] for (His) slaves"** (40:31). Allah said to Prophet Muhammad[PBUH]: **"We have sent you for no other reason but to be mercy for humankind"** (21:107). If Allah and Prophet Muhammad[PBUH] can only do justice, *is any Muslim scholar allowed to write an exegesis of the Quran or issue a fatwa that leads to injustice and zulm?*

Question 2: Have you spoken about *zulm* against women? For example, honor killing, child marriage, female genital mutilation, bride kidnapping (in Kyrgyzstan), wife beating, acid attacks, the imprisonment of rape victims, forced veiling, and restraining women from acquiring education and employment? If not, is this because the above actions are not *zulm,* or because you believe there is a justification for the above actions that has higher priority than avoiding *zulm*?

Please Guide Muslims:

- The Quran says: **"you shall not follow anyone blindly"** (17:36). Once an old woman publicly objected to a new command from Caliph Umar.

He heard her argument and withdrew the command. Similarly, today, if any scholar writes an exegesis of the Quran or gives a fatwa that could lead to *zulm,* then Muslims have the right to reject such exegesis or fatwa.

- Using the above word-count argument, please *repeatedly* guide all Muslims to abstain from cheating, lying, deceiving, hurting, or exploiting *anyone* (including women) because that is *zulm. By avoiding zulm and practicing justice, Muslims will obey the command of Allah as emphasized in the following 309 verses of the Quran. Many Muslims will re-learn an essential part of Islam, which they have forgotten.*

Verses that encourage ʿayn dāl lām (Justice)

4:3, 4:129, 5:8, 5:8, 6:152, 7:159, 7:181, 42:15, 2:282, 2:282, 4:58, 5:95, 5:106, 6:115, 16:76, 16:90, 49:9, and 65:2.

Verses that discourage ẓā lām mīm (oppression):

2:54, 2:57, 2:57, 2:59, 2:59, 2:150, 2:165, 2:231, 2:272, 2:279, 2:279, 2:281, 3:25, 3:117, 3:117, 3:117, 3:135, 3:161, 4:40, 4:49, 4:64, 4:77, 4:110, 4:124, 4:148, 4:168, 6:45, 6:160, 7:9, 7:23, 7:103, 7:160, 7:160, 7:162, 7:162, 7:165, 7:177, 8:25, 8:60, 9:36, 9:70, 9:70, 10:13, 10:44, 10:44, 10:47, 10:52, 10:54, 10:54, 11:37, 11:67, 11:94, 11:101, 11:101, 11:113, 11:116, 14:44, 14:45, 16:33, 16:33, 16:41, 16:85, 16:111, 16:118, 16:118, 17:59, 17:71, 18:49, 18:59, 18:87, 19:60, 21:3, 21:47, 22:39, 23:27, 23:62, 25:19, 26:227, 26:227, 27:11, 27:44, 27:52, 27:85, 28:16, 29:40, 29:40, 29:46, 30:9, 30:9, 30:29, 30:57, 34:19, 34:42, 36:54, 37:22, 38:24, 39:47, 39:51, 39:69, 42:42, 43:39, 43:65, 43:76, 43:76, 45:22, 46:12, 46:19, 51:59, 52:47, 65:1, 4:97, 16:28, 2:114, 2:140, 6:21, 6:93, 6:144, 6:157, 7:37, 10:17, 11:18, 18:15, 18:57, 29:68, 32:22, 39:32, 53:52, 61:7, 4:97, 16:28, 3:182, 8:51, 22:10, 41:46, 50:29, 3:108, 4:10, 4:30, 4:153, 4:160, 5:39, 6:82, 6:131, 11:117, 13:6, 16:61, 20:111, 20:112, 22:25, 25:4, 27:14, 31:13, 40:17, 40:31, 42:41, 14:34, 33:72, 2:35, 2:51, 2:92, 2:95, 2:124, 2:145, 2:193, 2:229, 2:246, 2:254, 2:270, 3:57, 3:94, 3:128, 3:140, 3:151, 3:192, 5:29, 5:45, 5:72, 5:107, 6:21, 6:33, 6:52, 6:58, 6:93, 6:129, 6:135, 7:5, 7:19, 7:41, 7:44, 7:148, 8:54, 9:23, 9:47, 10:39, 10:106, 11:18, 11:31, 11:83, 12:23, 12:75, 12:79, 14:13, 14:22, 14:27, 14:42, 15:78, 16:113, 17:47, 17:82, 17:99, 18:29, 18:35, 18:50, 19:38, 19:72, 21:14, 21:29, 21:46, 21:59, 21:64, 21:87, 21:97, 22:53, 22:71, 23:107, 24:50, 25:8, 25:27, 25:37, 26:209, 28:37, 28:40, 28:59, 29:14, 29:31, 29:49, 31:11, 34:31, 35:32, 35:37, 35:4, 37:63, 37:113, 39:24, 40:18, 40:52, 42:8, 42:21, 42:22, 42:40, 42:44, 42:45, 43:76, 45:19, 49:11, 59:17, 60:9, 62:7, 68:29, 71:24, 71:28, 76:31, 2:258, 3:86, 4:75, 5:51, 6:47, 6:68, 6:144, 7:47, 7:150, 9:19, 9:109, 10:85, 11:44, 23:28, 23:41, 23:94, 26:1, 28:21, 28:25, 28:50, 46:1, 61:7, 62:5, 66:11, 11:102, 21:11, 22:45, 22:48, and 17:33.

APPENDIX B

SERMON OF PROPHET MUHAMMAD[PBUH] AFTER SUCCESS IN TABUK

Verily the most veracious discourse is the book of Allah (the *Qur'an*). The most trustworthy handhold is the word of piety (*taqwa*). The best of religions is the religion of Ibrahim[PBUH]. The best of the precedents is the precedent of Muhammad[PBUH]. The noblest speech is the invocation of Allah. The finest of narratives is this *Qur'an*. The best of affairs is that which has been firmly resolved upon. The worst religions are those which are created without sanction. The best of ways is the one trodden by the Prophets. The noblest death is the death of a martyr. The most miserable blindness is waywardness after guidance. The best of auctions is that which is beneficent. The best guidance is that which is put into practice. The worst blindness is the blindness of the heart.

The upper hand is better than the lower (i.e. it is better to give than to receive). The little that suffices is better than the abundant and alluring. The worst apology is that which is tendered when death stares one in the face. The worst remorse is that which is felt on the Day of Resurrection.

Some men do not come to the Friday prayer, but with hesitance and delay. And some of them do not remember Allah but with reluctance. The tongue that is addicted to false expression is a bubbling spring of sins.

The most valuable possession is contentment of the heart. The best provision is that of piety. The highest wisdom is the fear of Allah, *the Mighty and Great*. The best thing to be cherished in the hearts is faith and conviction; doubt is part of infidelity.

Impatient wailing and fulsome praise of the dead is an act of ignorance. Betrayal leads one to the fire of Hell. Drinking amounts to burning. Obscene poetry is the work of the Devil. Wine (alcohol) is the mother of evils. The worst thing eaten is one which belongs to the orphan. Blessed is he who receives admonition from others.

Each one of you must resort to a place of four cubits (the grave).

227

Your affairs will be decided ultimately in the next life. The worst dream is the false dream. Whatever is in store is near. To abuse a believer is transgression. Raising arms against him is infidelity. To backbite him is a disobedience to Allah. Inviolability and sacredness of his property is like that of his blood. He who swears by Allah (falsely), in fact falsifies Him. He who pardons is himself granted pardon. He who forgives others, is forgiven by Allah for his sins.

He who represses anger, Allah rewards him. He who faces misfortunes with perseverance, Allah compensates him. He who acts only for fame and reputation, Allah disgraces him. He who shows patience and forbearance, Allah gives him a double reward. He who disobeys Allah, Allah chastises him.

I seek the forgiveness of Allah, I seek the forgiveness of Allah, I seek the forgiveness of Allah.[299]

NOTES

[1] Qtd in Russell, Bertrand. History of Western Philosophy. Unwin Brothers, 1946. Print., p58-59

[2] Tolle, Eckhart. A New Earth: Awakening to Your Life's Purpose. London. s.l. : Plume, a Penguin Group, 2005.

[3] J. B. Hare. The Internet Sacred Text Archive CD ROM 5.0 [CD-ROM] s.l. : The Internet Sacred Text Archive, 2005. ISBN-0-9709390-5-1.

[4] Encyclopedia Britannica. Hebrew patriarch. Encyclopedia Britannica [Online] 2016 [Cited: May 5, 2016.] read:http://www.britannica.com/biography/Jacob-Hebrew-patriarch.

[5] Telushkin, Joseph. Jewish Literacy page 22. New York: William Morrow and Company, 2008. ISBN 978-0061374982.

[6] The Free Dictionary. [Online] [Cited: 8 16, 2017] ww.thefreedictionary.com/Pluralis+majestatis.

[7] Quran verses 21:7–8

[8] The Concise Encyclopedia of Islam by Cyril Glasse, Page 141.

[9] Al-Mubarakpuri, Saifur Rahman. Ar Raheeq Al Makhtum. page 122.

[10] http://www.alim.org/library/quran/AlQuran-tafsir/MDD/1/0

[11] Hadees Qudsi #17

[12] Gary Miller, audio lecture "Islam and Christianity part 1," after about 33 minutes of play.

[13] The word Muslim in this book means only those who strictly follow the Quran and worship on one God.

[14] Al-Ghazali, Imam. BELIEF IN GOD. The Jerusalem Treatise Excerpt from the The Revival of the Religious Sciences (Ihya' 'ulum al-din) [Online] [Cited: 5 10, 2016.]

[15] Tindal. Christianity as old as the Creation.

[16] Fatwa No : 281311. www.islamweb.net [Online] [Cited: 5 28, 2016.] http://www.islamweb.net/emainpage/index.php?page=showfatwa&Option=FatwaId&Id=281311.

[17] The world's fastest-growing religion is . CNN [Online] [Cited: May 28, 2016.] www.cnn.com/2015/04/02/living/pew-study-religion/.

[18] Long history with Islam gives Indigenous Australians pride. *The Conversation US, Inc* [Online] [Cited: May 28, 2016.] read:http://theconversation.com/long-history-with-islam-gives-indigenous-australians-pride-3521.

[19] Islam on march south of border. wnd tv [Online] [Cited: May 28, 2016.] http://www.wnd.com/2005/06/30674/.

[20] moenssens andre a. Is Fingerprint Identification a Science? [Online] [Cited: May 11, 2016.] http://www.scafo.org/library/150401.html.

[21] Translation by Malik

[22] Holtzman, Livnat. " Anthropomorphism." Encyclopedia of Islam, THREE. Edited by: Gudrun Krämer, Denis Matringe, John Nawas, Everett Rowson. Brill Online, 2013. Reference. 19 January 2013 <http://referenceworks.brillonline.com/entries/encyclopaedia

[23] Quran Tafsir by Ibn Kathir [Online] [Cited: May 11, 2016.] http://www.qtafsir.com/index.php?option=com_content&task=view&id=1284&Itemid=124.Tirmidhi

[24] Schimmel, Annemarie. Islam: An Introduction. Islam, p32: An Introduction p32. Albany: State University of New York Press, 1992.

[25] Safiur-Rehman. Tajalliyat-e-Naboowat (Urdu) page 77-79. Islamabad: Darusslam.

[26] Kathir, Ibn. Tafseer Ibn Kathir verse [17:15] page 33 (Urdu). Delhi : Farid Book Dept. (P) Ltd.

[27] Ibid Page 33.

[28] Hadith Al-Tirmidhi #739.

[29] Albert Einstein Solves the Equation. LAPHAM'S Quarterly. [Online] [Cited: 7 23, 2017.] www.laphamsquarterly.org/religion/albert-einstein-solves-equation.

[30] Ash'ari, A. (n.d.). In al Maqalat (p. 291). As quoted in www.muslimphilisophy.com/hmp/14.htm by Hye, M.A.

[31] Sahih Al-Bukhari Hadith - 9.204

[32] Bukhari. Sahih Al-Bukhari 1.52 [CD ROM] Silver Spring, Maryland, USA : ISL Software Corporation, 1986-1999. Alim.

[33] Sahih Al-Bukhari 1.51.

[34] Sahih Muslim 884.

[35] Al-Tirmidhi hadith # 1422.

[36] Albert Einstein Solves the Equation. LAPHAM'S Quarterly. [Online] [Cited: 7 23, 2017.] www.laphamsquarterly.org/religion/albert-einstein-solves-equation.

[37] Bukhari [6.474]

[38] At-Tirmidhi. Question & Answers. Islamhelpline [Online] [Cited: May 15, 2016.] as recorded at http://www.islamhelpline.net/node/7905.

[39] A.A.Y. Qadhi, An Introduction to the sciences of the Qur'aan. P134,135. Al-Hidaaya Publishing. Birmingham, 1898649324.

[40] Siddiqi, Mohammad Zubair. Page 40. Hadith Literature: Its Origin, Development & Special Features . Cambridge : The Islamic Text Society, 2008.

[41] Ibid Page 6.

[42] Hofmann, Murad. Islam: The Alternative. Beltsville : Amana Publications, 1997.

[43] Kazi, Dr. Mazhar, page 17. 160 Miracles and Mysteries of the Quran. New Delhi : Islamic Book Service, 2003.

[44] "World Arabic Language Day". UNESCO. 18 December 2014. Retrieved May 15, 2016.

[45] The Amazing Quran by Dr. Gary Miller.

[46] Ibid.

[47] Abdul Malik Mujahid, Golden Stories of Umar Ibn Al-Khattab, p79, Darussalam Publishers, ASIN: B00DMI6XN0

[48] Miller, Gary quoted in Ahmad Imran, A perfect gentleman. Center Street. 978-1455508495.

[49] Dr. Gary, Miller. The Basis of Muslim Belief. *Islam the modern religion* [Online] [Cited: May 29, 2016.] http://www.themodernreligion.com/essays_Gary_Miller.htm#Jesus and Adam.

[50] Ibid

[51] Ibid

[52] Ibid

[53] In order to fully appreciate this chapter, the word Prophet is not used in some part of this chapter.

[54] Hart, Michael H. The 100: A Ranking Of The Most Influential Persons In History. New York : Citadel Press books, 2000. 9780806513508.

[55] Ibid.

[56] Hitti, Philip, quoted in Khan Wahiduddin. *Muhammad a Prophet For all Humanity.* Goodword Books. 2001. 81-85063842.

[57] Bodily Desecration Is Disturbing — But Why? Huffpost Religion [Online] [Cited: 6 13, 2016.] www.huffingtonpost.com/2012/01/23/bodily-desecration-disturbing_n_1224593.html.

[58] Islam and racism. *Islamcity* [Online] [Cited: 6 12, 2016.]
https://shahydcharming.wordpress.com/2015/03/12/islam-and-racism/.
[59] *Sahih Bukhari* 8.26
[60] Kathir, Ibn. Tafseer Ibn Kathir verse [81:8] page 22 (Urdu). Delhi: Farid Book Dept. (P) Ltd.
[61] Ashraf Ali, Thanvi. The Life of Rasul Allah SAW.
[62] Revolvy. Umamah bint Zainab [Online] [Cited: 6 13, 2016.]
http://www.revolvy.com/main/index.php?s=Umamah%20bint%20Zainab&item_type
=topic.
[63] Davis, Evan Grae. It's a Girl: The Three Deadliest Words in the World . 2012.
[64] Bukhari. Alim CD, *Sahih Bukhari*. 3:789.
[65] The Prophet Muhammad: A Mercy for all Creation. www.islamweb.net [Online]
[Cited: 1 1, 2017.] http://www.islamweb.net/en/article/134199/the-Prophet-
muhammad-a-mercy-for-all-creation.
[66] Bukhari. Alim CD, *3.778*
[67] Kaylani, M.I. Jihad ke masail, Page 157, 159. Riyad, Maktaba Darussalam. 1999.
[68] **Zahoor, Akram. Muslim History 570 - 1950 CE. Gaithersburg, MD : 0-9702389-0-8, 2000.**
[69] Animal Rights and Islam. *IFNA* [Online]
http://www.islamicedfoundation.com/askscholar/animal.htm
[70] Bukhari. Alim 2.399
[71] McDonald, M. V. (Translator), Montgomery Watt, W (Contributor). The History of al-Tabari:.
        New York : State University of New York, 1987, 0887063454
[72] Sahih Al-Bukhari 3.741
[73] Alim CD, Stories of the Prophet, Muhammad.
[74]Ashraf Ali, Thanvi.*The Life of Rasul Allah SAW*.
[75] Sahih Al-Bukhari Hadith - 3.251
[76] Seeartun-Nabee (Urdu) Vol. 2 page 174. S. Naumani, S. Nadvi, Maktaba Madina, Lahore.
[77] Beck, Julie. How to Get Better at Expressing Emotions. The Atlantic. [Online] [Cited:
6 10, 2017.] https://www.theatlantic.com/health/archive/2015/11/how-to-get-better-
at-expressing-emotions/416493/
[78] Maududi, Alim CD, Tafsir Maududi- Surah 109 Introduction.
[79] Hashmi, Farhat. Tafsir 7:33 (Al-A'raf 1-39)
www.farhathashmi.com/quran/tafsir/?giml-id=409 after 27 minutes of play.
[80] *Shirk* ke choore darwaze by Hamid Mehmood Khizri page 24.
[81] Sufism is not Islam page 180.
[82] Alim, Tafseer Ibn Kathir [11:118]

[83] al-Wahab, 'Abd as quoted by Qadhi, Abu Ammaar Yasir. A Critical Study of shirk page 118. 1-898649-62-6..
[84] Kamali Principles page 65-8, Azmi Schach's Origins page 65 Quoted by Siddiqi, Mohammad Zubair. Hadith Literature: Its Origin, Development & Special Features, Page 31. Cambridge : The Islamic Text Society, 2008. 9780946621385 .
[85] Introduction to *hadith* by John Burton page x.
[86] Nu'mani, Shibli. Sirat un Nabi, *From Modernist and Fundamentalist Debates in Islam, page 56: Reprint Idarah-i Adabiyat-i Delhi, reprint 1983 page 36-63. Translated by Tayyib Bakhsh.* Delhi : 0312215800.

[87] The Six Canonical Books of Hadith are: Sahih al-Bukhari, Sahih Muslim, Sunan Abu Dawud, Sunan al-Tirmidhi, Sunan al-Nasa'I, Sunan Ibn Majah.

[88] The Concise Encyclopedia of Islam by Cyril Glasse, Page 126.

[89] Glasse, C. The Concise Encyclopedia of Islam. Page 361. First HarperCollins. 1991. 0060631260.

[90] Khan, Wahiduddin. *Women between Islam and Modern society, page 230.* New Delhi : Goodword Books, 2002. 8185063753.

[91] Al-Qayyim, Ibn. I'laamul-Muwaqqi'een (4/261), Islambasics Library: The Path To Guidance. IslamBasics.com [Online] [Cited: June 19, 2016.] http://www.islambasics.com/view.php?bkID=37&chapter=12.

[92] S.R. al-Mubarakpuri. Ar-Raheeq Al-Makhtum.

[93] 4.12 Muslim Beliefs- Intercession . *Dr. Jamal Badawi* [Online] [Cited: June 21, 2016.] http://jamalbadawi.org/index.php?option=com_content&view=article&id=39:412-muslim-beliefs-intercession&catid=16:volume-4-muslim-beliefs&Itemid=17 .

[94] Qadhi, Abu Ammar Yasir *A critical study of shirk*, Page 137. Birmingham. Al-Hidaayah Publishing and Distribution. 2003.1898649626

[95] Muslim:396

[96] Fiqh-us-Sunnah - 3.107. *alim.org* [Online] [Cited: June 21, 2016.] http://www.alim.org/library/hadith/fiq/FQS/3/107

[97] Sahih Muslim 766.

[98] Qardi, Muhammad Tahir-ul. *Islamic concept of Intermediation (tawassul).* by page 24. Lahore. Minhaj-ul-Qur'an Publications. 2001.

[99] *Sahih Bukhari* 4.307

[100] Hashmi, Farhat. Audio. *AQ- Lecture FH 1402- Waseela Mashu'wasa'il* 17-5-2012 Islamabad." After 5 minutes of play.

[101] Ibn Khaldun, *Nabhani, Al- Majmua an nabhaniyya* 1:457. Quoted in A. Schimmel. *and Muhammad is His Messenger* page 88. Univ. of North Carolina Press. 1985. 0807841285.

[102] Alawi al-Maliki al-Hasani, Muhammad. *Notions that must be corrected* page 76. Rotterdam, Sunni Publications, 2010, 9789079294152.

[103] *Notions that must be corrected* page 74.

[104] Al-Nasai in *Kitab At-Tauhid* by Muhammad bin Abdul-Wahab. page 142.

[105] *Islamic concept of Intermediation (tawassul)* page 19.

[106] *Sahih Bukhari* 1:760.

[107] Considering only *Sahi Sitta* set of book of *Hadith.*

[108] Considering only *Sahi Sitta* set of book of *Hadith.*

[109] *Notions that must be corrected.* page 77.

[110] *Islamic concept of Itermediation (tawassul)* page 316.

[111] Fiqh-us-Sunnah - 4.136

[112] Dead Hear. Ahlus Sunnah Wal Jamah [Online] [Cited: July 2, 2016.] ahlussunnahwaljamah.blogspot.com/2008/02/dead-hear-4.html

[113] Bukahri Vol. 9, Number 172.

[114] *Islamic concept of Intermediation (tawassul)* page 177.

[115] *Notions that must be corrected page* 123.

[116] *Notions that must be corrected* page 90.

[117] "Islamic concept of Intermediation (*tawassul*)" by Muhammad Tahir-ul Qardi page 357.

[118] "Sufism in Bengal" by Enamul Haq, page 345.

119 Maariful Quran by Shafi Usmani, page 716, vol 1.

120 Islahi, A. A. Tadabbur e Quran (Urdu). jild 4, page 586. Lahor, 1983.
http://www.tadabbur-i-quran.org/text-of-tadabbur-i-quran/urdu-volume-4/urdu-surah-kaaf/37/

121 Rumi > Quotes > Quotable Quote. goodreads. [Online] [Cited: July 9, 2018, 2018.]
https://www.goodreads.com/quotes/8009645-the-moment-you-accept-what-troubles-you-ve-been-given-the.

122 Ibid.

123 Haykal, Muhammad Husayn. Translated by I.R. al Faruqi, page 453. *The life of Muhammad*. New Delhi. Millat Book Center. 1976.

124 CNN. Extremists destroy Jonah's tomb, officials say. [Online] [Cited: 7 28, 2020.]
https://www.cnn.com/2014/07/24/world/iraq-violence/index.html.

125 The Invocation of God. Ibn Qayyum al-Jawziyya. Translator: M. Abdurrahman Fitzgerald. The invocation of God by page 49. Cambridge. Islamic Texts Society. 2000. 0946621780.

126 Fadiman and Frager. Essential of Sufism. page 119. New York. HarperCollins. 1997. 0785809066.

127 Reality. Poet Seers [Online] [Cited: 1 2, 2017.] http://www.poetseers.org/spiritual-and-devotional-poets/sufi-poets/rabia-poems/reality/.

128 Abu-Dawood Hadith 991

129 Sahih Muslim 131.

130 37 Things Jalaluddin Rumi Can Teach You About Love. Purpose Fairy. [Online] [Cited: Oct. 7, 2019.] https://www.purposefairy.com/85691/things-jalaluddin-rumi-teach-love/.

131 Rumi, J. Trans. Helminski Kabir. The Rumi Collection, page 238. Shambhala. 2005. 1590302516

132 alim.org, Companions of the Prophet, At-Tufayl ibn Amr ad-Dawsi.

133 Attar. Trans. Fadiman and Robert Frager. Essential Sufism, page 118. Edison. Castle Books. 1997. 0785809066.

134 Sand, George. George Sand Quotes. Brainyquote. [Online] [Cited: 10 19, 2019.]
https://www.brainyquote.com/quotes/george_sand_154922

135 From *Hadith Qudsi* #32.

136 Sultan Bahu, translated by J. R. Puri and K. S. Khak page 358.

137 Ibn-Qayyim al-Jawziyyah from Al-Noonuyyah quoted 'Al-Walaa wal-Barra" of Mohammad Syed Al-Qahtani.

138 Rumi. Discourses of R*umi*. *Rumi* [Online] [Cited: July 9, 3016.]
http://www.rumi.org.uk/discourses.html

139 Taymiyyah, ibn. Being a True Slave of Allah . Aqeedah Of The Salaf AS-Salih [Online] [Cited: 7 9, 2016.] https://muslimscreed.wordpress.com/2011/12/07/being-a-true-slave-of-allah-by-shaykh-ul-islam-ibn-taymiyyah

140 Encyclopaedia of Islam, Second Edition. Zulm. *Brill Online* [Online] [Cited: January 19, 2013.] http://referenceworks.brillonline.com/entries/encyclopaedia-of-islam-2/zulm-COM_1393.

141 Ibid.

142 Ibid.

143 Lane, E.W. Arabic-English Lexicon. London. Willams & Norgate,1863. 9780946621033

[144] Dictionary of the Holy Quran by Abdul Mannan Omar page 351

[145] " Zulm." Encyclopaedia of Islam, Second Edition. Brill Online , 2013. Reference. Eeshat Ansari. 19 January 2013 <http://referenceworks.brillonline.com/entries/encyclopaedia-of-islam-2/zulm-COM_1393>

[146] al-Sheha Abdul-Rahma, Misconception on human rights on Islam, page 67. Riyadh.

[147] Abu Yousuf. al-Kharaj. p.144 Quoted in Human Rights in Islam And Common Misconceptions by al-Sheha Abdul-Rahma.

[148] Al-Tirmidhi 163.

[149] Sahih Bukhari 1.29

[150] Tirmidhi quoted in Islamic Tahdhib and Akhlaq. P138 Lemu, Aisha. Chicago, IQRA International Educational Foundation. 2001. 1563163209.

[151] Bukhari, Hadith no. 4.535.

[152] Muslim, Hadith no. 910.

[153] Mariful Quran. English. 4:105. Page 565,

[154] Maududi, A.A. Human rights in Islam. page 36,37,38. Narobi, The Islamic Foundation, 1990. 0950395498.

[155] Abu Dawud as quoted in Human rights in Islam p 36

[156] Human rights in Islam by A. A. Maududi page 37

[157] Bukhari 7.1.

[158] Bukhari 8.380

[159] *Sahih Bukhari* 5.701

[160] Chase-Dunn, C. Review of Ross Hassig, Aztec Warfare. *The Institute for Research on World-Systems* [Online] [Cited: July 24, 2016.] http://irows.ucr.edu/cd/bookrevs/hassig.txt.

[161] Shahi Bukhari 3.624.

[162] Mujahid, Abdul Malik. Ali (rta) vs. a Jew. *Hiba* [Online] [Cited: 1 23, 2017.] http://www.hibamagazine.com/ali-rta-vs-a-jew/.

[163] Farooq, Mohammad Omar. Rape and Hudood Ordinance: Perversions of Justice in the Name of Islam. *Social Science Research Network* [Online] http://papers.ssrn.com/sol3/papers.cfm?abstract_id=1525412

[164] Ibid

[165] Ibid

[166] Tafseer Ibn Kathir, Urdu, Vol.3, Para 18, page 38. Delhi, Fareed Book Dept.

[167] Farooq, Mohammad Omar. Rape and Hudood Ordinance: Perversions of Justice in the Name of Islam.

[168] *The Law, Patriarchy and Religious Fundamentalism- Women's Rights in Pakistan.* Corrieri, Liliana. Hong Kong : Asian Legal Resource Center (AHLC), 2013. 978-962-8314-65-2

[169] Farooq, Mohammad Omar. Rape and Hudood Ordinance: Perversions of Justice in the Name of Islam.

[170] Alim.org-Al-Muwatta Hadith-15.41

[171] Poliomyelitis. *WHO* [Online] [Cited: 1 4, 2017.] http://www.who.int/mediacentre/factsheets/fs114/en.

[172] Bukhari 3.592

[173] Muslim 910.

[174] Bukhari 8.111

[175] Ibn Taymiyyah quoted by Ibn ul Qayyim, Madaarij as-Saalikeen (The State of Repentance).

176 Al-Dawoody, Ahmed. The Islamic Law of War: Justifications and Regulations. Page 56. New York : PALGRAVE MACMILLAN, 2011. 978–0–230–11160–8.

177 Ashraf, S.M., Studies in Muslim Philosophy page 2. Lahore, 1997, 9694321565.

178 Jihad. Encyclopedia of Britannica. [Online] [Cited: August 8, 2016.] https://www.britannica.com/topic/jihad.

179 Maududi quoted in *Rise of Radical Islamic Fundamentalism: Mawdudi, Qutb and Faraj.* Lane, Jan-Erik. ISSN(e):2411-9458.

180 Qutb, Syed, Quoted by Loboda. The Thought of Sayyid Qutb. Ashbrook Statesmanship Thesis, 2004.

181 Maududi, Abul Ala. Jihad Fi Sabilillah.

182 Maududi, Abul Ala. Tafhim al-Quran footnote of verse [42:13].

183 Ibid.

184 Khan, Wahiduddin. Tabeer ki Ghalti. P112, 130. New Delhi. Al-Risala Books. 2002. 8185063745

185 Ibid P219 to 224.

186 Qutb. In the shade of the Quran [42:13].

187 Alim.org Maududi Introduction to Surah 9.

188 Ibid.

189 Ibid.

190 Safi A. Mubarakpuri. Tajalliyat-e-Naboowat. Page 432. Darussalam. Riyad. 9699134461.

191 Lewis, Bernard, Arabs in History. p. 57. Oxford University Press, 2002. 9780191587665.

192 Genghis Khan: The daddy of all lovers. Daily Mail.com [Online] [Cited: 8 7, 2016.] http://www.dailymail.co.uk/news/article-456789/Genghis-Khan-The-daddy-lovers.html.

193 Maududi, Abul Ala. Tafhim al-Quran footnote of verse [42:13].

194 *Sahih Bukhari* (4:59)

195 Tafseer by Arberry.

196 Ali, Geragh. A Critical Exposition Of The Popular *Jihad.* Page iii. Dodo Press. 9781406568301.

197 "Sealed Nectar" by Saifur Rahman al-Mubarakpuri

198 Salahi, A. Muhammad: His Character and Conduct. The Islamic Foundation, Leicestershire, 0860375617.

199 al-Mubarakpuri, The Sealed Nectar

200 Persian Royal Ancestry. *AncestryFootprints* [Online] [Cited: 2 10, 2017.] http://www.ancestryfootprints.com/sites/default/files/Authenticated/Lars/Genealogy/Royal%20Ancestry%20Books/Persian%20Royal%20Ancestry.pdf?443

201 http://www.alim.org. Umar bin al-Khattab History.

202 Picktal, Marmaduke. Causes of rise and decline of Islam.

203 Herschensohn, Bruce. Across the Taiwan Strait: the bridge between mainland China and Taiwan. page 23. Lexington Books. 2002. 0739103423.

204 Ibn Kathir. Life of the Prophet Muhammad.

205 Depending upon the state.

206 William Muir, The Life of Mahomet, vol. 3, chapter 14, page165.

207 *Sahih Bukhari* 5.619.

[208] Sunan ibn Majah. Vol. 3, page 413. Maktaba Dar-us-Salam, 2007. 9960-9881-3-9.

[209] Al-Risala, September 2005, page 16.

[210] For example, Jamat-e-Islami introduced a constitution in Pakistan in 1956.

[211] Milestones by Sayyid Qutb

[212] Ibid

[213] Ibid

[214] Ibid

[215] Ibid

[216] El-Gamal, Mahmoud A. Islamic Finance : Law, Economics, and Practice. s.l. : Cambridge University Press, 2006. 978-0521741262.

[217] Khan, Wahiduddin, Al-Risala, Urdu magazine. April 2005, page 23-35.

[218] Ibid.

[219] Ibid.

[220] Ibid

[221] Only few Muslims remained in Mecca.

[222] www.alim.org/library/quran/surah/introduction/48/QSI

[223] Lings, Martin. Muhammad. s.l. : Inner Traditions International, 1983. 0-89281-170-6. Page 248.

[224] With very few exceptions.

[225] Saifur Rahman al-Mubarakpuri, Ar-Raheeq Al-Makhtum (The Sealed Nectar), page 156.

[226] "Jihad in the Quran" by Louay Fatoohi page 37. Birmingham, Luna Plena Publishing. 2009. 9781906342067.

[227] Fatoohi, Louay. Jihad in the Quran. page 34.

[228] Maududi, Abul Ala. Jihad Fi Sabilillah.

[229] Brill's encyclopedia of Islam, *Fiqh* by Goldziher,I.; Schacht, J.; J. Schacht

[230] Maududi. Let Us Be Muslim Part-V.

[231] Ibid

[232] Abul Ala Maududi. Encyclopedia of the Middle East. [Online] [Cited: 7 28, 2017.] http://mideastweb.org/Middle-East-Encyclopedia/abul-ala-maududi.htm.

[233] Maududi - Tafhim al-Qur'an. 42. Surah Ash Shura. englishtafsir.com. [Online] [Cited: 7 28, 2017.] http://englishtafsir.com/Quran/42/index.html.

[234] Milestones by Sayyid Qutb page 243-245

[235] Milestones by Sayyid Qutb page 15

[236] Milestones by Sayyid Qutb page 32

[237] Milestones by Sayyid Qutb page 233

[238] Al-Mubarakpuri, Saifur Rahman. Ar-Raheeq Al-Makhtum . s.l. : Maktaba Dar-us-Salam.

[239] Al-Risala page 16,17. Oct. 2007.

[240] Khan, Wahiduddin. *Women between Islam and Modern society, page 230.* New Delhi : Goodword Books, 2002. 8185063753.

[241] Ghazali, Abdus Sattar. ISLAMIC PAKISTAN: ILLUSIONS & REALITY. [Online] [Cited: 3 3, 2019.] http://ghazali.net/book1/index.htm.

[242] Qutb. Milestone page 88.

[243] Qamaruddin Khan quoted by Piscatori & Eickelman. Muslim Politics. Priceton : Priceton University Press, 1996.

[244] Ayubi, Nazih N., Nader Hashemi and Emran Qureshi. Islamic State. Oxford Islamic Studies Online. [Online] [Cited: 9 1, 2019.] http://www.oxfordislamicstudies.com/article/opr/t236/e0394.

245 Tirmidi and Ibn Majah (quoted in *Essays on Islam*), page 32. London. FOSIS. 0860372596.

246 The Vanguard of the Islamic Revolution. [book auth.] Seyyed Vali Reza Nasr. s.l. : University of California Press, 1994, 978-0520083691, Page 13.

247 Qutb, Sayyid. "The America I Have Seen" (New York, 2000), pg.11 as quoted in The Thought Of Sayyid Qutb by Loboda.

248 Sarton G. Introduction to the history of science. www.usc.edu/. History of Islamic Science [Online] [Cited: 10 5, 2016.] www.usc.edu/schools/college/crcc/private/cmje/heritage/History_of_Islamic_Science.pdf.

249 Hofmann, Murad. Islam the Alternative page 2. Beltsville. Amana Publications. 1992. 0915957663

250 Lewis Bernard. Muslim discovery of Europe page 1. W. W. Norton & Company. 0393321657.

251 Lewis Bernard. What went wrong. Page 7. Oxford University Press. 2002. 0060516054.

252 Bonner Michael. Jihad in Islamic History page 158, 159. Princeton University Press. 2006. 0691125740.

253 Naipaul, VS. Among the Believers. Page 82. Vintage. 1982. 0394711955.

254R.J, Woolsey. Defeating the Oil Weapon. *Commentary Magazine* [Online] [Cited: 10 5, 2016.] https://www.commentarymagazine.com/articles/defeating-the-oil-weapon.

255Meiji Period (1868 - 1912). *japan-guide.com* [Online] [Cited: 1 11, 2017.] http://www.japan-guide.com/e/e2130.html.

256 The Meiji Restoration Era, 1868-1889. *About Japan* [Online] [Cited: 1 11, 2017.] aboutjapan.japansociety.org/content.cfm/the_meiji_restoration_era_1868-1889.

257Meiji Constitution Goes Into Effect. *History Channel* [Online] [Cited: 1 12, 2017.] http://www.historychannel.com.au/this-day-in-history/meiji-constitution-goes-into-effect/

258Religion in Japan Fast Facts. *ReligionFacts* [Online] [Cited: 1 12, 2017.] http://www.religionfacts.com/japan

259Estimated War dead WW II. War Chronicle [Online] [Cited: 1 12, 2017.] http://warchronicle.com/numbers/WWII/deaths.htm.

260Muslim-Majority Countries. Pew Research Center [Online] [Cited: 12 4, 2016.] http://www.pewforum.org/2011/01/27/future-of-the-global-muslim-population-muslim-majority/.

261Iran-Iraq War. infoplease [Online] September 2016. http://www.infoplease.com/encyclopedia/history/iran-iraq-war.html.

262 Taiwan's government calculated its HDI to be 0.882, based on 2010 new methodology of UNDP

263Revolutionary Association of the Women of Afghanistan. *Prostitution Under the rule of Taliban* [Online] [Cited: 10 5, 2016.] http://www.rawa.org/rospi.htm

264Shelton, E. Transformational Leadership, Page 192. Trafford Publishing, 2012. 1466958502

265 The Daily Star. [Online] 3 31, 2007. [Cited: 11 16, 2019.] archive.thedailystar.net/2007/03/31/d7033101033.htm.

266 Daily Mail. [Online] [Cited: 8 20, 2017.] www.dailymail.co.uk/news/article-2135434/Egypts-plans-farewell-intercourse-law-husbands-sex-DEAD-wives-branded-completely-false.html.

267 Breastfeeding fatwa causes stir. *BBC News.* [Online] [Cited: 8 20, 2017.]
http://news.bbc.co.uk/2/hi/middle_east/6681511.stm.
268 Umar Marries A Milkmaid To his Son. *Alim.* [Online] [Cited: 6 13, 2017.]
http://www.alim.org/library/biography/khalifa/content/KUM/17/20.
269 Alcohol In Islam. The religion of Islam [Online] [Cited: 1 14, 2017.]
http://www.islamreligion.com/articles/2229/alcohol-in-islam/.
270 Jerusalem And Umar Ibn Al-Khattab. Lost Islamic History [Online] [Cited: 1 17,
2017.] http://lostislamichistory.com/jerusalem-and-umar-ibn-al-khattab/.
271 Mosque of Omar. *Lonely Planet* [Online] [Cited: 1 12, 2017.]
https://www.lonelyplanet.com/the-palestinian-
territories/bethlehem/attractions/mosque-of-omar/a/poi-sig/451497/361063.
272 http://www.alim.org/library/biography/khalifa/content/KAB/7/pdf/4
273 Bukhari 7.206.
274 Biography of Khlifa Umar bin Khattab in Alim software.
275 Awad, Abed. Does Islam really condemn converts to death?
http://religion.blogs.cnn.com. [Online] 7 18, 2018.
http://religion.blogs.cnn.com/2014/06/06/does-islam-really-condemn-converts-to-
death/.
276 Ibid.
277 Ibid.
278 Ibid.
279 Quoted in Islam and Women - Sources of Influence. [Online] [Cited: 10 13, 2016.]
http://www.liquisearch.com/islam_and_women/sources_of_influence.
280 Budge, E.A. Wallis. The Kebra Nagast. Internet Sacred Text Archive. [Online] [Cited:
12 23, 2018.] http://www.sacred-texts.com/index.htm.
281 *Sahih Bukhari* [4,25].
282 Tirmidhi Sunan #148.
283 Prophet Muhammad's Last Sermon. IntroductionToISLAM.org. [Online] [Cited: 7 16,
2016.] http://www.introductiontoislam.org/Prophetlastsermon.shtml.
284 Translation by Mohsin Khan.
285 Translation by Asad.
286 In Asad's foot note of the exegesis.
287 Bukhari, no. 853 and Muslim, no. 1829.
288 Haeri, Shahla. " Temporary Marriage." Encyclopaedia of the Qurʾān. Brill Online,
2013. Reference. 20 January 2013
<http://referenceworks.brillonline.com/entries/encyclopaedia-of-the-
quran/temporary-marriage-SIM_00415>
289 Ibid
290 Ibid
291 "Muta." Encyclopaedia of Islam, Second Edition. Brill Online, 2013. Reference. 20
January 2013 <http://referenceworks.brillonline.com/entries/encyclopaedia-of-islam-
2/muta-COM_0819>
292 Ibid
293 Al-Nasr, Tofol Jassim. Gulf Cooperation Council (GCC) Women and Misyar
Marriage: Evolution and Progress in the Arabian Gulf. *http://vc.bridgew.edu/* [Online]
[Cited: 10 17, 2016.] http://vc.bridgew.edu/jiws/vol12/iss3/4/.
294 " Muta." Encyclopaedia of Islam, Second Edition. Brill Online, 2013. Reference. 20
January 2013 <referenceworks.brillonline.com/entries/encyclopaedia-of-islam-2/muta-
COM_0819>

[295] Women and Misyar Marriage.
[296] Gulf Cooperation Council (GCC) Women and Misyar Marriage. Article 4, Issue 3, Volume 12
[297] Chapter Four: Qur'anic evidences for the legitimacy of Mut'ah. Shia Pen [Online] [Cited: 1 29, 2017.] http://www.shiapen.com/comprehensive/mutah/quranic-evidences.html.
[298] Mission Delhi – Zubeida Bano, Pahari Bhojla. *The Delhi Walla* [Online] [Cited: 12 10, 2016.] http://www.thedelhiwalla.com/2011/06/27/mission-delhi-%E2%80%93-zubeida-bano-paharji-bhojla/.
[299] The Orations of Muhammad. Compiled by Akbar. Page 52. MMA. Sh. Muhammad Ashraf. Lahor, 1954. 9694320240.